University of Southern Denmark Studies in History and Social Sciences vol. 253

Party Sovereignty and Citizen Control

Party Sovereignty and Citizen Control

Selecting Candidates
for Parliamentary Elections
in Denmark, Finland, Iceland and Norway

Edited by

Hanne Marthe Narud

Mogens N. Pedersen

Henry Valen

University Press of Southern Denmark 2002

Party Sovereignty and Citizen Control
Published with the generous support from
Riksbankens Jubilæumsfond, Sweden

© the contributors and the University Press of Southern Denmark
Set and printed by Narayana Press
Cover design by UniSats

ISBN 87-7838-692-6

Printed in Denmark 2002

Customers in the United States and Canada please contact:
International Specialized Book Services
5824 NE Hassalo St-Portland, OR 97213
Phone: +1-800-944-6190

University Press of Southern Denmark
Campusvej 55
DK-5230 Odense M
www.universitypress.dk

Content

Preface 7

1 Parliamentary Nominations in Western Democracies
HANNE MARTHE NARUD, MOGENS N. PEDERSEN AND HENRY VALEN

Introduction 9
The Process of Nominations 11
The Role of Nominations in the Chain of Parliamentary Delegation 16
Bringing the Perspectives together 19
Research Questions 21
Plan of the Book 25

2 Denmark: The Interplay of Nominations and Elections in Danish Politics
MOGENS N. PEDERSEN

Introduction 29
The early history of nominations and elections 30
An illustration from the 1998 election 34
The role of the state 37
The role of the parties 38
Who are the candidates? 43
Proper behavior during the electoral campaign 45
The changing role of the voters 47
A special case: the increasing success rate of female candidates . . 54
Turnover and recruitment 58
Concluding comments 60

3 Finland: Formalized Procedures with Member Predominance
SOILE KUITUNEN

Introduction 63
The nomination system 65
The role of the party 71
Criteria for candidate selection 78
Sanctions and rewards 92
Conclusions 100

4 Iceland: From Party Rule to Pluralist Political Society
SVANUR KRISTJÁNSSON

Introduction 107
The nomination system 110
Sanctions and rewards 138
Nomination method, turnover and main characteristics of MPs:
 The question of causation 153
Conclusions 161

5 Norway: Party Dominance and Decentralized Decision-Making
HENRY VALEN, HANNE MARTHE NARUD AND AUDUN SKARE

Introduction 169
The new system 174
The organizational process 177
Candidate selection 183
Sanctions and rewards 202
Nominations and the electorate 210
Conclusions 214

6 Conclusions
HANNE MARTHE NARUD, MOGENS N. PEDERSEN AND HENRY VALEN

The institutional setting 217
How are nominations organized? 218
What are the mechanisms for screening? 219
What is the outcome of the screening process? 222
What is the level of parliamentary turnover? 223
The multi-leveled network of principals and agents 224
Citizen control over candidate selection 226

Notes 229
References 237
Contributors 246
Index 247

Preface

This book is based upon a project started in 1997. The original plan was to analyze parliamentary nomination in all the five Nordic countries. However, due to unexpected tensions between members of the research group, the book was seriously delayed. Faced with the choice between terminating the entire project, or proceeding to publish it in a curtailed form, we have chosen the latter course. We regret that the Swedish contribution could not be included.

The editors wish to thank the Bank of Sweden Tercentenary Foundation for its generous support. By providing the editors with financial support in 2001, the Foundation was highly instrumental in bringing the project to a conclusion. We should also like to express our gratitude to NOS-S, which not only provided the funds for the initial stages of the project, but also gave useful advice along the way. In addition, the editors wish to thank the Danish *Udvalget til beskyttelse af videnskabeligt arbejde (UBVA)* for its legal advice.

A final word of thanks should go to Jan Johansson, who originally took the initiative to launch this project, and to those contributors who had to wait patiently for a conclusion.

Hanne Marthe Narud
Mogens N. Pedersen
Henry Valen

1

Parliamentary Nominations in Western Democracies[1]

HANNE MARTHE NARUD, MOGENS N. PEDERSEN AND HENRY VALEN

Introduction

This book is about the selection of candidates at parliamentary elections. The topic is indeed an important one in the study of representative democracy. Nominations are the first step – and the primary screening devices – in the process of representation. Forming a crucial part of the electoral process, they are mechanisms both for electing delegates to parliament and for holding them accountable. Hence, the concept of "political representation" concerns the relationship between candidates/representatives and their voters (Pitkin, 1967). While originally individual candidates appealed directly to the electorate of their respective constituencies, the emergence of organized political parties has greatly affected the character of elections as well as that of representation. Today the political parties have become the main actors in modern elections. The competing parties present their candidates and platforms, and they organize the electoral campaigning. The delegates are only indirectly involved in this process. Being responsible to their respective parties, they are committed to the party platform and policies, and politically they operate within the framework of the party's organization. Yet, since the prime purpose of the election is the selection of delegates, the choice of candidates that each party can offer to the electorate is – at least theoretically – of importance to the electoral contest.

What do we know about nominations? Information is available in a few countries in which the topic has been studied, particularly in the United States. But little is known of a general character. This scarcity of knowledge is amazing considering the fact that the study of elections has attracted great academic interest from historians, political scientists, sociologists, psychologists and lawyers. Characteristically, one of the few existing books on nominations carries the subtitle "the secret garden of politics" (Gallagher and Marsh, 1988). Except for the United States (e.g. Ranney, 1977; 1978; Reiter, 1985), the scarcity of any systematic knowledge is universal. Why should we pay any attention to this process?

We have already suggested the answer, but will elaborate the argument somewhat further. Nominations are important events because they are closely linked to the power structure of democratic societies. The nominating procedure is "one of the best points at which to observe the distribution of power within the party", to use a widely cited statement by Schattschneider (1942:64). Nominations are instrumental to parties, because they provide a linkage between the interest and preferences of the party and various subgroups of the electorate. By balancing the list, the party is able to create an image and to appeal to specific categories of voters and interest organizations. In short, by selecting candidates for public office parties build a bridge from politics to society, and back again.

Our main theoretical concern with this book is to evaluate nominations as instruments of democracy. That is, as mechanisms for the selection of political leaders, and as devices for control of the elected representatives. We do so by comparing the institutions, procedures and norms shaping the nominations in four countries in Northern Europe: Denmark, Finland, Iceland and Norway. We address two empirical questions. First, what is the impact of system-specific factors on the nomination of candidates? And second, how are nominations influenced by within-country variations? We confine the latter question to the impact of party-specific conditions. We will expand on these points later in this chapter.

A four-country study

A Nordic comparison of this kind is particularly tempting, because these countries are well suited for comparative research. They share several politically relevant characteristics, e.g. the party systems and patterns of voter alignments, which facilitates the sorting out of potential explanatory factors (see Lane et al. 1993; Sundberg, 1999). For this reason, in comparative research they have commonly been treated as "most similar systems" (Przeworski and Teune, 1970). At the same time these countries differ with regard to some of the institutional arrangements that form the framework of nominations. They differ with respect to geographic location and territorial size, and important variations exist in their electoral systems. Most relevant for the process of nomination is the extent to which the electoral law allows for voting in terms of individual candidates. The potential for voting for individual candidates has been greater in Finland, Iceland and Denmark than in Norway (see e.g. Helander, 1997, Pedersen, 1966). Hence, the impact of these differences for the nomination procedure will be a major concern in the analysis.

We believe that the comparison of our four countries offers valuable information about the functioning of small democracies in the process of representation, and in addition, it provides a contribution to the general study of party organization. The subsequent part of the chapter first gives a summary of previous studies of candidate selection. It then elaborates the theoretical concerns of the book, leaning on the prominent and growing literature on delegation and accountability drawn from the principal-agent theory. We subsequently use some of the insights from agency theory to discuss the various dimensions of candidate selection in parliamentary democracies. In so doing, we define our specific research questions. At the end of the chapter we sketch out the plan for the book.

The Process of Nominations

Candidate selection has long been a favorite topic for American political scientists (see e.g. Key, 1968:370-453). Possibly, one reason is that in the US institutional arrangements for nominations have been highly disputed, and as a result, legal regulations have been introduced.[2] As a first attempt outside the US Austin Ranney (1965) published a book on nominations in Great Britain. Previous research has largely neglected the impact of political institutions, in particular multiparty systems and proportional electoral systems. The most notable exception is the book edited by M. Gallagher and M. Marsh (1988), in which they compared candidate selection in nine different countries, among them Norway. The scant existing literature does, however, allow us to identify some aspects of the nomination process.

Dimensions of candidate selection

In his comparative chapter on candidate selection in 24 democracies, Ranney (1981) outlined the main methods by which parties select candidates for national legislatures. He made a distinction between formal rules on the one hand and actual procedures on the other. Ranney observed (1981:76) that only three countries, the former West Germany, Turkey and the US, had their nomination procedures regulated by written laws. Norway and Finland fell into this category as well, even though in these cases the law is not mandatory. In other nations selection procedures were – and still are – governed by rules that are made and enforced by the parties themselves. Concerning informal rules for candidate selection, Ranney (1981:82) found a good deal of variation from one country to the next and even between parties within given countries.[3] We shall here emphasize two main dimensions:

(i) The first is the degree of *centralization*. This factor has been given considerable attention in the literature, (cf. Gallagher and Marsh, 1988, Katz and Mair, 1992; Ware, 1996; Norris, 1997; Pennings and Hazan, 2001). Power over candidate selection is distributed between national, regional and constituency agencies, and the level of system centralization depends upon the degree of supervision exercised by these agencies over the selection. Ranney (1981:82-83) concluded that by far the most common pattern is: "selection by constituency party agencies under some form of supervision by national or regional agencies, and the next most common is selection by national agencies after considerations or suggestions made by constituency and regional agencies."

(ii) The second dimension is the degree of *inclusiveness* in the process. In most countries participation is restricted to party members according to the internal party rules. The notable exception, Ranney (pp. 85-86) observed, is the officially regulated primary system of the United States. In contrast to the European parliamentary systems, candidate selection in the US is by far the most inclusive, since party agencies or party officials have virtually no say in who participates in the selection process. It is important to note, however, that the primaries in the US, which are run by the state government, are not directly comparable to the European ones. The US has "open primaries", which in practice means that they are open to a wide range of people who are not necessarily members (Ware, 1996:260). "Closed primaries", which are used by some of the European parties, are restricted to party members and involve some kind of internal party elections to pick out the preferred candidates. A recent comparative study by Bille (2001) suggests that democratization of candidate selection has indeed taken place among Western European parties, although for the most part on a modest scale.

In combination, these two dimensions include four distinct varieties of nomination systems. At one extreme is found an inclusive, yet central, process: Participation is open to many individuals, though the outcome of the process is decided at the central level – not in the local branches of the party. An alternative nomination system is one that is decentralized and open at the same time. But we may also envisage decentralized and closed systems, where the decisions are made in the local party branches by a small group of "gatekeepers". A fourth type would be one with centralized nominations restricted to a few party members. However, "real-world" systems will mostly be of a mixed character. A complete control by central party elites is rare, as is a complete absence of such control. A notable exception is to be found in Greece, in which case the PASOK has proven extraordinary in the power granted to the party leaders in selecting candidates. Alan Ware (1996:262) explains the Greek case as resulting from the country's specific historical experiences.

Selection criteria

In a classic article from 1967 Lester Seligman (1967) distinguished between two stages in the recruitment process. The first stage provides the *certification* of candidates, i.e. a process of social screening and political channeling that results in eligibility for candidacy. At this stage, the aspirants' personal abilities are evaluated, e.g. their professional and political competence (see e.g. Norris and Lovenduski, 1995; Valen, 1988). The next stage consists in the *selection*, the actual decision on who is going to represent the party in the election. The number of office-seeking aspirants tends to be higher than the actual number of available "openings". Many aspirants are eliminated during the first pre-selection screening that takes place in the parties beforehand, and the collective profile of the population will change along the way. The characteristics of the successful candidates differ from those of the unsuccessful ones, but empirically it is not easy to pinpoint exactly how. Some qualities may, however, be identified. The five most prominent ones are the following:

1) *Incumbency*. By far the most widely prized – or criticized – characteristic of selected candidates is incumbency. The fact that incumbent candidates have legislative experience makes them valuable professionals to the party. Not only are they likely to make better candidates than non-incumbents, but they are also known to the voters and to the selectorates, a fact that may constitute an electoral advantage to the party (Ranney, 1981:98-102). Ambitious aspirants may see this differently.

2) *Local connections*. Most parties in most countries favor candidates with strong local connections (Gallagher and Marsh, 1988). Even though the Constitution of the US and a handful of parties elsewhere have local residence requirements, it is not common that parties have formal rules concerning the residence of the candidate. It is, however, a widespread norm in many parties to favor local candidates. Also Ranney (1981:99) noted that: "strong local connections – such as long-standing residence in the district, activity in local party affairs, holding local public office, or activity in some local

union, business, or civic affairs – is second only to incumbency as a trait widely valued by those who select parliamentary candidates".

3) *Interest group affiliation.* Many parties nurture visible affiliation with key interest groups. To select candidates with membership background in e.g. labor unions, ecclesiastical organizations etc. is quite common in many countries. Balancing the list with organized interests may give the party electoral as well as economic advantages.

4) *Factional affiliation.* The balancing of particular factional interests is also an important criterion, at least for some parties. Factional affiliation, if organized, may be seen as a subcategory of interest group affiliation, but most commonly they are of a more informal nature. Valen (1958) has made a distinction between ideological factions on the one hand and interest factions on the other. Ideological factions are not considered legitimate by the parties, since they represent an ideological constraint and may threaten party unity. Interest factions, on the other hand, are more acceptable, since they constitute a link between parties and organized interests in the community. The important point is that most parties to some extent face the problem of keeping its major factions sufficiently happy. By balancing the lists in terms of gender, age, occupation, etc., the parties attempt to satisfy intraparty factional demands. In addition, list balancing is expected to satisfy certain segments of the electorate.

5) *Above average socio-economic and educational status.* This point has to do with the end-result of the process rather than the selection criteria as such. Political parties have a strong tendency to recruit candidates whose income, level of education and occupations are higher than that of the average voter. This "iron law of social bias" is a common characteristic of all Western legislatures (Valen, 1966; Putnam, 1976; Norris, 1997; Narud and Valen, 2000). The reasons for social bias in political recruitment, Norris and Lovenduski (1995) argue, may have to do with institutional features (e.g. the election system), party-specific features (e.g. the party statutes), and/or individual features (various background characteristics and personal skills).

Since the conditions listed above tend to vary from one country to the next, they are all relevant for comparative analysis. However, some theoretical notions may be helpful for understanding how the selection of candidates is related to elections as well as to other institutions of representative democracy. For this purpose, let us lean on some arguments from the principal-agent literature.

The Role of Nominations in the Chain of Parliamentary Delegation

In recent years a new theoretical vocabulary drawn from economic theory has gained prominence in the study of representational linkages. It is now customary to describe the linkage in terms of *delegation* from a principal to an agent. Delegation takes place in several stages of the political process: from voters to parliamentary candidates, from parliament to government, from government to the bureaucracy and so on. The first stage in this process of delegation is the selection of parliamentary candidates and the succeeding parliamentary elections.[4] *Accountability*, which is the other important element in the chain of delegation, reverses this relationship, and involves requirements for reporting back and the possibility for sanctions and rewards (e.g. removing someone from office). When delegation takes place, there is always a danger of opportunistic behavior on the part of the agents, in the literature referred to as so-called "agency losses" (Kiewiet and McCubbins, 1991). Agency losses occur when for example a conflict of interest arises between the principal and the agent, and the agent acts contrary to the will of the principal.[5] To control such problems, principals may place certain restrictions on agent actions. These control mechanisms may be put in place *ex ante*, i.e. before the principal delegates to an agent, or *ex post*, i.e. after authority has been delegated (Kiewiet and McCubbins, 1991; Strøm, 1999; 2000). Let us illustrate the relevance of these concepts for the question of parliamentary nominations.

There are two types of control mechanisms that are placed *ex ante*. The first is the so-called *contract design*, that is, the set of rules on which the principal "hires" the agent. In the process of candidate selection these are the set of institutions that regulate delegation from voters to representatives, i.e. the electoral laws and/or the nomination laws (Mitchell, 2000). One important question is to which extent the electoral laws allow for a personal vote, or at the other extreme, whether voters are faced with a closed list system. Another is the level of institutionalization of the procedure, that is, whether nominations are structured by formal regulations, or whether they are governed by rules and procedures that are decided by the parties themselves.

The other ex-ante control mechanism is the *screening and selection devices* applied by the principals to sort out the "good agents" (Strøm, 1999:67), that is, candidates with the qualifications and characteristics preferred by the selectorates. With relevance to the nomination process, these are the demands for group affiliation, local connections and other characteristics that help "balancing" the list with a variety of economic, demographic and social interests.

Ex post control mechanisms, on the other hand, are the ways in which the principals are able to *monitor* and *sanction* the agents at a later stage. *Monitoring* is obviously constrained by the nature of parliamentary affairs, which take place on a scene that is fairly remote from the attention of the mass public. In most systems the ability – and even the interest – of individual voters to keep an eye on the actions of their MPs is very limited. To most people the media would be the most important source of information – particularly before election time. It is during the electoral campaign that the candidates take their case to the electorate, thereby providing an incentive to the public to think about governmental matters (Riker, 1986). Hence, the voters' perception of their agents' performance will most likely be colored by the incumbents' performance at election time.

The ability to *sanction* individual candidates is related to the character of the election system as well as to formal and informal rules of the nomination procedure. Elections, as a means of control, offer many complex considerations. First of all, in the case of multiple principals (as indeed voters are), we face the problem of preference aggregation. Electoral accountability in a situation of multiple preferences is difficult, since the agents will have problems in defining the true preferences of the principals. And second, elections may be seen as devices for *selecting* agents as well as mechanisms of political accountability. Defined retrospectively, they are the most important sanctioning devices that voters can use to secure responsiveness from their leaders. But defined prospectively, they are mechanisms for the selection of "good" agents. These two understandings of elections, as Fearon (1999:57) points out, are by no means incompatible. Elections are means for both selection and sanctioning, and the extent to which these interact or dominate is highly conditional upon certain mechanisms of the electoral law.[6] Election systems in which candidates have the incentive to seek a personal vote, for instance, offer a direct and much stronger sanctioning mechanism to the voters than a strictly party-centered system. Closed list systems, therefore, put the sanctioning devices in the hands of the party activists.[7] Here, the effective principals may be the national, the local, or the provincial party branches – conditioned upon the level of centralization of the process.

What does the principal-agent literature contribute to the general knowledge of candidate selection? What do we gain by bringing this perspective into the analysis? At least three achievements spring to mind: First, the basic concepts of the agency model offer a good supplement to the conventional literature on nominations, since it takes into consideration how institutions shape the strategic context of parties and candidates. Second, it illustrates that nominations take place within a complex network of multiple principals and multiple agents, and that decisions have to be made concerning "who" is accountable to "whom". Third, and because of the former, this particular framework clarifies the dilemmas facing incumbent candidates seeking re-selection. The question of electoral accountability is more complex than is assumed in the traditional literature, as it involves several levels of the party hierarchy to be considered. Bringing in the "old" perspectives discussed initially, and combining them with the arguments from the principal-agent literature, are the best means of clarifying these arguments.

Bringing the Perspectives together

We have sketched two theoretical traditions for the study of candidate nominations, an older and a brand new one. They are clearly related, which can be seen when we ask questions about the relationship between their main concepts, on the one hand, *centralization* and *inclusiveness*, and, on the other, *delegation* and *accountability*.

First of all, the level of centralization and inclusiveness has a bearing on who is responsible to whom in the process of delegation. The party hierarchy consists of at least five levels:

- Central party leadership
- Regional party leaders/activists
- Local party leaders/activists
- Party members
- Party voters

Each one of these levels encompasses a set of principals as well as agents who are accountable to one another. The ultimate principal, of course, is the individual voter, but the institutional setting determines his/her ability to sanction the elected agent, and consequently, the electoral focus of the incumbent candidates. For example, in a decentralized and party-centered system in which nominations are restricted to convention delegates, the candidates have little incentive to search for personal votes. When seeking reselection, the focus of the incumbent would be on the local party leaders, since they control the "key" to his/her success. By contrast, in an open system with party primaries or preferential voting, voters are able to control reselection, and the incumbents have the incentive to seek personal votes. These factors imply that taken *collectively* incumbent agents would feel accountable to those who control reselection.

Second, the level of inclusiveness has an impact on the outcome of the selection process. Open primaries, as opposed to closed list systems, are likely to promote candidate-centered politics, in which personal qualities, and not group affiliation, are the most important criteria for selection. In the former the ability to attract voters is an important criterion for candidate selection, promoting aspirants with certain personal qualities and professional skills. By contrast, in closed list systems, the selectors employ criteria like age, gender, social status, race, religion, group affiliation and locality, aiming for a ticket that "balances" certain ascribed characteristics, and then use achievement criteria to pick the individuals (Gallagher, 1988; Valen, 1988).

Third, the picture becomes further complicated as we take into account the demands put forward by the selectorates during the nomination procedure. When considering the various aspirants for nomination, the selectors tend to calculate the possible effect of individual candidates on the voters. When screened in the selection process, the candidates most likely to be nominated are the ones possessing certain qualities of importance to the selectors. As elected agents they have mandates reflecting demographic, social and ideological interests in society. Hence, *individually* they may face a dilemma as regards which principals to represent. Securing the representation of group interests has an important theoretical bearing upon the question of accountability. By linking the candidates to certain sub-groups of society, expectations are created as to "who" represents "whom" in the legislative body.

Taken as a group, the elected MPs represent a collection of interests that the parties would like to include, but considered individually, different MPs are related to different segments of interest representation. In addition, they are constrained by the questions of formal party positions and constituency control. In this respect, a dilemma may arise between constituency interests and a parliamentary career. If sitting in committees basically dealing with nation-oriented or international issues, MPs often meet demands for a generalist focus. However, a national focus does not travel well with local expectations. In highly decentralized systems with emphasis on district representation, such demands may be at odds with the incumbents' chances of reselection.[8]

In this book we attempt to study the various dimensions of the nomination process by defining a "linked" set of principal-agent relationships. They are "linked" in the sense that, during the process of candidate selection, a number of principals (voters, members, activists, central leaders), on different levels (local, provincial, national), delegate authority to several agents on the basis of a variety of selection criteria. These agents are accountable to their (multi-level) principals.

Hence, all the principals, per definition, possess the authority to remove the agents if they do not serve the principals' objectives (see Matthews and Valen, 1999, for similar arguments). Their incentives to do so are structured by institutional constraints, formal procedures, and informal norms.

Research Questions

Given the overall theoretical framework, three general questions may be formulated:

- How does delegation take place?
- How is control exercised?
- Do delegation and control matter?

Linking these questions to the dimensions of candidate selection discussed initially, we may formulate five empirical questions:

1) What is the institutional setting for selecting candidates?
2) How are nominations organized?
3) What are the mechanisms for screening?
4) What is the outcome of the screening process?
5) What is the level of parliamentary turnover?

What is the institutional setting?

Each country chapter begins with a historical description of the nomination system in which institutions and norms have been molded. It provides an account of the various electoral reforms that have taken place and identifies the actors involved in the process of delegation and accountability. Here, the level of centralization and inclusiveness are important factors, as these dimensions define "who" is involved "when" in the nomination process.[9] One of the questions we raise is the extent to which demands for democratization have been put forth, in the sense that more people should have a direct say in the selection process.

How are nominations organized?

In some systems the voters determine the relative strength of the parties in parliament, but in practice, "who" is going to have access to the political elites is decided by a small segment of party activists. In other systems the voters have more direct influence upon the question of candidate selection, either via the electoral system (e.g. preference votes) or simply via open party primaries. Since agency losses from voters to MPs are most likely when incumbents are independent of voters' preferences for reselection, we are preoccupied with the influence of individual voters, direct or indirect, on the composition of the list. To what extent does the electoral system allow for a personal vote?

With regard to the legal system, the following sets of questions are analyzed: What are the legal procedures governing candidate selection? Do any written rules concerning nominating procedures exist? Multimember constituencies and proportional electoral systems, for example, tend to make the individual candidates for parliament less visible, whereas single-member constituencies and plurality elections have the opposite effect. In the latter, the media tend to play a more significant role than in the first, thus, actively playing a part in the process. The various country chapters therefore describe the sets of formal and informal rules governing the process as well as the role of "external" factors, e.g. the media. In this context, we are particularly preoccupied with knowing how rules provide a constraint for the process of delegation, and if variations may be detected between different party families in how the process is organized.

What are the mechanisms for screening?

This part of the analysis gives attention to the devices for "screening and selection" in the process of delegation, i.e. the two stages of the nomination process, which were identified by Lester Seligman (1967), certification and selection. The focus is on the screening and selection criteria applied by the parties. The following norms will be examined:

(i) *Territorial representation*. To what extent are local ties and political experience a prerequisite for the selection of candidates? How important are constituency bonds for candidate recruitment?

(ii) *Group representation*. Which social, economic and demographic groups are represented on the list? To what extent have women's quotas been introduced? And are attachments to specific social organizations valued as a criterion for selection?

(iii) *Personal qualities*. What is the importance of political and professional competence, political experience and education? To what extent are platform abilities (e.g. charisma, eloquence, the ability to perform in the mass media) important screening mechanisms?

(iv) *Political (ideological) factions*. What is the nature of the ideological factions? To what extent do policy considerations have an impact on the balancing of the list?

We expect the application of these criteria to be influenced by institutional variations as well as by party-specific mechanisms, e.g. the size of the party and its ideological leaning.

What is the outcome of the screening process?

By "the outcome" of the selection process we mean the social and demographic outlook of the "agents" selected for political office. The social bias of modern legislatures has been mentioned already, and the Nordic democracies are no exceptions (Valen, 1966). The socio-economic status of the Nordic political representatives lies well above that of the average voter in terms of both income, job background and education. In a long-term perspective the predominant trend has been the replacement of farmers and blue-collar workers by career politicians (see e.g. Pedersen, 1972, 1977; Eliassen and Pedersen, 1978; Esaiasson and Holmberg, 1996; Narud, 1999; Matthews and Valen, 1999; Narud and Valen, 2000). However, in a comparative context the Nordic countries have also been renowned for the high number of women in their legislatures, nowadays maybe their most outstanding feature. We are therefore especially interested in the impact of specific reforms on the outcome of nominations. At which stage of the recruitment process does the "representative distortion" occur: at the stage of the nominations or at the stage of the elections? How much of the recent success of women can be traced back to improved conditions during the nomination procedures, bringing more women forward, and granting them "quotas" on the electoral lists? To what extent does preferential voting affect the outcome of the process?

What is the level of parliamentary turnover?

How do we know that delegation works? One indication, albeit a weak one, is the rate of parliamentary turnover. The most effective "control" mechanism possessed by the principals is the power to reselect and re-elect incumbent candidates. Comparative studies demonstrate that the record for incumbent candidates has been quite favorable, as most party organizations have let interested parliamentarians accumulate up to several terms of seniority. However, electoral fluctuations and increased volatility have increased the uncertainty of incumbent candidates as to their chances of re-election. In addition, their options for reselection are constrained by factors like internal party struggles, the political agenda, contacts with groups and organizations at the local level, and formal party positions. Hence, the question of candidate turnover should be examined at the nomination stage as well as at the election stage. First, is turnover a result of electoral defeat? Or is turnover a result of deselection at the nominating stage? Second, does turnover affect certain groups more than others? Regarding the latter question, our focus will be on incumbents and women.

Plan of the Book

The four country chapters have been organized according to the five research questions discussed above. Hence, the first three parts describe the political institutions and organizational procedures relevant to the nomination process of each country. A distinction has been made between *formal institutions*, on the one hand, embodied at the system level, and *informal procedures and norms*, on the other hand, embodied at the level of individual parties. The first aspect refers to the "contract design," e.g. the written constitution or the rules of the electoral system. The more informal aspects refer to the norms, procedures, and traditional practices that govern the process of candidate selection in each party. Informal rules – like formal ones – constrain the options available to the actors, and have therefore an impact upon the outcome of the process. The second two parts of the analyses focus on the impact of formal institutions and party procedures on the outcome of the process, more specifically on the composition and turnover of the legislative elites.

As to the Nordic countries, only a few studies have previously been conducted (see e.g. Valen 1956; 1965; 1988, Sköld 1958, Brändström 1972, Johansson 1999). However, a systematic comparison of these countries has never been done. In a recent book on political recruitment edited by Norris (1997), only Finland was included, and in the extensive study edited by Gallagher and Marsh (1988) only Norway was represented. In the latter Henry Valen's (1988) analyses demonstrated that the nomination system in Norway is a decentralized one, and that little tolerance exists among the local constituencies for national leaders interfering with the selection of candidates. His conclusion is that, in general, the system of nomination is well adjusted to the requirements of other political institutions, particularly the electoral system. Moreover, ticket balancing, which is the dominant pattern of candidate selection, appears to be an adequate method for intraparty conflict resolution. Hence, the extent to which these are common features of a more general nature is a question of great interest.

For the purpose of this book the authors had neither the opportunity nor the means to collect one joint data set. The results of the various chapters were generated on the basis of data already available in each country. In some cases, however, new data have been collected in order to meet the demands of the overall research design, particularly regarding information on parliamentary composition and turnover. In addition, the level of analysis differs somewhat between individual countries. The analyses of Finland, Iceland and Norway have been done on the basis of nationwide nomination studies, whereas the results for Denmark are generated primarily on the basis of local constituency studies. However, despite these differences, the information available in each country is quite sufficient to answer our basic research questions.

2

Denmark: The Interplay of Nominations and Elections in Danish Politics

Mogens N. Pedersen

Introduction

Every electoral system that allows for some degrees of freedom with regard to the nomination and selection of candidates and legislators has to strike a balance between three sets of interests, all of which have some legitimacy in a modern party-based regime. First, the interests of the "ordinary" voters, who as the formal principals want to have a say with regard to the selection – among candidates nominated by the parties – of those who should enter parliament. Most voters may not care, but some, who are conscientious and informed, do. They want a candidate with some special qualities. They may even set aside their party preference for a preference for a special candidate. Second, the national party leadership has an interest in the composition of the party's group in parliament. Most party leaders do not want to see too many mavericks, nor too many unqualified members. On the contrary the leadership will often wish to push the candidacy of obviously talented political recruits. They also know, how important it is that the lower ranks in the party feel that they "get something", at least the feeling of having some influence with regard to nominations. Third, the local party leadership and the rank-and-file members may wish to see a close link between "their" member and "their" constituency, for such close relations may not only give political status to the constituency, but "bacon" as well.

Thus we have at least three groups of interests, all of them legitimate, but not always coinciding. They may even be in direct conflict. Every system of nomination and election will create a certain balance between these interests. Thus there may exist a balance within the individual party, allowing for considerable differences across the party spectrum. In some cases the entire "national" party system may be characterized by solid patterns of nominations and selection outcomes. Sometimes this balance may, however, be an unstable one, undergoing change in the short as well as in the long term.

Among the Nordic political systems Denmark stands out with a nomination and selection system that has undergone considerable change with regard to the power balance between the three above-mentioned interests. The change apparently for a long time has moved the system away from a once quite stable situation in which the parties – locally and/or nationally – controlled the entire process of nomination and electoral selection. The direction of change is towards a situation in which the individual, mostly unorganized, voter has much more formal influence, which he – or she – also tends to use. At present the situation nationwide is in fact one of a rather unstable balance between the three interests, even if the situation also tends to differ considerably from one party to another. The evolving situation is only partially researched by Danish political scientists, for which reason the following analysis should be considered an attempt to "freeze" the picture at the turn of the century. But since the situation is changing, and since furthermore the measuring instruments are not optimal, the reader should not expect the picture to stand out as clear and focused as one could wish for.

The early history of nominations and elections

From the very early days of Danish democracy nominations and their outcomes have been discussed and have been seen as a matter of concern. The following story brings us directly into the problem.

Already during the elections for the Constitutional Assembly in 1848 a spectacular episode developed, when in one of the constituencies in Zealand two candidates were nominated in sharp and fundamental opposition to each other. One candidate was a prominent professor of theology at the Copenhagen University. He had been serving as a representative already during the period of waning royal absolutism, when the King had allowed elections for Consultative Provincial Assemblies. Now he was being nominated by a group of bourgeois voters in the small town of Præstø, and it was widely expected that he would win the seat. But he had displeased some of the leading notables, and they had another candidate nominated, a local cotton weaver and smallholder. After a dramatic and slanderous campaign in which the weaver was attacked for some alleged juvenile crimes, he was nevertheless elected in the public election, and even elected with a comfortable majority. However, a few days later he had to resign, because his influential backers decided to withdraw their support. The event was immediately seen as a symbolic political event and has even been immortalized in a poem by one of the finest Danish poets.[10]

This story encapsulates the class conflict of the middle 19th century, which was predominantly a conflict between the well-educated and academic class and the lower classes. It also tells about the cleavage between Town and Village, and between the national Center (Copenhagen) and the provinces – that part of the country that in other Nordic countries is called the Periphery. And finally it also reminds us of the potential conflict between the local favorite son and the intruder who "parachutes" in from outside the constituency. These cleavages and potential conflicts have survived until today.

It was only during the late 19th century that parties emerged as playing a role in the nomination process.[11] The gatekeepers during the first decades after 1849 were local notables who, due to their position in local and national networks, were able to facilitate, and certainly often also control, the process. The members and especially the leaders of the emerging party groups in the *Folketing* played an important role in these networks (Larsen, 1979). Gradually these individual notables were replaced by the collective party organization, especially so in the towns, where the Social Democratic Party towards the end of the century made inroads. But it was only well into the 20th century that the mass party organizations became the dominant structural form in the four, so-called "old", parties.

Three characteristics about the early period in the history of nominations deserve to be mentioned here, because they point towards the present situation.

First, the elections were, until 1901, held publicly in 100 single-member constituencies. In most cases townspeople and farmers from the countryside met at the town hall square; prospective candidates were presented and introduced themselves to the audience, and the election took place by a show of hands. In case of doubt about the election it was admissible to make a formal count. By giving the act of election this public character, the constituency also became a central political arena. Many of the early traditions have lived on, even if the act of voting under the PR system has changed its character and its meaning, and even if – as we shall see shortly – the concept of constituency has undergone profound change. The candidate still will have to search for and/or be called to participate in nominations in a district, and a certain amount of openness in the nomination process is considered appropriate.

Second, often close links developed between the individual member and his constituency. As most parties had strongholds in various parts of the country, their influential politicians naturally developed special affiliations with these strongholds, often relations that lasted for decades (e.g. Hatting & Winding, 1950). *Folketing* members still think of themselves as representing a locality, and this locality mostly is the district in which they are nominated. And the boundaries of the district will in many cases be traceable to the electoral system of the 19th century.

Third, and most important for understanding the present state of affairs, the central party organization did not play a decisive role in nominations in any of the parties. This was especially the case with the Agrarian Liberal Party that, by the way, had a very weak national organizational setup before 1929, when the present organization was formed (Larsen, 1979). It was also true about the Conservatives, named *Højre*, before the formation of the modern form of a Conservative People's Party in 1915. The old *Højre* was a national frontrunner with regard to the formation of a viable network of organizations in Copenhagen as well as in the provincial towns, but these organizations played mostly a supportive, social role. The party, which was forming the government until 1901, was controlled by its – mainly aristocratic

– national leaders with regard to policy formation, and by the local notables with regard to the nomination process. As far as is known the executive board of the national organization did not try systematically to exert influence upon nominations. It may from time to time have helped local organizations to find suitable candidates, a task which, however, became increasingly difficult as the party approached extinction in the *Folketing* (Dybdahl, 1969:141;179f.).

The Social Democratic Party was formed outside parliament and only gained its first two representatives in 1884. From the very beginning the by-laws required that local nominations had to be accepted by the Executive Committee of the party. There was, however, widespread opposition within the party to this regulation, and it was discussed at most of the party congresses. In 1913 the Executive de facto gave up its sole right to veto nominations by allowing the party congress to make decisions. It is, however, a matter for further research to find out to which extent the veto of the central executive was practiced. Informal tri-partite negotiations between local party and union leaders, members of the national leadership and the prospective candidate may have been common practice. In a few known cases the Executive recommended a certain nomination, but it did not always succeed. The local candidates were heavily favored all over the country, and most sources point in the direction of the local initiative as the decisive influence (Dybdahl, 1969:232-43).

One reason why it is difficult to establish the power balance between the central and the local party organization at this early stage has to do with the possibility of forming electoral alliances. In a three-to-four party system as it existed before 1915, it happened that two parties, primarily the Social Democrats and the Radical Liberals, formed alliances, meaning that they decided to nominate only one candidate from one of the parties in several constituencies. In such cases the central-local conflict theme could easily be about the decision to enter the alliance, rather than a decision about nomination of a candidate for the party. In such situations national coordination was mandatory, and hence the national party leadership often had a hard time in convincing the local leaders that they had to support a candidate from another party. The coordination problem was most severe in the Radical Liberal Party in which the local organization was keen on its autonomy (Rasmussen & Skovmand, 1955), but even among the Social Democrats occasional conflicts are reported.

This historical introduction leads the author to restate his main thesis about what makes the Danish case interesting in a comparative and especially in a Nordic perspective: The central leadership of the parties have over the last decades increasingly lost control of the selection process, and they never were in complete control. But the local branches of the parties have in many instances also experienced a certain curtailment of their influence. They still to some degree control the nomination proper, but they have more and more to take into account the somewhat unpredictable behavior of the voters as well as some of their own members. This is the main topic that will be developed in this chapter.

An illustration from the 1998 election

Since the Danish electoral system as well as the nomination procedures are quite complicated, it may be useful to begin this chapter with a few notes about a single case. I have decided to provide a bare minimum of factual information about the constituency of Funen, one of the 17 constituencies within the Danish electoral system. I will let this constituency stand as an example or illustration of the general situation. A more detailed description of the nomination procedures and the procedures for preferential voting will be provided further on in this chapter. At this juncture we only take a look at the numerical distributions.

In the 1998 *Folketing* election no less than 96 candidates were running for election in this constituency. Funen is a reasonably big island in the middle of the country. Its approximately 360,000 voters elect 15 members, a number which is predetermined by the electoral law. Apart from one candidate who was running as an independent, a party had nominated all the candidates. On Funen as in the rest of Denmark eleven parties were competing for votes, meaning that each of the parties had nominated – on average – nine candidates. The constituency itself is divided into nine nomination districts, and thus most of the candidates are nominated in just one such district.

Denmark: The Interplay of Nominations and Elections in Danish Politics

Figure 2.1 Map of Funen. The division into nomination districts.

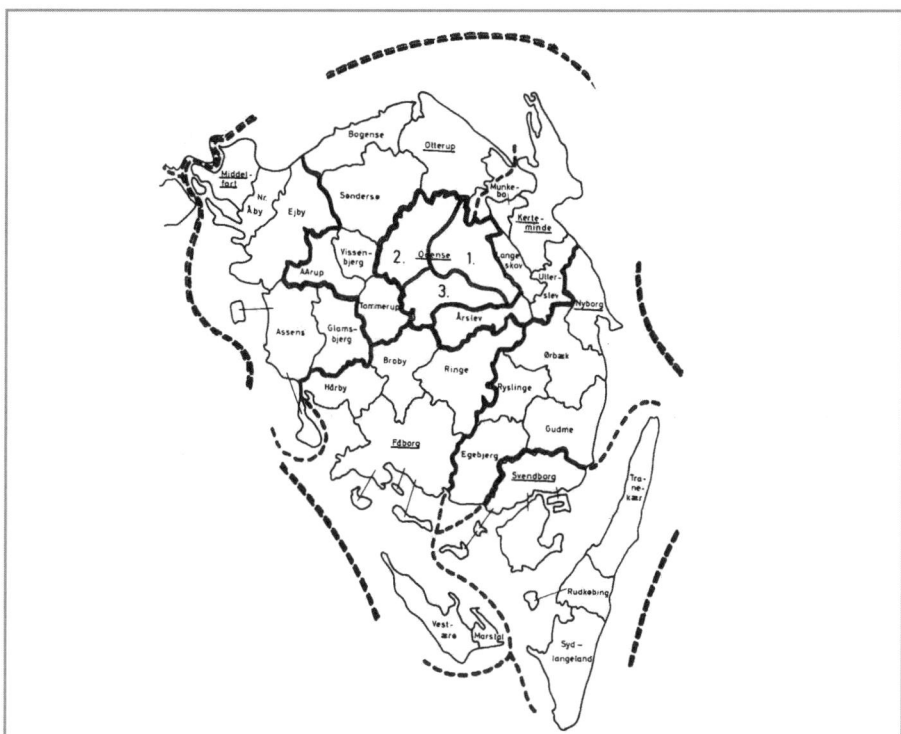

Among the fifteen members elected in the previous election of 1994 a few – four – had for various reasons stepped down before the recent election. Of the remaining eleven incumbents two were defeated in the election, and nine thus were returned to parliament for a new term. This means that only six new candidates passed the threshold, and one of these had even been a substitute member of the outgoing *Folketing*.[12]

If a count is made of the number of preferential votes given to the candidates, a very clear rank order emerges. The absolute winner, with a total of almost 18,000 personal votes all over Funen, was a young female candidate, who happened to be nominated in one of the smaller districts, i.e. a district in which her party, the Social Democrats, only gained a total of approx. 12.000 votes, of which a bit more than a third were personal votes for this local candidate. The candidate, who had never been nominated before, thus was dependent upon votes from all over the island for her electoral success.[13]

More typical were the following 10 names on the rank order list. These were the ten candidates who had run from a seat in parliament. Most of them had even improved their results (in terms of personal votes) compared to the previous election. Thus only two of the elected candidates on Funen – from two small parties – did not figure among the top-20 on the rank order (*Fyens Stiftstidende*, March 13, 1998).

These proportions – many parties, many candidates, few elected, and even fewer newcomers, of which a few will enter the political arena with great success – are typical of all Danish constituencies. So is the tendency for incumbents to be favored by the preferential voting. Apart from one, maybe two, of these items, they are also typical of constituencies all over the world, at least of those of the multi-member, multiparty kind. The proportion of newcomers to the Danish parliament tends to be 25-30 percent of the total membership (Pedersen, 1994). "From the Many Are Chosen the Few" reads a chapter title in a classical book (Prewitt, 1970). The situation under scrutiny in this chapter does not differ.

The election of a few members of parliament from among a pool of candidates, who are selected from among a pool of aspirants, recruits and apprentices, who themselves emanate from a pool of activists in the population of eligible persons, constitutes a continuous process which can only for analytical purposes be broken down in sequential segments. Each sub-process is linked, not only to the preceding sub-process, but also to the following one. Analytical concentration on the nomination itself, for example, will at best only provide a partial picture of the entire process of elite recruitment. Recruitment and derecruitment processes are closely linked together, as are the processes of nomination and election.

Given this problem one has to identify the different institutional actors and, next, to describe the contributions of each of these actors to the entire process. Thus the role of the state will be briefly outlined, followed by a description of the role of parties at the various levels, with special focus on the relationship between the central party organization and the local branches. Finally, the active role of the electorate will be described and discussed, preceded by a few remarks about the norms that regulate the behavior of the candidate during the electoral campaign.

The role of the state

The first important fact to note about the Danish system of nomination is the relative lack of legal regulation. The Danish Constitution itself does not deal with nominations; it does not even mention political parties. The electoral procedures are laid down in great detail in an act of parliament,[14] and in this act a chapter is devoted to "Electoral parties and Candidates". But only the following rules are stipulated:

- which parties, incumbent and new ones, are entitled to participate;
- specifications for registration and monitoring of new parties;
- formal requirement for candidates (150-200 recommendations in writing from voters in the constituency);
- specifications for registration as a candidate and for the endorsement procedures of the nominating party;
- limitation with regard to nomination (only possible in one constituency (*Amtskreds*) and only for one party).

It is noteworthy that many relevant activities are not regulated in the electoral law, or in any other public act. There do not exist codified rules of proper conduct for parties and candidates during the campaign, rules concerning conduct and publication rights for pollsters during the campaign, rules concerning the conduct of the mass media etc.[15] Very few stipulations are thus laid down in the Act of Parliament and in the various annexes to that Act.

One important regulative intervention has, however, in recent times been added to the legal complex, and this concerns the introduction of public financial support for political parties as well as candidates, an issue of only secondary importance for the matters dealt with here.[16]

Although nominations proper are not treated at length in the legal texts, several other legal stipulations are, however, relevant for the way in which the nomination process is conducted, for the outcomes of this process, and for the subsequent election. These rules are mentioned briefly in the following sections. The most important part of the legal framework deals with the procedures of preferential voting, and these rules will be presented, when we discuss the impact of the voters on election day.

The process of nomination takes place within the individual party according to the by-laws of that party. The public authorities are only monitoring the formal registration of parties and candidates. The Ministry of the Interior through its election office will control this monitoring, and the *Folketing* itself will confirm the final election results and all the details.

The role of the parties

Danish parties are organized in the same way as parties in most other countries (Katz & Mair, 1992; Bille, 1997). They differ widely in size, from the biggest, the Social Democratic Party, which still counts approx. 60,000 members, to several small parties like the Center Democrats with a membership in the vicinity of 1,200 members nationwide. Older and bigger parties have experienced considerable, not to say dramatic, decrease in their membership numbers; the newer parties, i.e. those which have surfaced since about 1970, have never been able to – or wanted to – build up strong organizations (Pedersen, 1987).

In terms of their organizational structure, the components tend to be the same. At the local level, typically within the individual municipality, the party will have a branch organization in which most of the local activities will take place. In several cases there will be more than one branch per municipality.[17] These local branches will, for purposes of national elections, coordinate their efforts within the organizational framework of a nomination district organization. There are 103 such nomination districts in Denmark, but not all parties will have sufficient strength to maintain organizations in every district. The nomination district organization is the traditional center for nomination activities.

Corresponding to the constituency in each party a constituency organization will coordinate activities at this level, often playing an important role in the organization of the election as well as the nominations.

One level up we find in each party a central national organization: a general assembly/congress-like body, which only meets once in a while; an intermediate board of representatives; and a small executive board which runs the day-to-day affairs of the party, supported in most cases by a secretariat and a secretary general.

Danish parties differ considerably with regard to the role of each of these bodies in the nomination process. The variation comprises several dimensions:

- The potential influence of rank-and-file members vis-à-vis the local branch and/or nomination district leadership;
- The potential influence of the constituency leadership vis-à-vis the leadership at lower levels of the organizational hierarchy;
- The potential influence of the leadership of the central party apparatus vis-à-vis the constituency and/or nomination of district leaders.

In general the current situation with regard to the distribution of influence on nominations within the parties reflects past experiences and conflicts within the parties. Rules are changed quite often in response to alterations in the balance between the rank-and-file and the central leadership, and thus the variations across time as well as across parties are only understandable, when they are seen in a time perspective. This perspective will not be developed here (but see for example Bille, 1997). Only a crude map will be provided of the actual configuration.

At one end of the spectrum we find the situation in one of the parties that nowadays claims to represent the ideas that became popular in Danish politics in 1973 with the meteoric rise to prominence of Mogens Glistrup and his Progress Party. In the 1998 election two parties were campaigning on this platform, ideologically more or less identical. In the more prominent of the two, the Danish People's Party, the central leadership, not to say the party leader herself, was in complete control of the nominations. The central executive board of the party *(Hovedbestyrelsen)*, under the leadership of Pia Kjærsgaard, selected the top candidates for each of the 17 constituencies. Furthermore the executive decided to use the so-called "party list option" in the nominations (cf. below), thus taking all precautions to have the first 17 candidates to be elected in case of victory rank-ordered. The party leader proclaimed that this strict procedure was a provisional safeguard, which would only be in force at this first election (*Fyens Stiftstidende*, Nov. 2 1997). The main rationale for the centralist procedure was to avoid the mistakes of the earlier Progress Party, and to make sure that the candidates were loyal, cooperative – "and not too queer" – as the party leader expressed it.

In the other parties the national party leadership may sometimes wish that it could impose the same procedures, but in practice the situation is very different.[18] In several, but not in all parties, the central leadership will have a kind of veto right vis-à-vis the local organization, but it will not be able to impose a candidate against the will of the local majority. The central organization may suggest names, and it may try to convince and persuade, but very often it is without luck. Plenty of stories are known in which an unlucky candidate, often a candidate of some national prominence and endorsed by the central leadership, is defeated by a local favorite.[19] Some observers even suggest that it comes close to political suicide to attempt a "parachutage", as the French call it. "There is a difference in coming from the outside, saying, "I really understand you well!", and then to be a daily part of the local problems", is a typical argument used by a local "favorite son" against a "top-hung" candidate (*Weekendavisen*, March 19-25, 1999). There are, of course, also a few instances of – indirect – exceptions to the rule of local autonomy. Thus the party leader and maybe also other "top brass" may be given preferential treatment, if they wish to move from one constituency to another. They may – like all other members – wish to do so, either in order to safeguard their incumbency, or because they find it preferable to seek nomination closer to their home or to the seat of parliament.[20] But party leaders definitely find it easier to move than the ordinary member. It is probably considered an honor to host a party leader or an influential minister. By doing so the local organization will make the political platform better for the incumbent leader, and in return the leader may eventually provide some services for the region or town in question. In such cases the local autonomy, and especially the preferences for the local favorite, may move into the background. But these are the exceptions.

The formal right of the central leadership to reject a proposal made by a local nominating agency exists in several parties, as said. But in three of the older parties, the Agrarian Liberals (*Venstre*), the Radical Liberals (*Radikale Venstre*), and the Conservatives (*Konservative Folkeparti*), as well as in one of the newer parties, the Center Democrats (*Centrumdemokraterne*), the autonomy of the local organization is totally undisputed. What shall be understood by "the local organization" may, however, differ. In most cases it means the party organization within the nomination district (*opstillingskreds*). But in some instances the organization at the higher level of the county – and thus the constituency (*Amtskreds*) – plays an important role, because it is exactly at this level that the placement of the candidates within the individual nomination districts takes place. To give just one example: In the organization of the Center Democrats the nomination process is carried out at the level of the constituency, using an internal ballot among all members of this very small party within the constituency. The candidates subsequently decide, according to their ranking in the ballot, in which nomination district they would like to become nominated. In this case, the role of the party organization at the lowest level of course may become very marginal.

Until the 1960s the nominations mainly took place in the party organization of the nomination district, and the nomination proper was conducted some time ahead of the expected election. The formal decision was made by the General Assembly of the organization or by a specially called meeting. Two major modifications have been made to this arrangement in recent times, not in all, but in several parties. These modifications have had important consequences for the entire process and its outcome.

First, it has now become the rule in some parties that the nomination, at least formally, has to be made once every year. Thus a kind of "exam" may take place every now and then. In other parties the nominating organization only has to make sure that a candidate is nominated and thus "in position" in time, before the election is called.

Second, and much more important, is the introduction of a decisive ballot in connection with nominations. Four parties, the Socialist People's Party, the Social Democrats, the Center Democrats, and the Agrarian Liberals use this device. The ballot is carried out either at the level of the constituency (*vide* the Center Democrats) or, as in the Social Democratic Party, at the level of the nomination district in cases when more than one candidate is proposed.

The combinations of these dimensions produce a complex picture that is summarized in Table 2.1. But one has to emphasize that there is much greater variety to be found when also intraparty variations are taken into consideration.

Table 2.1 Who are in Control of Nominations in the Danish Parties?

Party	Centralized Control	Approval by Central Apparatus	Local/regional autonomy	Mandatory or optional decisive ballot
Unity List	No info.	No info.	No info.	No info.
Socialist People's Party	No	Yes	No	Yes
Social Democratic Party	No	Yes	No	Yes
Radical Liberals	No	No	Yes	No
Center Democrats	No	No	Yes	Yes
Christian People's Party	No	Yes	No	No
Agrarian Liberals	No	No	Yes	Yes
Conservatives	No	No	Yes	No
Progress Party	No	Yes	No	No
Danish People's Party	Yes	No	No	No

Source: Based upon information in Katz & Mair, 1992, cf. also Bille, 1997.

At the opposite side of the spectrum from Pia Kjærsgaard's party with its completely centralized nominations we thus find the situations, most notably in the Agrarian Liberal party, where the local rank-and-file is in complete – or almost complete – command, because the nomination is carried out at the lowest local level, utilizing some kind of ballot procedure and without possibility of interference from the central organization within the party. It is important to emphasize also that the nomination procedures within the Danish People's Party constitute a clear exception to the general picture, which is that party members, the rank-and-file, are able to exert considerable influence on the selection of candidates in most parties.

It can be argued that this description of the procedural variation at best provides a somewhat formalistic picture. Thus it does not take into consideration that the party organizations vary widely, from fairly big ones to very small groups. A general assembly, not to speak about a ballot, is not the same kind of political arena in a very small party and in a bigger urban party organization. A meeting or a ballot in a party like the Center Democrats, with approx. 1,200 members nationwide, but scattered across 275 municipalities, 103 nomination districts, and 17 constituencies, is, in quantitative as well as qualitative terms, very different from a gathering in a big Social Democratic organization in a major city. The dramatic decline in the party membership figures in the older parties is bound to have had an impact on the organization cultures. Very little is known about these matters.[21] Much more research is needed in order to make it possible for us to understand the rich variety of influence patterns.

Who are the candidates?

There does not exist any recent study of the socio-economic composition of the total universe of candidates. An older study from the early 1970s is, however, probably still relevant to some extent.

In connection with the 1973 election a study was made of all candidates for elections between 1960 and 1973 (Foverskov, 1979). Among the findings was the observation that the distribution of candidates on a number of relevant dimensions tended to be stable over time. The profiles also differed considerably from one party to another. The following figures give a summary description, see Table 2.2.

Table 2.2 *The Percentage Share of Specific Social Categories among the Candidates for Five Parties. The Folketing Election of 1973.*

Party Category	Social Democrats	Conservatives	Center Democrats	Christian People's Party	Progress Party
Academics, all Categories	17	25	15	18	10
Public Sector Employees	22	12	23	32	4
Independent urban sector	2	23	19	9	37
Workers of all categories	9	0	2	4	9
Women	16	21	13	19	8
N=	104	95	103	57	195

Source: Foverskov, 1979.

The result of the nomination processes within the various parties tended to be a distribution of candidates, which although varying across the left-right spectrum of parties was also marked by the general appearance of considerable numbers of academics and public sector employees, these two categories often combined in the very same person. The Progress Party as a new protest movement differed conspicuously in this respect. Its main base was the small-scale employer or tradesman from the cities.

Since no studies have been conducted of the results of the nomination process since the early 1970s, it was necessary for this chapter to carry out a small analysis. The previously mentioned 96 candidates in the Funen constituency at the 1998 election have been tabulated according to gender, age, occupation, educational level and information about home address. Although the sample is not statistically controllable, and although the information is not in all cases sufficiently precise, the distribution of the candidates on various dimensions may still tell a story, see Table 2.3.

Table 2.3 The Candidates in the Funen Constituency in the 1998 Folketing Election. Distributed by Party and Various Social Categories. Absolute Numbers.

Party Label	Women	"Locals"	Academic Education	Younger (<40 y)	Public Sector empl.	First nomination	All candidates
A	3	8	0	3	4	3	9
B	3	7	7+	2	6	6	9
C	3	8	3+	4	5+	5	9
D	4	7	1	1	3	4	9
F	3	7	1	2	5+	4	9
O	1	5	1	3	1+	5(6)	6
Q	2	6	1+	3	3+	4	8
V	1	7	3+	1	3+	4	8
Z	-	4	0	2	2+	9	9
Ø	3	7	3+	1	4+	3	8
U	1	10	2+	2	4+	11	11
Other	-	-	-	-	-	1	1
ALL	25	76	22	24	40	59	96

Source: Based upon unofficial statistics, Fyens Stiftstidende, March 13, 1998.

Note: "+" in connection with a figure indicates that the estimate may be on the low side.

A quarter of the Funen candidates were women; a quarter were younger candidates, i.e. below 40 years of age. Approximately one in four had an academic education, and a little less than half of the candidates were employed in the public sector. If candidates who are students or who live off social benefits are included, a majority of the candidates could be characterized as being affiliated with or dependent on the public sector. Finally it is noteworthy that approximately 60 percent of the Funen candidates were running for the first time in this constituency.

Even more interesting is the observation that among the 96 candidates the great majority, i.e. 79 percent were local candidates in the sense that they lived within the boundary of the constituency of Funen. The constituency also tended to elect local candidates: 10 out of 15 elected were "locals". Whether this is a characteristic feature of all constituencies still needs to be analyzed, but it is somewhat in doubt (cf. Pedersen, 1975).

Proper behavior during the electoral campaign

Once nominated a candidate is expected to serve his nomination district and the wider constituency. As a minimum he is expected to participate in meetings locally.

If he or she behaves well, renomination is probable, but as in most other countries it now and then happens that a candidate is forced to resign. This may even happen to a candidate who has become elected. It also happens that a competitor is nominated in another nomination district within the constituency with the – more or less explicit – purpose of defeating an incumbent who may have "run out of steam". But if the candidate, especially the incumbent, behaves, he (or she) is pretty sure of renomination.

All candidates will carry out meetings within the party on a regular basis. For those candidates who are nominated outside the Metropolitan Copenhagen constituencies this can be quite a burden, involving considerable amounts of travel. Between elections the heaviest burden is, however, laid on the incumbent members of parliament. They are expected to act as agents for the local area, sometimes the nomination district, mostly the constituency, but sometimes also the wider region. With the emergence of local and regional television channels as well as regionally oriented newspapers, the local pressure put on members of parliament can be considerable and felt even by the non-incumbent candidates.

As soon as the *Folketing* election is called, a set of informal norms is activated. Within the wider constituency the candidates of any party are expected to fight together against the candidates from other parties and, explicitly, not to compete among themselves. This means that they will normally only campaign within the boundaries of their own nomination district. In some instances constituency-wide agreements to this effect are even made explicit within the party. The norm will in particular stipulate that a candidate will normally put up posters, circulate leaflets, and canvass voters only in his "own" nomination district, unless explicit agreements have been made to act otherwise.

There are two modifications to this norm. First, prominent members or leaders in the party may carry out meetings nationwide, but still they will respect their colleagues in their home constituency and not interfere with these "neighbors". Secondly, if the party cannot at all expect to elect a member from the entire constituency, or if only one candidate has a chance to get returned, the candidates may behave in a more relaxed way.

This norm of "non-intervention", which has been especially strong in the Social Democratic Party, is sometimes broken by young candidates or by mavericks.[22] It is increasingly being called into question, especially in those parts of the country where the old-fashioned electoral district is no longer considered a "natural" political unit, i.e. where e.g. candidates *de facto*, if not *de jure*, are nominated in the wider constituency, cf below.

The changing role of the voters

The most remarkable aspect of the Danish nomination system is the role played by the ordinary voter on election day. Whereas voters in many countries, when they stand in the polling booth, are presented with a *fait accompli* in the sense that they are not given a meaningful choice among the candidates from any given party, the situation is different in Denmark. Without turning the election into a pure choice between individuals, Danish voters are in most parties given a possibility to choose among several candidates, and they often exercise their choice in such a way that it influences the final selection.

It is hardly possible to understand the rather complicated system of preferential voting in Denmark unless one sees it as an emergent institutional order, which took its beginning in the early 20th century and gradually developed into the present format. What has emerged is a situation that was not at all envisaged by the inventors of the electoral system as a realistic outcome, but which was, nevertheless, always present as a hypothetical option. We shall follow the historical development for a while.

Between 1915 and 1920 the Danish electoral system underwent the change from a plurality/first-past-the-post-system to a proportional representation system. The political decision that was made constituted a compromise in many ways, not least in the sense that the parties in parliament tried to preserve at least some of the perceived qualities of the plurality system at the same time as a full-fledged PR-(list) system was introduced. There was among most politicians a wish not to break entirely with the old electoral system.

What the politicians had in mind was that they wanted to preserve the close relationship between the candidates and their local supporters. It was felt that the voter's personal knowledge of and confidence in the local candidate of *his* party was an asset for Danish democracy.[23] This linkage between voter and candidate could be preserved by allowing the voter the option of voting not only for the party, but also, eventually, to cast a vote directly for the candidate who was nominated in the nomination district, in this way demonstrating an appreciation of the candidate himself.

As part of the political compromise it was, however, also decided that the voter should not be forced to vote for the local candidate. An option should exist to cast a vote for one of the other candidates for the party within the wider electoral constituency. "The electoral law should be such that the voter, without forsaking his party, has a choice among more people", was a major aim for one of the political architects of the compromise that introduced PR in Denmark.[24]

During the debates in the parliament a few speakers expressed a fear that such a personal option might eventually lead to "unhealthy competition" among the candidates of the same party, but no serious criticism was voiced against the new arrangement, and no one tried – in public at least – to analyze the various scenarios that were possible within the new framework. Apparently the preferential vote option was mainly considered, firstly, as a way in which to show loyalty for the local candidate, and only secondly as a safety valve for dissatisfied voters. From the very first genuine PR-election in 1920 it was obvious that the parties agitated for a vote for the party and decidedly not for utilizing the option to vote for a candidate from outside the nomination district.

The preferential voting system introduced in 1920 is very complicated, and we need not examine it in detail. Let it suffice to say that it was – and still is – easy to understand how it works, as long as we observe it from the perspective of the individual voter. The voter, when coming into the polling booth, may *either* give his vote to the party, *or* to the candidate nominated in his "own" nomination district, *or* to a candidate for the party in one of the neighboring nomination districts within the constituency.

The complications arise when we look at the options open to the nominating parties. The party in the individual constituency was – and still is – given an option between three main ways in which to present the candidates to the voters, and in which to regulate the way in which votes are counted and distributed among the candidates. Since, however, these three basic options can be combined in many different ways within the constituency, a comprehensive description is well beyond the scope of this chapter.[25]

Figur 2.2 A ballot paper.

Fyns Amts 1. opstillingskreds

Folketingsvalget 1998

A. Socialdemokratiet
Else Marie Mortensen
Poul Andersen
Lotte Bundsgaard
Erling Christensen
Michael Gammelgaard
Carsten Hansen
Frederik Nørgaard
Grete Schødts
Hans Stavnsager

B. Det Radikale Venstre
Claus Brodtkorb
Mogens Godballe
Dorit Myltoft
Erik Persson
Niels Helveg Petersen
Kristian Thorup-Kristensen
Lise Tofthøj
Jan Tønnesen
Hedvig Vestergaard

C. Det Konservative Folkeparti
Per André Andersen
Bendt Bendtsen
Lars Christensen
Jørgen Colding
Anne Henriksen
Niels Jørgen Langkilde
Jan Møller
Pernille Weiss-Pedersen
Annette Winther

D. Centrum-Demokraterne
Elisabeth Nørgård Nielsen
Lis Albertsen
Aksel Hundslev
Ebbe Kalnæs
Ingolf Knudsen
Kim Slott Nielsen
Olaf Nielsen
Anne-Mia Palmer
Susanne Uhre-Prahl

F. Socialistisk Folkeparti
Steen Gade
Torben Andersen
Karsten Hønge
Hanne Lauritsen
Peter Madsen
Inga-Britt Olsen
Pia Olsen
Kaj Stillinger
Leif Søndergaard

O. Dansk Folkeparti
Ib Dalsfledt
Kristian Thulesen Dahl
Svend-Aage Nielsen
Morten S. Petersen
Bjarne B. Tychsen
Tina Petersen

U. Demokratisk Fornyelse
Kresten Bjerre
Niels Bondo
Michael Christensen
Lars O. Grønborg
Erik E. Jungsholm
Mogens Keinicke
Henrik Madsen
Ole Arne Monrad Møller
Leif Nybo
Inge Sørensen
Poul Veppler

V. Venstre, Danmarks Liberale Parti
Arne Skipper
Mariann Fischer Boel
Peter Brixtofte
Erik Larsen
Lars Chr. Lilleholt
Ove Erling Mortensen
Niels Ingolf Rasmussen
Jørgen Schleimann

Z. Fremskridtspartiet
Peter Hartvig
Erik Dissing
Jørgen Kramsbjerg Hansen
Jens Munk
Bjarne Nissen
Klaus Nymark
Lillian Olsen
Benny Sasser
Søren Eliot Sørensen

Ø. Enhedslisten - De Rød-Grønne
Søren Kolstrup
Jesper Kiel
Bernard Jeune
Stine Johansen
Knud Clemmensen
Inger Christensen
Anne Grethe Toksvig
Regnar Hansen

Uden for partierne
Svend Jensen

If a party organization wants to be as much as possible in control of who gets elected within the constituency, it will try to minimize the effectiveness of the voters' behavior. This is done by putting up the candidates for the party in a "party list order", decided entirely by the party organization. This format creates a definite rank order, in which the party wants to see the candidates elected. The voter may vote for the top candidate or for one of the other candidates on the list, but very many "undisciplined" voters are required in the constituency to change the rank order. This way of composing the list was until some years ago not only used by the small parties on the left wing, but was also the preferred practice of the Social Democratic Party. In recent elections the "party list" has only been used by the Socialist People's Party and the left-wing party, *"Enhedslisten"*, and in both parties only in some of the constituencies. This practice apparently is decreasing in importance.

Until a few decades ago the predominant option used by the parties consisted in nominating one candidate in each of the nomination districts within the constituency and letting the candidates be elected in the order of their total number of votes, this sum being defined as the sum of votes for the party in the nomination district, the personal votes received by the candidate in the nomination district, and the personal votes received from voters in other districts within the constituency. When this option is used, and this is still the case in the Socialist People's Party as well as in a few other instances, the electoral fate of the candidate is mainly influenced by the relative size of the electorate in his "home" nomination district, but in some cases the net number of personal votes received from the outside may be of importance. For this reason this last type of personal votes have been named "effective personal votes" in contrast to the "ineffective personal votes", i.e. those personal votes cast within the "home" district for "its" candidate. The latter votes do not play a separate role from that of ordinary votes cast for the party in the district (Pedersen, 1966).

The third option is the so-called "simultaneous list organization". In this option the candidates for the party are only in a formal way – if at all – nominated in a nomination district. In practice they are running at the same time and on equal terms in all the nomination districts within the constituency. They are elected in a rank order determined predominantly by their relative number of personal votes.

Table 2.4 The Utilization of Main Options of Nomination Within Parties in the Election of 1994: All 103 Nomination Districts.

PARTY	Party List Option	Nomination District Option	Simultaneous Nomination Option	Total Number of Candidates
Social Democrats	0	0	106	106
Radical Liberals	0	0	98	98
Conservatives	0	0	103	103
Center Democrats	0	0	96	96
Socialist People's Party	71	9	23	103
Christian People's Party	0	0	104	104
Liberals	0	4	95	99
Progress Party	0	0	103	103
Unity List	34	54	11	99
Total Number of Candidates	105 candidates	67 candidates	739 candidates	911 candidates

Source: Own calculation based upon Table 21 in Folketingsvalget, September 21, 1994.

Table 2.4 summarizes the patterns of utilization of these options in the election of 1994. The information given only maps the major patterns of nomination, but does not contain details about the many different variations that are possible, when these three options are combined with other possibly varying parameters, for example the number of candidates nominated in each constituency, the relationship between candidate and district, etc.[26]

As mentioned earlier the present pattern of nominations is fairly new. In 1960 90 percent of all nominations belonged to the "nomination district option"-type, and "simultaneous nominations" were used in a mere 6 percent of all cases. This situation started to be reversed rather dramatically in the late 1960s and early 1970s. After a stable situation in the 1980s it apparently has started to change again. Thus in the 1994 election the reversing was complete – with only 15 percent "nomination-district"- type nominations and no less than 82 percent "simultaneous nominations".[27] It is rare in an otherwise fairly stable political system to see a similar fundamental change.

Before we take a closer look at some of the effects of this change, a few more words are needed about the voters' utilization of their right to cast a preferential vote.

During the 1920s, immediately after the right to cast a preferential vote had been introduced, most voters tended to vote personally for the candidate who was nominated within their "own" nomination district. Relatively few voted for the party itself, and even fewer would cast a vote for a candidate from one of the other nomination districts. Thus the vote was "ineffective" in the sense that it was given to the candidate who would also have gained it if a party vote had been cast instead. Right up until 1939 the "ineffective" votes made up 80-90 percent of all votes.

Gradually this situation changed, and it did so in two different directions. First, the voters' preference for casting personal votes decreased, from about 70 percent in 1945 to about 40 percent in the 1960s. Second, during the same period the amount of "effective" personal votes tended to increase somewhat.

Writing in the mid-1960s about this tendency, this author suggested that the development was indicative of a loosening of the traditional bond between the voters and the nomination district. The preferential vote option makes it possible for the voter not only to avoid supporting the "local" candidate, but also to give specific support to special candidate categories, highly visible candidates, and, first and foremost, incumbent members of parliament (Pedersen, 1966).

On the other hand a full-scale analysis of all candidates for election in the four elections 1960-68 demonstrated that the selection of candidates by the party organizations, and in particular the nomination in various types of more or less "safe" districts, was a much more influential factor in the recruitment process than the use of the preferential vote for "effective " personal voting. The voters tended to cast their personal votes on those candidates who had already been favored by the nominators. In a way the voters with their vote "approved" the choice made by the party organization (Johansen & Kristensen, 1979).

In 1971 some important changes were made in the Danish electoral system. In connection with a major municipal reform, the number of nomination districts was lowered from 126 to 103, and the number of constituencies was also lowered from 23 to 17. At the same time a new option was made available for the nominating party organizations. They might in the future use the so-called simultaneous nomination option, but combine it with nomination of each candidate in a separate nomination district. Thus the link between the candidate and the district could be preserved, but at the same time the party's candidates within the constituency would be given an almost equal standing in the competition for votes.

These changes in the legal institutions and the political options, together with the dramatic increase in the electoral volatility during the early 1970s and the ensuing breakup of the traditional party system, had far-reaching effects upon the nomination processes and upon the role of the voters. Thus it has been thoroughly documented that "safe" constituencies tended to disappear as the predictability of electoral success diminished, but it has also been suggested that the effects of the personal votes continued to be that those social categories among the candidates who were already favored in the nomination process proper continued to be favored by the voters. In this respect the pattern of the 1960s continued into the 1970s (Johansen & Kristensen, 1979).

Unfortunately the research just mentioned has not been continued. Until a new analysis has been done, we will have to do with a small, partial analysis, done explicitly for this chapter. Since the most conspicuous change in Danish political recruitment in recent times consists in the considerable increase in the nomination of, and election of, women, this partial analysis will deal with this issue.

A special case: the increasing success rate of female candidates

In 1966 as well as in 1988 the women's share of the Danish population was 51 percent. But in the same years the share of female legislators was changing from 11 percent to 31 percent (Christoffersen, 1992: 346). Ten years later, in the 1998-election, the women's share reached 37 percent. Although there is still a long way to go before the magical 50-50 distributions have been achieved, the change is impressive and is given a great deal of attention in the media.

Much less interest has been given to the women's share of the candidates and to the dynamics of women's representation, including the effects of the various institutional arrangements on the change.

In the older studies it was found, again and again, that female candidates often had a hard time. During the pre1971/73 regime they were disfavored during the nomination process, but they were also quite often disfavored in the election itself. Thus, when a woman was nominated in a certain district, she eventually received many personal votes from (women in) other nomination districts within the constituency. But relatively more voters in her "own" district might abandon her by voting for a candidate for the party from one of the other districts. The net result of these tendencies was not necessarily to the advantage of the female candidate (Pedersen, 1966; Johansen & Kristensen, 1979).

In a special analysis of these mechanisms Peter Foverskov found that female candidates were disfavored during the 1960s, but that the situation later approached a balance. In the elections of 1971 and 1973 the proportion of female members of parliament was equal to the proportion of female candidates, whereas it had been much lower during the 1960s (Foverskov, 1979: 216). Writing about the beginning of a period when women started to make considerable progress as candidates and as members of parliament, this author may just have caught the first glimpse of a more fundamental change in the interplay between nominations and elections; it was exactly in the election of

1971 that the percentage of women elected rose from 11 percent (reported for 1968) to a new high of 17 percent.

How much of the recent success of women can be traced to improved conditions during the nominations, bringing more female candidates forward, and entering them into favorable, even "safe", nomination districts? And how much is an effect of preferential voting in a situation, when four out of five candidates are competing for votes in the so-called simultaneous nomination option, thus in a situation that should give the ordinary voter a maximum of influence on the election? These are difficult questions to answer, and only some preliminary answers can be given.[28]

Our first observation will be that the number of female members has grown conspicuously since 1971, but so has the number of nominated female candidates, see Table 2.5.

Table 2.5 *Female Candidates and Folketing Members as Percentage of all Candidates, resp. Members. 1971-98. Grouped Data: Averages over Three Elections.*

Election Periods	Female Candidates (Pct.)	Elected Females (Pct.)
1971-1975	16.6	16.2
1977-1981	22.3	21.7
1984-1988	29.3	29.3
1990-1998	29.4	35.0

Source: Calculations based upon data from Folketingsvalget, March 11, 1998.

The growth rates were almost identical during the first two decades, suggesting that the advance of the women happened during the nominations, but also suggesting that female candidates were not favored additionally during the election proper. In other words a plausible hypothesis would be that the effect of preferential voting did not favor the female candidates in particular during the elections of the 1970s and the 1980s, but may have done so in recent elections.

Upon closer inspection this suggestion can be made more precise. The elections during the 1990s (1990, 1994, and 1998) saw at the same time a considerable growth in the percentage of women elected – from

34 to 38 percent) and a considerable decrease in the percentage of female candidates (from 31 to 28 percent), suggesting that the voters gave a relative preference to female candidates.

This kind of reasoning is, however, only suggestive, since it is based upon an observation of highly aggregated data. A breakdown of the 1998 data on regions and constituencies tells us that the geographical variations are very large, from constituencies with zero female members to a Copenhagen constituency, in which two thirds of all elected members were women. A comparison across parties also indicates that the party voters are more influential in some of the small parties (Radical Liberals and Center Democrats), where the women outnumber the men in the parliamentary groups, than in the bigger parties. Again one has to warn against hasty conclusions, since these observations are made on an aggregate level as well.

It is possible to dig a bit deeper by looking at the relative positions of the women within the constituencies. An analysis of a partial set of data from one election – the 1994 election – and four parties (Social Democrats, Radical Liberals, Conservatives, and Liberals) has been done. In this analysis male and female candidates have been compared with regard to the position they reached during the election, see Table 2.6. Of a total of 406 candidates 124 were women, and it is seen that these women did quite well in the election. They did not finish in the hopeless positions nearly as often as the men did. They did, in relative terms, more often end up in situations where they would be "first substitute" in the constituency, or where they would be among the elected, if not as the first one in the constituency. Their share of the very top positions was, however, almost as high as that of the men.

Such a picture lends itself to various interpretations. Are the party organizations nominating women in positions with a higher probability of election, *ceteris paribus*, or are the female candidates helped to their better results by a lion's share of preferential votes? It looks as if the women are mostly placed – and maybe also tending to place themselves – in nomination districts that are not entirely hopeless. On the other hand they are not given preferential treatment in the competition for the very top slots, those coveted "safe seats" that still exist in some of the parties.

Table 2.6 The Distribution of Female, Male and All Candidates by Their Position in the Election of 1994.

	Male Candidates	Female candidates	All candidates
Elected as no. 1 in constituency	15.2	12.9	14.5
Elected, lower positions	16.0	27.4	19.5
Substitute no. 1 in constituency	13.5	23.4	16.5
Substitute, lower positions	55.3	36.3	49.5
All	100.0	100.0	100.0
N	282	124	406

Source: Own calculations, based on Folketingsvalget, September 21, 1994.

An even more impressive picture of the changing placement of female candidates can be found in Table 2.7.

Table 2.7 The Distribution of Female Candidates with Regard to Their Rank Order in the Election. Percentage of All Candidates for the Four "Old" Parties. Selected Sessions.

a) Percentages

	1920 (April)	1935	1950	1964	1994
Elected as no. 1	0.3	0.5	0.9	1.4	3.9
Elected, lower pos.	0.5	0	1.1	1.9	8.4
Substitute no. 1	0.5	0.2	1.9	2.3	7.1
Substitute lower pos.	3.1	2.4	7.9	5.7	11.1
All Women	4.4	3.1	11.8	11.3	30.5
N=	380	415	457	477	406

b) Index values (1920 = 100)

	1920 (April)	1935	1950	1964	1994
Elected as no. 1	100	167	300	467	1300
Elected, lower pos.	100	50	220	380	1680
Substitute no. 1	100	40	380	460	1420
Substitute lower pos.	100	77	255	184	358
All Women	100	70	268	257	693

Source: Pedersen, 1965; Folketingsvalget, September 21, 1994.

In this table it is possible to follow the share of female candidates and their distribution with regard to elective position, and to do so over the entire period since 1920. The growth in the relative share is clearly visible, as is the tendency for women to end up in better positions in the elections. The figures have been transformed into indices in order to make the growth rates comparable. The figures speak for themselves. Dramatic change has taken place since the women obtained the right to vote and to serve as candidates and as members of parliament.

Turnover and recruitment

The amount of – or level of – membership turnover in a parliament is a crucial variable in any study of nominations. Voluntary resignations as well as not quite voluntary resignations from the position as member make room for new recruits. Often such resignations are prompted by the loss of incumbency. The member is defeated in an election and decides immediately thereafter, or after some hesitation, eventually even after unsuccessful attempts to win back the seat, that the time has come to resign from candidacy. It probably also happens from time to time that the incumbent politician gets ousted brutally by the local party organization. Such situations are, however, difficult to find and to verify.

But there are other good reasons for terminating one's career. Death or illnesses are obvious reasons. Retirement due to old age is also an obvious reason. Promotion to higher political office, e.g. in the EU, may happen to a few. What these situations have in common is that they open up a position for a new political recruit.

In Danish legislative politics turnover was quite high during the 19th century. In a situation with amateur-politicians, a majority electoral system and a weak and turbulent party system, careers were often quite short. As the party system matured and regular career routes and patterns developed, the turnover rate gradually dropped, from 30 percent during the first 30 years after 1849 to approximately 20 percent over the next eight decades. The average age of the career termination during the same period rose from 50 years in the early decades to almost 60 years around 1960. Even more conspicuous is the observation that almost a third of the legislators had their careers terminated due to death, illness or old-age retirement, i.e. "non-political" reasons, during the early 1960es. The corresponding figure for the first decades after 1849 was a mere 12 percent. This development has been analyzed in terms of institutionalization processes, closely related to the "freezing" and "frozen" party system (Pedersen, 1977; Eliassen & Pedersen, 1978; Pedersen, 1994).

Stability was interrupted, first by a generational upheaval in some parties during the late 1960s, second, and more effectively, by the 1973 "Earthquake"-election, which, for good, perhaps, changed the Danish party landscape in terms of the number and character of the parties. In the longer run the recruitment patterns did, however, gradually return to or approximate their older shape. The development is visualized in Table 2.8.

Table 2.8 Indicators of Legislative Turnover in Denmark 1947-1998. Grouped Data: Averages over Three Elections.

Elections	Retirement Rate(*)	Incumbents' Success Rate(**)	Turnover Rate(***)
1947-53	8	81	26
1953-60	10	90	24
1964-68	10	87	22
1971-75	11	72	35
1977-81	13	78	30
1984-88	7	84	23
1990-98	11	81	28

Source: Pedersen, 1994 for the period 1947-88. For the last three elections author's own calculations.

* Retirement Rate defined as retiring incumbents as a percentage of all seats in parliament
** Incumbents' Success Rate defined as re-elected incumbents as a percentage of all incumbents running for re-election
*** Turnover Rate defined as newcomers as a percentage of all seats in parliament.

Although it is difficult to tell if it is good or bad for a democratic party system to live with a high or a low rate of turnover, we may dare to say that an overall success rate of approximately 80 percent leaves room for renewal of parliament without opening up the doors widely. The party leaderships are still able to control to some extent the entry. The kind of new recruitment, which the French aptly characterize as *parachutage*, is possible, but not likely. But it has indeed happened in connection with the emergence of *flash parties* (like the *Fælles Kurs* party which with short notice entered the parliament in 1987); the various splinter parties of the Progress Party, as well as that party itself, also have seen several instances of nominations of completely inexperienced political activists who were then catapulted into the *Folketing*, mostly for short and undistinguished legislative careers.

Careful selection and grooming of ambitious activists is, however, more common, and in some of the parties it may require a long apprenticeship before a chance to get nominated turns up, even a longer time to get a nomination in a constituency which promises election. When a party is increasing its parliamentary strength, it is easier to start a political career. The opposite situation characterizes small parties that are stagnating or contracting. In such parties new recruitment may for several election periods be out of the question, if the incumbent and leading politicians are occupying the – still – safe seats.

These statements are not very precise. The reason for the vagueness is the scarcity of documentation in the Danish case.

Concluding comments

At the entrance into the 21st century a complex pattern has developed with regard to political recruitment to the Danish parliament. Some features look stable, others are in flux.

The initial mobilization, socialization, and prescreening of ambitious individuals still take place in parties, but these parties are not the same organizations as in earlier times.

Some parties belong to the group of "new" parties. They have only weak membership organizations. In order to become a candidate, one has to be a member of the party, and only members nominate candidates. With relatively few party members the nomination process tends to "degenerate" into the same kind of "nomination by notables" that characterized the popular movements and nascent political parties during the 19th century. The obvious difference is that in the latter situation notables were "status notables"; in the new parties one obtains political status by becoming a member of the party organization. It is relatively easy to move ahead in the party, from being an ordinary member, to becoming a party official, and, eventually, a candidate for some kind of political office – sublocal, local, or national. But due to the smallness of the party, the final step into serious national candidacy is an obstacle of considerable proportions. Unpredictability is, however, an important feature in these parties.

In the traditional parties, dubbed the "old parties", emphasis is still on the popular basis of the organization. Even if membership has dived, these parties can still function as mass parties, with an organized training of new recruits and with possibilities of genuine screening of candidates. In at least 3-5 parties it is possible to maintain a proper *cursus honorum*, including the notion of movements from "hopeless" candidacy, over "possible/risky" nominations, and forward to more and more "safe" constituencies. In these parties the prospective and ambitious individual may still dream about – or plan – an orderly political career.

So much said about the early stages of the recruitment process and the process of nomination. The picture becomes more complex when we look at the way candidates are being treated in the election proper. At present it is, however, possible to state as a conclusion that the party organizations and their leadership – nationally as well as locally – have lost some of the gatekeeping control. The rank-and-file members, and often a small minority only, have become more influential during the nomination process. The ordinary party voters, organized or not organized, have gained more influence on election day, simply by their increasing use of the option of casting a preferential (personal) vote. But for a more precise evaluation of the relative influence of party leadership, rank-and-file membership, and the voters, we will have to await new research in which the distinction between small/new and big/old parties undoubtedly will be of crucial importance.

3

Finland: Formalized Procedures with Member Predominance

SOILE KUITUNEN

Introduction

In Finland, as in many other European countries, political parties organize the process of nominating parliamentary candidates. A firm indicator of party dominance both in nominations and elections is that outside the party lists, without party sponsorship, only seven candidates have been elected to parliament during the time period from 1945 to 1995 (Tarasti & Taponen 1996, 86). The chain of delegation operates at several stages in the candidate selection process. Firstly, the decision-making power over candidate lists is delegated mostly from voters to local and district party organizations and, as a consequence, only a small minority, about 10 percent of the Finnish population, is entitled to act on behalf of the whole electorate in nominations.[29] Secondly, local party branches along with local party members are acting as principals in delegating authority to their agents, the members of parliament. As a result of this chain of delegation, MPs act on behalf of two major groups of principals: parties and electors. Electors may exert control over agents' actions at a later stage by removing unwanted legislators. Likewise, local party branches and party members are able to intrude into this selection process, but at an earlier phase, by refraining from voting for incumbents or previous candidates in party primaries.

Certain elements in the Finnish nomination system contribute both to its formalization and decentralization. Finland is one of the few countries along with Germany, Norway and the United States in which law to a certain extent regulates candidate selection, even if the provisions of law are not always binding (Gallagher 1988c, 257). For example, in Finland electoral laws constitute only a loose framework for a process in which party rules dominate by directing how delegation of authority is to be conducted and how candidates are to be selected for parliamentary elections (see Tarasti & Taponen 1996; Timonen 1981). On the other hand, it is apparent that the nomination system in Finland is highly decentralized. Since authority over nominations is mostly delegated from the electorate to local party members and party branches, national party leadership has only limited and theoretical possibilities to involve itself in the selection of candidates. Nevertheless, in the case of severe internal conflicts within the party, the party center may wield some influence over the otherwise locally centered nominations.

The following sections give an outline of the Finnish nomination system in parliamentary elections especially from the principal-agent viewpoint. Firstly, the historical development of the candidate selection system is traced by describing the major reforms in electoral law on parliamentary elections, as well as in party statutes and in procedures used during the twentieth century. It will be shown that the Finnish system has gradually evolved from a pure Scandinavian list system to a system in which ordinary voters are able to prioritize both individual candidates and parties. Secondly, the aim of the study is to outline the current context for candidate nomination shaped by the party and the electoral system, and thirdly, by drawing upon survey data gathered from district party organizations, to present nomination practices and procedures used in the 1995 elections. Furthermore, the more informal aspects of the nominations have been illuminated by studying party district officials' evaluation of the essential qualities sought in candidates.[30] In addition, in order to determine the effects of nominations and election on the socio-demographic representation, background characteristics of the aspirants, candidates and legislators are scrutinized.

In the final part of this study, the employment of sanction and reward mechanisms presented for the ordinary voters and party selectorates are examined by analyzing the rate of turnover among deputies and candidates along with the reasons for turnover. Moreover, the turnover effects on two distinct groups, incumbents and women, will be explored by means of three indicators: by comparing the numbers of newcomers, past and old deputies. Finally, on the basis of the main results obtained in individual sections of this chapter, some general conclusions are drawn particularly with respect to institutional arrangements apparent in nominations as well as to delegation and accountability mechanisms utilized by both party selectorates and electors.

The nomination system

Historical development

In many European countries, including Finland, the nomination system is shaped by legal, electoral and party systems, which together constitute the broad context for activities of individuals, parties and other recruitment agencies. This socio-political context has often been called an "opportunity structure" (Norris & Lovenduski 1995; Schlesinger 1994). According to the principal-agent model, the contract design governing the delegation of decision-making power over candidate selection from voters to representatives, i.e. electoral laws and nomination laws, is of great importance. The transformation of the nomination system in Finland has been substantially influenced by alterations made in the law concerning parliamentary elections and, more generally, by reforms in the electoral system (see Tarasti & Taponen 1987). During the 20th century five points in time are of particular relevance in this respect: 1935, 1955, 1967, 1969 and 1975 when the current Electoral Act came into effect. In the following sections these major modifications and their influence on the nomination procedures of the parties will be outlined and the consequences of these reforms for both the evolution of the nomination system and the process of delegation in particular will be analyzed.

Although parties did not have any official status in Finnish politics until the late 1960s, they in practice dominated electioneering by carrying the main responsibility for putting forward candidates, constituting associations of individual eligible voters and establishing electoral alliances (see Nousiainen 1992, 161). During the time period from 1906 to 1935, electors were entitled to vote for a maximum of three candidates with the same ballot. Furthermore, voters were able to make use of the right both to alter the order of the candidates on the lists and to add a candidate not on the previously drawn up lists. (Tarasti & Taponen 1990, 88) Even if the latter option was very rarely used among the electorate, it actually did have some impact on election results when employed (Tarkiainen 1971, 163-164).

In the early 20th century the nomination procedures of the political parties varied considerably according to the party in question. In addition, these practices were highly informal and unstandardized. Open primaries, as employed in the United States, were used in the northern constituencies of the country and by recently formed parties in particular, but they were given up later due to firm criticism against their undemocratic and unofficial nature (Tarkiainen 1971, 249-255). At the same time the process of candidate selection was also highly centralized, since all campaigning activities and most of those related to candidate selection were directed by the national party leadership (Tarkiainen 1971; Sundberg 1995, 46). Nevertheless, local party members were actually involved in this process since the right to nominate candidates belonged not only to municipal and district organizations but also to local party branches.

A standard became established according to which the name of a particular aspirant should be introduced officially at a formal party meeting, even if the decision about candidates was often made in a highly informal manner at a party meeting at some level of the organization. Examples of the centralism of the nomination system are cases in which all decision-making power was delegated from local party members to local party leaders. (Tarkiainen 1971, 253 & 257-258) With the intention of reducing these oligarchic characteristics of the nomination system, closed party primaries, as opposite to open ones, were introduced. In reality, they were rarely used during the early 1900s except in the Social Democratic Party (SDP), which quite consistently applied this method even before primaries were made obligatory. (Tarkiainen 1971, 261-263)

In the electoral reform of 1935, the number of candidates the voters were permitted to vote for was reduced to two. Though the opportunity to alter the order of candidates was withdrawn, voters still had the right to write the name of their own candidate outside the official lists. The system was altered more profoundly in 1955, when the remaining features of the long-list system were rejected. Since this reform candidates have been selected without a ranking order, and voters have been able to vote for only one candidate. (Tarasti & Taponen 1996, 83-84; Sundberg 1995, 51)

Prior to the changes made in the late 1960s it was quite common for the party center to intervene in candidate selection in order to resolve internal party conflicts, to form electoral alliances or to prevent them (Koskiaho 1972, 218; Timonen 1981, 32; Tarkiainen 1971). Almost all parties had a provision in their statutes that the direction of nominations and electoral campaigns was one of the responsibilities of the national party headquarters (Koskiaho 1972, 218-224). As Timonen (1972, 256) has noted, both the regionally-centered procedure used in non-socialist parties and the primaries used in socialist parties contributed to the centralization of candidate selection even though opportunities for the party center involvement were somewhat more circumscribed in the latter than in the former case. An interesting feature in party statutes was that most parties, except the SDP and the SDL (the Social Democratic League of Workers and Smallholders), did not have any detailed instructions on how candidate selection was to be conducted in a constituency. An extreme case in this respect was the Christian League, the party rules of which not only made no references to candidate nominations but also none to parliamentary elections in general (Koskiaho 1972, 217-223).

In comparison with the previous reforms, the nomination system was to a substantial degree transformed in the late 1960s when several reforms concerning candidate selection were introduced. These included the Party Act (1969), the Decree on Public Party Subsidies (1967) and the Electoral Act (1969). According to the Party Act, a party can be registered provided that its internal decision-making and other activities are congruent with the basic principles of democracy (Tarasti & Taponen 1996, 241). The Electoral Act had at least two outstanding consequences for electors and parties: the right to vote for a candidate outside the official lists was withdrawn and, more importantly, the

Electoral Act did not allow parties to nominate one candidate for more than one constituency, a practice which had earlier enabled parties to use popular leaders as vote collectors in several constituencies. Furthermore, according to the 1969 Electoral Act, only registered parties were entitled to put forward the number of candidates equaling the number of seats in a multi-member constituency, which gave the parties the monopoly over nominations after 70 years of informal dominance in parliamentary elections.

These modifications in legislation in the late 1960s actually contributed to narrowing the disparity between the parties and to reducing the old form of authoritarian control of the party center (Helander 1997; Tarasti & Taponen 1990, 91-92; Sundberg 1995, 46). According to the new electoral law, parties were, through their own statutes, entitled to regulate the nomination process in each constituency. Despite this reform some disparities between party statutes still remained. Three Left Wing parties, the SDP, the SDL and the FPDU (the Finnish People's Democratic Union), as well as the Liberal People's Party (the LIB) regulated their nomination activities in more detail compared to other parties. When the socialist parties and the liberals used primaries regularly, other parties hardly ever employed them. One striking feature in party statutes was that some parties, such as the NCP (the National Coalition Party) and the SPP (the Swedish People's Party), still allowed their party center to direct the nomination activities and electoral campaigning in parliamentary elections. (Koskiaho 1972, 218-224)

The current legal system

Mainly due to strong criticism leveled against the informalized nature of the nomination system, a new electoral reform was introduced in 1975. This law still lays down certain principles about candidate selection, thus providing a loose framework for the nomination processes of political parties. The new Electoral Act included two primary changes that also influenced parliamentary nominations. Firstly, the Election Act of 1975 required parties to select their candidates through primaries, which were to be conducted according to electoral law and internal party rules. Party statutes, however, took precedence in relation to provisions of law. Secondly, the right to present candidates was restored to the electors' associations. (Tarasti & Taponen 1990, 93)

Even though some minor modifications have been introduced in the electoral law since the 1975 reform, the basic features of the system have remained unchanged. The Electoral Act of 1975 and section 26 in particular deal with the four stages of the nomination process (see chapter 3.2.4). Only the first two paragraphs of section 26 are mandatory upon parties, while others are to be followed in the event that there is no reference in the party statutes to the particular issue in question. The first phase in the candidate selection process is the nomination of people wishing to be considered for candidature (here, aspirants), which is delegated to local party branches comprising individual members. In addition, a group of 15 party members or more belonging to the same branch, or 30 members belonging to different branches, are entitled to nominate their own aspirants. One peculiarity in the Electoral Act is that no party membership is required for the proposed aspirants, whereas it is a requirement for enfranchisement in the primaries. Despite this, one may assume that the membership is regarded as a basic criterion for selection in most parties.

The second stage is the actual selection of the candidates. According to the Electoral Act, parties are obliged to conduct a primary that is secret and based on equal suffrage. Party members living in a constituency as well as members of party branches are entitled to participate in the primaries. In the event that there are fewer aspirants than can be selected as candidates in a constituency, primaries are not mandatory. Otherwise primaries should be conducted according to party statutes and when no provisions exist on the particular matter in question, the Electoral Act sections 26b through 26f are to be followed. The third and fourth phases of the nomination process concern the final decision about candidates. If no primary was held, nominated aspirants or some of them are selected as candidates. In addition, the district party organization is entitled to replace up to one quarter of the candidates with the lowest proportion of the votes in the party primaries. (Tarasti & Taponen 1996, 250-264) Thus, the right of list manipulation serves as a legitimization for the involvement of the district organization in the nomination process.

Finland is divided into 15 electoral districts, each of which constitutes a separate electoral unit. The number of seats for each district is based on the size of its electorate, with the range from 7 to 31. Parties are entitled to nominate up to 14 candidates in each district, or, if more than 14 MPs are elected in a constituency, an equal number of candidates may be nominated. There are some noteworthy features in the Finnish electoral system that quite dramatically deviate from their Nordic counterparts and, more importantly, account for the variation in their nomination systems. Contrary to other Scandinavian countries, the Finnish electoral system allows voters not only to determine the number of seats for each party in a constituency, but also to decide on the ranking order of the candidates within the party lists. With respect to delegation mechanisms, the final phase of the nominating process is delegated to the voters instead of to the political parties. In the Finnish preferential system, parties are entrusted with the task of nominating candidates, whereas voters decide, by their use of preference votes, who will be elected. Unlike other Scandinavian voters, Finnish voters are able to prioritize both the candidate and the party. Besides this, the tendency towards focusing on candidates in the voting system is emphasized by the fact that the majority of the Finnish voters prefer nowadays to vote for candidates instead of parties (Borg 1997, 106).

Another striking difference between Finland and the other Nordic countries is that Finnish candidates have, in a purely theoretical sense, the same opportunity to be elected. In the Finnish open list system, the position on the lists does not have any influence on the election results. This in turn implies that the Finnish parties are not able to make use of electorally hopeless seats on the lower part of the lists as instruments for ticket balancing, but have to consider the representation of the list as a whole. In other words, party officials are not obliged to think in terms of safe, combative and hopeless list positions, but have to pay attention to the entire list being as representative as possible in relation to the proportion of important sub-groups in the society. There is one exception, the SDP, which ranks its candidates not in alphabetical order but according to candidates' success in the primaries, which may also be conducive to the election results. It has been claimed that the electorate of the Social Democratic Party is perhaps inclined to vote for a candidate appearing at the top of the candidate list (Timonen 1972, 270).

The role of the party

Current party statutes

Although parties are allowed to deviate from most of the stipulations in the Electoral Act, they have chosen to follow the legal text almost verbatim, and the variation between parties and constituencies is not very substantial (Helander 1997b, 59; Kuitunen 1997; Sundberg 1995, 47). There are still some differences between parties as well as deviations from the Electoral Act to be observed (Table 3.1.)

Table 3.1 Some characteristics of the party nomination statutes and the Electoral Act (four largest parties).

	Electoral Act	LWA	SDP	CP	NCP
Nomination of the aspirants	Party branches, party members' associations	Party branches, party members' associations	Party branches, party members' associations	Party branches, party members' associations	Party branches, party members' associations
Party members' association	» 10 members of the same party branch, or, » 30 members from different party branches	» 10 members of the same party branch, or, » 30 members from different party branches	» 5 members of the party branch	» 10 members of the same party branch, or, » 30 members from different party branches	» 10 members of the same party branch, or, » 30 members from different party branches
Enfranchisement in primaries	Members	Members	Membership for 4 months before primaries	Members over 15 years Membership for 2 months before primaries	Members
Eligibility requirements for candidacy	None	None	Membership for 4 months before primaries	None	None
Manipulation of lists	« 1/4 of the total number of candidates	« 1/4 of the total number of candidates	« 1/5 of the total number of candidates	« 1/4 of the total number of candidates	« 1/4 of the total number of candidates
Confirmation of the list	Party executive	Party executive	Party executive	Party executive	Party executive

» larger, « smaller.

Firstly, according to the statutes of the SDP only five members are required for an association of individual party members, compared to 10 party members needed in the other major parties. Secondly, an interesting feature is that the rules set very few requirements for candidacy and enfranchisement, which in turn are relatively easy to meet. In the LWA (Left Wing Alliance) and in the NCP, all party members are eligible and enfranchised, but in the CP (the Center Party), and in the SDP a more long-term commitment is required: two months in the case of the former and four months for the SDP. The Social Democrats differ from other main parties with respect to eligibility requirements for candidature as well since four months' prior membership is required of aspirants seeking candidature in parliamentary elections. This is in accordance with the former results indicating that Left Wing parties tend to make more rigorous demands on their candidates than parties on the right-wing of the political spectrum (see Gallagher 1988), even if this in Finland holds true only for the SDP and not for the LWA.

Thirdly, an interesting finding is that the CP allows its members from the age of 15 to take part in primaries, whereas other parties comply with the minimum age of 18 determined by law. Fourthly, only the SDP and the LWA have chosen to make their own regulations for the procedure exercised in primaries. For example in the SDP the number of votes available for voters is dependent on the proportion of the candidates selected from a constituency. The Social Democratic Party deviates from other parties also in respect to the list manipulation. It allows a maximum of only ⅕ of the total number of nominated candidates to be replaced, whereas the LWA, the CP and the NCP rely on the provisions of the Electoral Act and allow a maximum of ¼ of the candidates to be removed from the lists.

Nomination procedures

Considering the relatively partial picture that party statutes are capable of giving of nominations, it is evident that one should consider the genuine party procedures enforced in nominations as well. The following section contains a comparison of the four major parties on the issues of the frequency of using party primaries, the participation rates of local party members and branches in proposing aspirants, and the frequency of replacing candidates.

Party primaries have become a more common procedure in Finnish nominations since the late 1960s and early 1970s. The Social Democrats have applied this method more often than the other parties. This observation was made also in the 1995 parliamentary election. The SDP arranged a primary in every constituency, whereas the LWA applied this method in only half of the districts. The Center Party selected its candidates by primaries in almost half of the constituencies and in the remaining districts candidates were nominated by party conventions. In these conventions branch delegates represent local party branches. Conventions usually attract tens or even hundreds of participants to vote for the names put forward by the delegates (Helander 1997b, 69). One interesting feature in Table 3.2. is that the left-right spectrum no longer accounts for the discrepancies between parties making use of party primaries; for example, the NCP applied primaries more often than the LWA. As far as the smaller parties are concerned, it is quite natural that primaries are rarely used. There are two main reasons for not holding a primary: either the recruiting potential of these parties is modest in comparison with large parties or small parties are inclined to enter electoral alliances in order to gain advantages in terms of votes and seats.

Previous studies (Sundberg 1996) have shown that the capacity for nominating candidates varies somewhat between parties according to their size and the strength of their organization. Between 1962 and 1995, the CP, the LWA, the NCP and the SDP have been able to nominate candidates in each district, while the small parties have not managed to put up candidates in all constituencies (Sundberg 1996, 162). Unsurprisingly, the number of candidates in the largest parties is greater than in the small ones even if the tendency of some major parties, for instance the CP, to join electoral alliances has reduced the maximum number of candidates supplied by each member party.

Participation rates may vary not only due to the party size but also to the political situation, which is reflected in the result showing that local party branches are more passive in proposing candidates and attending primaries if electoral defeat is more probable than success (Timonen 1981). According to a Finnish nomination study carried out by Helander (1997b, 71), the inability of the CP to mobilize its members to participate in nominations may be due to the party's position as the leading party in the government during 1991-1995, which made substantial cuts in the state budget. The degree of participation may vary also within one party according to municipality. This was apparent in the 1979 election in which small, rural party branches were far more passive than their counterparts in the cities. On the whole, ⅕ to ⅖ of branches of the four major parties proposed aspirants with the lowest average being 25 percent in the NCP, and the highest average, 42 percent, among the branches of the CP. (Timonen 1981, 5-6)

Variation in participation rates between different parties and between municipalities within a particular party proved to exist in the 1995 nominations as well. Data do not suggest declining participation rates, but rather that variation between parties has increased since the late 1970s. In the 1995 nominations approximately 31 percent of local party branches proposed aspirants with variation from 15 percent at the lowest to 40 percent at the highest. The most passive party branches were those of the CP, where only 15 percent supplied aspirants for nomination. By contrast, the involvement rate was over twice as high in the LWA, and exactly twice as high both in the SDP and the NCP, in both of which 30 percent of the branches offered aspirants. Along with local party branches, associations of individual party members are entitled to propose their own aspirants as well, an opportunity which has not remained a mere formality. Since the number of candidates put forward by the associations is restricted to one, their role appears to be somewhat limited. The associations' proportion of the total number of aspirants was relatively small, only four percent, though there were such associations in almost half of the constituencies. Members of the four major parties turned out to be more anxious to make use of this possibility than members of all the political parties on average. The most active members were found among districts of the SDP in which 70 percent chose to set up associations in order to nominate candidates. The method was not unknown for the LWA either, since 50 percent of its districts had at least one members' association.

In general, participation rates in party primaries may be regarded as surprisingly low with respect to the significance of the party functions in question. In the 1979 parliamentary election the turnout varied from 39 to 45 percent among the four largest parties (Timonen 1981). In the 1995 election the variation between parties turned out to be even greater, from 11 percent at the lowest to 67 percent at the highest with the average being approximately 50 percent. The SDP proved to be the most successful party in mobilizing its members with a 63 percent turnout rate on average. In some of the districts of the SDP the turnout reached as high as 67 percent. In the NCP turnout rates varied from 35 to 54 percent, with the average being 43 percent. The same participation pattern, as shown before with respect to the nominating activity, proved to exist with regard to turnout rates as well. The CP turned out to be the party with the most difficulties in mobilizing its members to both putting forward candidates and voting in party primaries. The most passive districts of the CP reached a proportion as low as 11 percent with the average being 20 percent in all the districts under consideration.

Despite these relatively low figures in some of the constituencies and certain parties, participation rates in Finland seem to be relatively high when compared to some other European countries (see de Winter 1988, 26; Gallagher 1988c, 246; Valen 1988, 214). The great differences in participation rates between countries may naturally result from the different procedures used in candidate selection; involvement is expected to be at a higher level when primaries are used, which can be discerned in Finland and in several other countries applying this method (Gallagher 1988c, 246-247).

A striking feature in the otherwise highly decentralized Finnish nomination system is that, although candidates are nominated and selected by local party members, the party district executive is allowed to change one quarter of the aspirants placed on the list produced by the primaries. As the results presented in Table 3.2 show, the claim to manipulate lists is very often applied in order to correct certain biases apparent on the lists. In the 1995 nominations, as many as one half of the party districts of the four major parties adapted this method with the average being 50 percent. Lists were not, however, very drastically transformed, since the average change was only two per persons constituency and in over 90 percent of the districts with manipulated lists, changes only concerned one to three persons. The LWA turned out to be more enthusiastic about removals than the SDP or the non-socialist parties. According to party respondents, changes were in most cases due to candidate refusals and relatively many replacements were made in order to constitute a more balanced list in which the candidates' place of residence was of primary interest. Furthermore, in some cases the district organization made use of this right to correct the occupational bias of the candidates. Quite surprisingly, although almost every second district official considered women to be under-represented on the lists, improvements as to the representation of female candidates were seldom mentioned.

Despite the fact that the selection of parliamentary candidates is delegated to local party members and to district party organizations, the national party center may still try to influence this process. Due to the lack of relevant data, we are not able to answer this question in a fully detailed fashion. Nonetheless, some general notions concerning the interferences of the party center can be made. According to the survey addressed to party district organizations only two cases of this type of center involvement were enumerated. The media also reported a couple of cases in which the national party leadership was anxious to drop some names from the candidate lists. The rationale behind these attempts was to avoid selection of persons with a suspicious past in business and thus keep the party reputation as clean as possible. (Helander 1997b, 72)

The decline of the political parties

In Finland, as in other developed countries, the question about party decline has attracted much attention in the academic world. Besides the academics the media has also been very eager to deal with this topic, which has been more or less on the agenda for twenty years now.[31] Different surveys have established the fact that the inclination of the voters to join political parties has diminished considerably. This has been reflected in the shrinking numbers of party members during 1970-1996. The same declining trend, but not as sharp, is to be observed with respect to the number of local branches. (Sundberg 1996)

Table 3.2 Some characteristics of candidate selection practices within the four major parties and all parliamentary parties 1995.

	LWA	SDP	CP	NCP	All Parties
Average number of aspirants proposed by party branches	19	41	18	30	22
Share of party-branch proposed aspirants (%)	40	32	15	30	31
Share of constituencies where non-partisan aspirants were proposed (%)	75	-	30	-	30
Share of constituencies where individual party members proposed aspirants (%)	46	69	14	25	25
Share of constituencies where party primaries were held (%)	55	100	57	75	49
Average turnout in the party primary (%)	49	63	20	43	45
Proportion of party district organizations where lists were manipulated (%)	100	69	75	80	78
N	11	13	14	12	84

How have these tendencies along with the institutional changes affected the candidate selection process? Although no relevant long-term data are at our disposal, some general conclusions may be drawn on the basis of results gathered in this study.

At large, the institutional and procedural changes seem to have reinforced the dominant role of the parties in nominations, even when their formal power over candidate selection has been reduced by reform of the law. This was apparent in the 1975 Electoral Act reform, in which the right to put up candidate lists was restored to the electors' associations. The reform did not, however, threaten the informal monopoly of political parties in nominations. The 1975 reform was pivotal for parties in other respects, too. By introduction of closed primaries, the position of party institutions was highly recognized; their internal activities became more transparent and widely known to the public. One may assert that the overall formalization and standardization during the 20th century has reinforced the credibility of political parties by establishing their role as the legitimate recruiters and promoters of the national political elite.

Turning to the probable effects of party decline on the nomination activities, we may try to respond to a particularly interesting discussion evolved recently in the Finnish media. According to this debate, candidate selection is "doomed" to be centralized due to the shrinking number of party members (*Helsingin Sanomat* 7.7.1998). In reality, the Finnish data gathered from nominations do not confirm this hypothesis. Conversely, the candidate selection process has become more decentralized since the golden years of the political parties. What is more, the decline in party membership has not resulted in the decline of participation figures in nominations. In reality, the involvement rates of local branches in proposing aspirants and the turnout in primaries were identical in 1979 and 1995. By and large, the organizational strength of the party is not a very good predictor for the participation rates. In 1995 the incomparable organizational strength along with the large number of party members of the Center Party were of no help in mobilizing its members to nominations.

Criteria for candidate selection

Group representation
Selection criteria

Many previous studies on political recruitment have established the fact that certain groups are favored over others in the parliamentary selection processes. Women, young people, blue-collar workers and rural inhabitants are perceived to be discriminated against with a relatively low share of candidatures and legislative positions as a consequence (Czudnowski 1975; Matthews 1985; Valen 1988, 225-228). Selectorate preferences, namely those of the party members and party executives, are pivotal in this respect since these groups are able to not only to determine the array of the candidates but also to a considerable extent the caliber of the parliamentarians. These selection criteria are not always explicitly defined in party statutes, but are mainly implicit in nature (see Gallagher 1988a, 6; Kuitunen 1997b, 132-133; Valen 1988, 220).

Some scholars have used Seligman's (1961) distinction between subjective, achievement-related criteria and objective, ascriptive criteria in order to determine the influence of different background characteristics on the nominations in a more systematic manner. The former group refers to characteristics such as ideological orthodoxy, party record, expertise in organizing, and bargaining abilities, whereas the latter includes age, family, social status, religion, locality and group affiliation. Correspondingly Bochel and Denver (1983, 53) and de Winter (1988, 37) have distinguished between objective and subjective criteria, but have also added political characteristics as a third category affecting candidate selection.

Several studies concerning the nomination system in Finland suggest that emphasis is usually placed on both subjective and objective criteria: candidates are to be representative of the electoral demography of the constituency, for example, in aspects such as gender, profession and domicile (Noponen 1964, 320; Tarasti & Taponen 1996, 262-263; Tarkiainen 1971; Sundberg 1995, 47). The parties' primary aim seems not to be ticket balancing according to the political characteristics of the candidates, but according to their socio-demographic composition instead (Sundberg 1995, 50). Unfortunately there is a dearth of empirical works dealing with the Finnish party members' evaluations of the ideal candidate and legislator as their basic target. However, some light on this topic can be shed by looking at the party district officials' responses about the most essential qualities sought in aspirants.

Table 3.3 presents several interesting features. Firstly, the most decisive characteristic of the aspirant proved to be her or his domicile, a fact that was mentioned by an overwhelming majority regardless of the party. In contradiction with some former results presented in the literature on nominations, the results do not give substantial support to the idea that political characteristics are unimportant in nominations. On the contrary, political characteristics were valued relatively highly as a requirement for selection, though they were not as strongly emphasized as objective characteristics.

Results reveal some interesting differences between parties when it comes to the magnitude of subjective and political characteristics. Previous studies such as Valen's (1966) and Czudnowski's (1975) have suggested that social position is the most prominent quality for right-wing parties, whereas socialist parties are said to lay more stress on party loyalty and record. In the data for Finnish nominations, the former held true as far as the NCP was concerned whereas the latter proved to be valid only for the Social Democrats. Taken as whole, intraparty variations were not logically positioned along the left-right division line. One may conclude that there is a relatively wide consensus of opinion among the Finnish party officials about qualities preferred in parliamentary candidates.

Table 3.3 Characteristics considered important for selection (percentage of party district officials).[1]

	LWA	SDP	CP	NCP	All parties
OBJECTIVE CHARACTERISTICS[2]	18	46	43	25	25
Domicile	64	85	64	83	64
Sex	82	69	64	42	60
Age	27	62	71	75	50
SUBJECTIVE CHARACTERISTICS[2]	-	8	7	-	2
Social position	36	31	14	42	26
Communication skills	27	8	7	0	18
Marital status	-	15	7	-	5
POLITICAL CHARACTERISTICS[2]	-	8	7	-	2
Party record	9	31	29	8	31
Party activity	9	39	14	17	25
Party loyalty	9	8	7	-	6
N	11	13	14	12	84

1 Respondents were asked to mention the three most important characteristics.
2 Considering that all the qualities are important.

Ticket balancing

Parties are inclined to balance their lists according to the socio-demographic composition of the selected candidates. By using this strategy of *ticket balancing*, parties try to appeal to as many voters as possible and consequently to maximize both their votes and seats in parliament. In addition, a balanced candidate list may perform certain functions inside the party; by selecting candidates who represent influential internal party factions, conflicts between these groups may be avoided and their commitment to the list ensured (Gallagher 1988c, 253; Ranney 1981, 101).

Several aspects in the Finnish voting and nomination systems may produce severe hindrances to the realization of group representation. The selection and nomination are left in the hands of the local party members and party branches which may not prioritize ticket balancing through socio-demographic characteristics but rather seek other qualities in the candidates, such as speaking abilities or knowledge about political issues. Therefore, in order to correct biases in the candidate lists, party district executives are permitted to remove a certain number of candidates and replace them with others who are considered more representative or otherwise better qualified for the party's electoral purposes.

Sometimes ticket balancing can lead to odd and unexpected results as for instance in the candidate selection of the Social Democratic Party in the 1966 parliamentary election. The leaders of the SDP altered the list produced by party primaries in order to balance the representation of women and young people on the lists. Under Finland's preferential system, votes tend to be split between candidates in these particular categories and thus actually reduce the possibilities of women and young people being elected to parliament. (Pesonen 1972, 224; see also Ruostetsaari 1998)

In the theory of group representation four groups are of primary importance, namely territorial groups, women, young people and occupational groups (see Sundberg 1995; Valen 1988). As far as territorial representation is concerned, no residential requirements are stated in the Finnish Electoral Act. In the long run, the number of candidates and legislators selected outside their own constituencies has been notable, approximately one fifth of the deputies. This tendency has proved to be disappearing after 1962, and with the introduction of the 1969 Electoral Act the disposition of recruiting outsiders lost much of its relevance since a candidacy was limited to only one party and one constituency.[32] (Noponen 1989, 144-145)

One of the established features in the Finnish nomination system is the overrepresentation of the cities in parliament during the 20th century (Noponen 1989, 145-146; Nousiainen 1992, 26-27). In the beginning of the century, almost 50 percent of legislators were elected from the countryside and the relatively high proportion of rural legislators was discernible even after the Second World War. This has been explained by the capability of the Center Party to mobilize the largest part of the agrarian population. However, the trend towards urbanization is reflected in the fact that the composition of legislatures has been transformed from dominance by the agrarians to an overrepresentation of deputies recruited from the cities. For example, data from 1984 display that only one fourth of deputies actually lived in the countryside even though the majority was born in rural communities. (Noponen 1989, 145-146)

Despite the overrepresentation of major cities in the Finnish *Eduskunta*, territorial interests may be articulated and mediated through the individual candidates and deputies holding local positions of trust. In Finland a double mandate, a seat in the legislature and in the local government, is a common, even though sometimes a firmly criticized phenomenon. Approximately two thirds of the deputies hold a local position of trust (Noponen 1989, 134). For many parliamentarians, local positions of trust are the first stage in their political career, which lead to more pivotal political posts. In his study on political recruitment in Finland, Ruostetsaari (1998) found that the number of Finnish deputies trained in local politics has been steadily increasing since 1907, whereas the number of the legislators holding a leading position of trust in a party organization has dramatically decreased since 1962. There has occurred a polarization among Finnish legislators. While the proportion of parliamentarians with no positions of trust before recruitment has increased during the time period from 1966 to 1995, lack of training in political parties and in labor unions has been compensated by increased formal education and by experience in local offices. (Ruostetsaari 1998)

The data gathered from the constituency of Helsinki designate the magnitude of local confidential posts in the recruitment process. Only 16 percent of those not selected as candidates had acquired a local elective office or other political position at a municipal level, while as high a proportion as 56 percent of those selected as candidates had such local experience. Of the elected deputies, a majority, 60 percent, had at least one position of trust at the local government. The overrepresentation of local politicians is distinct if compared to the equivalent proportion in the whole electorate. (Paltemaa 1997) A similar conclusion about the magnitude of local positions of trust in seeking parliamentary candidature was drawn on the basis of interviews accomplished with party district officials.[33] Almost all the respondents perceived the achievements and performances of the parliamentary candidates in municipal politics as being one of the pivotal criteria while assessing the competence and capability of previous candidates in the recruitment process. Correspondingly, some officials considered poor performance as being one of the main reasons for the deselection.

Helander's (1997a, 1997b) study of parliamentary candidates corroborates the general trend by showing that patterns of legislative recruitment produce political élites that clearly link together local and national political power. According to results drawn by Helander, as high a proportion as three fifths of the candidates in the constituency of Turku actually held seats on municipal councils. The candidates in the parliamentary parties proved to be particularly anxious in this respect, whereas the majority of non-partisan candidates and parties attending parliamentary elections for the first time did not in fact have this kind of resource at their disposal. (Helander 1997a, 155-156; 1997b, 63)

Considering the strong territorial orientation in the Finnish system, it may be anticipated that even the parliamentary candidates give high priority to the interests of their own district. The study by Helander (1997a) does not reassert this general picture. In fact, only every tenth parliamentary candidate saw the advancement of her/his own geographical constituency as the primary commitment. Candidates on the left side of the political spectrum put most weight on party representation whereas the non-socialist candidates prioritized the idea of being a spokesperson for the whole country. This difference has been identified by former studies as well (see Oksanen & Pitkänen 1989, 238). In general, both the left- and right-wing candidates showed a clear pattern of including the promotion of multiple interests in their role orientation, a result that implies that loyalty to the party or to the entire nation may not constitute a severe hindrance for the advancement of other interests at the same time.

The second aspect, representation according to gender, is deeply rooted in representational theory. As early as the first decades of independence, Finnish parties established a strategy of nominating at least one woman for each constituency for parliamentary elections. After the early 1900s, the idea of recruiting one female candidate has been transformed into a more or less formalized norm of achieving an equal number of both genders among the candidate lists and deputies. In contrast with some other Nordic parties, Finnish parties have not been particularly eager to establish official quotas, but have adapted more informal procedures instead. From the perspective of ticket balancing, the third decisive criterion is the number of young people among both candidates and parliamentarians. Along with that of young people, the parliamentary representation of older people may also be given some attention. In Finland one may expect professional representation being substantial in the strategy of ticket balancing as well. The traditional class cleavage between blue-collar workers and white-collar workers has not totally disappeared but it is still present in people's conceptions, which direct at least to a certain extent their political choices (Sundberg 1995, 50; Sänkiaho 1995, 90-91).

Due to the prominent function candidate selection plays in the internal party activities, the appearance of disputes between different sub-groups is highly probable. Unfortunately no systematic evidence of these kinds of conflicts and their occurrence has been gathered in Finland. As the interviews conducted with the district officials indicate, territorial conflicts are almost unavoidable in the nominations due to the high priority put on the equal representation of the different sub-areas. Nevertheless, data from municipal nominations in Finland suggest that conflicts between different territorial as well as other factions such as occupational and age groups were rare in the 1996 local elections. According to municipal party officials, the frequency of internal conflicts was somewhat higher between men and women, even though disputes were exceptional also in this respect. (Kuitunen 1997c, 329-330) Results are consistent with those gathered elsewhere (see Barkfeldt et al. 1971; Wallin et al. 1981), which indicate that nominating candidates has more to do with anticipating the wishes of party members than realizing them. In any event, considering the lower status of local politics, it is highly questionable whether one can generalize these results far enough to be applied to the national level.

Based on the 1995 nomination study, we can make some indirect conclusions about how essential group-related criteria are in nominations. Empirical evidence supports the idea that territorial representation is prominent and in fact is more essential than other representational foci in nominations. As was already shown in Table 3.3, there were interesting intraparty differences especially as far as gender and age were concerned; gender was supported more among the LWA respondents, whereas age was not as significant a factor as for other parties. To test the support for different aspects of group representation, three indices were constructed: indices of objective, subjective and political characteristics. The weight placed upon these indices was compared within the four major parties. Demographic group qualities, age, domicile and gender were perceived as important by one quarter of the party district officials in comparison with only two percent emphasizing the magnitude of social or party-related qualities. Regarded also from this viewpoint, no clear signs of the distinctive socialist and non-socialist recruitment patterns were to be detected among the major parties.

Socio-demographic characteristics of aspirants, candidates and legislators

Studies on political élites have established the fact that the composition of legislatures is far from being representative; legislators tend to be men more often than women, highly educated, usually middle-aged and drawn from a higher social stratum than the electorate (Czudnowski 1975; Matthews 1985; Putnam 1976). In the recent past, some scholars have found it more interesting to take a step backwards and try to account for these élitist biases in terms of the processes through which deputies are recruited. Several studies have indicated that the selection processes of political parties rather than the electorates as such cause the underrepresentation of certain groups (Helander, Kuitunen & Paltemaa 1997; Loewenberg & Patterson 1979, 111; Noponen 1989, 116 & 121).

In the following analysis the socio-demographic background characteristics of aspirants, candidates and legislators are compared in order to determine which one of the recruitment stages, nominations or election was more decisive regarding the élitist biases. These three groups were composed as follows. Aspirants consisted of all party members seeking party candidature in the 1995 parliamentary elections. The group of candidates was composed of aspirants selected as candidates by party primaries as well as those who were put on the party lists after primaries by the party district executive. The third group, legislators, refers to elected deputies. The following analysis is based on data gathered from only the four largest parties and from those constituencies where party primaries were arranged.

As can be discovered in Table 3.4, candidate lists produced by party primaries and by list manipulation were far from being representative when it came to the proportion of women, non-university graduates, people under thirty years of age, as well as over sixty, and those living in the countryside. Compared to the socio-demographic composition of the electorate as a whole, the most underrepresented group on the lists was non-graduates. They were underrepresented by a factor of 1.7 (89%/52%), whereas the equivalent factor indicating electoral bias was at its smallest for blue-collar workers, namely 1.1 (17%/16%).

What is more interesting, however, is the fact that these socio-demographic biases were sizable already at the first phase of the nomination process, in which party members offered aspirants for the primaries. The next stage of the candidate selection consolidated the élitist characteristics of aspirants even though the inclination towards élitism was not as clear as one could expect. On the contrary, the number of candidates from underrepresented groups, such as non-graduates, rural inhabitants and older people, roughly corresponded to the situation before the primaries. What is more, the proportion of women actually increased as a result of the nominations. These changes were partly due to the list manipulation.

In general, the last phase of the recruitment process turned out to be more decisive than the one preceding it. Electors were more inclined than the party selectorate to vote for highly educated middle-aged urban residents as well as males and those in white-collar occupations. Although they actually fortified the élitist characteristics of the candidate supply, the changes made by the electorate were not as preponderant with respect to the outcome as the élitist biases apparent from the very first stage of the nominating process would lead us to suspect.

As far as incumbents are concerned, the results are consistent with previous studies indicating the incomparable success of incumbents in candidate nominations and election (see Ranney 1981; Somit et al. 1994). Party selectorates were not as firmly in favor of previous legislators or candidates as voters as a whole. As the results point out, some of the aspirants were victorious enough to gain a candidacy even without previous experience from campaigning, an observation which did not, however, hold true at the next stage of the recruitment process. In fact, only 14 percent of the elected deputies were without previous experience of the candidate position.

It appears to be the case that the major biases in the Finnish parliament are a reflection not so much of the party selectorate or voter preferences for certain well-off groups as of the pool of applicants offered by party members. Thus a major revision to alter the situation would be not to actuate the party selectors' preferences but to affect the factors related to the supply of the aspirants (see also Helander 1997b, 73 & 75).

Table 3.4 The social and demographic background of aspirants, candidates and legislators in the 1995 election (% four major parties).

	Whole population	Aspirants (1,073)	Candidates (515)	Legislators (113)
Men	48	62	59	67
Women	53	38	41	33
18-29	34*	12	13	5
30-44	29	37	35	27
45-59	23	47	51	68
60 +	23	3	1	1
Large city	37	43	42	61
Small town	28	34	36	28
Countryside	35	23	22	12
Blue-collar workers	17	19	16	11
Lower-level white-collar workers	18	18	19	19
Upper-level white-collar workers	10	39	43	61
Others (students, businessmen/women, etc.)	55	25	23	11
Graduates	11	45	48	59
Non-graduates	89	55	52	41
No previous candidature	-	75	56	14
Previous candidature	-	15	25	19
Previous legislator	-	2	3	5
Current legislator (1991-95)	-	9	17	63

This category also includes the age-group 15-17.

To determine the effects of different background characteristics on the candidate selection and election, two separate multivariate regression analyses were run. The first one was run for the nomination process, from aspirant to candidate, and the second one for the step from candidate to legislator. Analysis of the data suggests that the aspirants least likely to be selected as candidates included those without previous experience of candidacy or legislative work as well as elderly aspirants (Table 3.5).

Table 3.5 *The impact of the different background characteristics on candidate nominations and elections (standardized beta coefficients).*

	Nominations: From aspirant to candidate	Elections: From candidate to legislator
Gender	.07*	-.11*
Age	-.09*	.11
Place of residency	-.06	.08
Occupation	.01	.08
Education	.09*	-.02
Previous experience	.37***	.21***
Adj. R²	.15	.08

In the analysis all the variables were recoded from zero to one. Gender: 0 = male, 1 = female. Age: 0 = < 30 years of age, 1 = > 60; a total of four categories. Place of residence: 0 = countryside, 1 = large city; a total of three categories. Occupation: 0 = non white-collar worker, 1 = white-collar worker. Education: 0 = non-graduate, 1 = graduate. Previous experience: 0 = no experience from candidature/legislature, 1 = previous/sitting MP, a total of three categories.

Note: According to general wisdom, OLS regression analysis should not be used when the dependent variable is a dichotomous one. In order to verify the results gathered in the above analysis, the logistic regression was run. There were no major differences between the results of these two analyses. Significance is illustrated by asterisks * < .05, ** < .01 and *** < .001.

Gender and education displayed an almost significant impact on candidate nominations by promoting the selection of female aspirants as well as those with university degrees, whereas occupation emerged not as a significant predictor of demand denoted in the candidate selection. Evidently, the previous experience turned out to be the most essential entrance requirement not only for candidacy but also for legislative position. In the election gender was almost a statistically significant variable, and women were a slightly disadvantaged group in relation to male candidates. Taken as a whole, the empirical evidence corroborates the view that the sanctioning mechanisms put into practice by both the party selectorate and the entire electorate are conditioning first and foremost the victory rates of freshmen and women, not so much those of other social and demographic groups.

In order to assess the character of the recruitment patterns in a more detailed fashion, we will run separate analyses for both men and women. These separate regression runs allow us to test whether the determinants of recruitment performance are similar for both of these groups (Table 3.6.).

Table 3.6 The impact of the different background characteristics on candidate nominations and elections (standardized beta coefficients).

	Nominations: From aspirant to candidate		Elections: From candidate to legislator	
	Men	Women	Men	Women
Age	-.04	-.15*	.11	.00
Place of residency	-.04	-.07	.07	.09
Occupation	.05	-.02	.12	.05
Education	.01	.18**	-.08	.06
Previous experience	.36***	.38***	.24**	.12
District	-.08	-.02	.00	-.15
Party background	.06	.01	-.09	.14
Adj. R²	.13	.17	.09	.01

Significance is illustrated by asterisks * < .05, ** < .01 and *** < .001.

The selected variables are the same as used in the section 3.3.2. In the following analysis, however, two additional variables are included: the district and party variables. Region is said to be decisive in promoting the recruitment of women into parliament. Women have shown to be more successful in eastern than western parts of the country (Haavio-Mannila 1979). The party variable (socialist/non-socialist party) has also proven to have significance in relation to the recruitment of women into candidature and legislature. Traditionally, women have gained more candidatures and parliamentary seats in socialist than non-socialist parties.

In considering coefficients for all variables in the first regression analysis, from aspirant to candidature, it is evident that previous experience from legislature and candidature displays a more significant impact than any other variable. This observation holds true for both men and women. Quite interestingly, age and education proved to be significant explanatory variables for the selection of female, but not male candidates. Women aspirants least likely to come forward included those without university degrees as well as elderly members.

Opposite to expectations, the coefficient of the previous experience lost its significance for the election of female deputies, whereas it was a significant predictor of being elected for the male candidates. In comparison with the first regression analysis, the background variables explained a far lower degree of variance (adj. R2 = .09 and .01).

What the results appear to suggest is that the increased proportion of women candidates may not increase the number of two remarkably underrepresented groups, namely the elderly and non-academics, in candidature positions and parliament. As to the norms for eligibility applied in nominations, these appear to be relatively similar for both men and women aspirants; party selectors seek middle-aged, highly educated male and female aspirants with upper-status occupations. When it comes to election, we find an interesting difference between the male and female recruitment model. What the electors primarily seek in female deputies is neither the incumbency nor any other factor included in the model.

In large, the representation of Finnish women signifies a steadily increasing trend from 1945 to 1995. The same kind of trend upward is to be observed with respect to the share of female candidates as well. From 1945 to 1995 the representation of women deputies has become four times larger, and the share of female candidates has more than doubled since 1954. The relatively high proportion of Finnish women in the parliament and candidature positions has been explained by three inter-related factors. The multi-member PR-system, women's high educational level and the notable proportion women in the labor force along with a "female-friendly" society are said to be the most important means to enhance women's entrance into the political arena (see Haavio-Mannila 1979).

A particularly relevant question is what kind of effects, if any, has the candidate-centered system with preferential voting had on the representation of Finnish women? The answer may be twofold. At large, voters have become more positive towards female candidates. A slight majority of women vote for female candidates, whereas an overwhelming majority of men (74%) still casts its votes primarily for male candidates. This tendency along with two additional trends – an expanded share of women taking part in elections and the increased number of female candidates – appear to be important factors in explaining the more balanced female representation in the Finnish parliament. Conceivably, the changing role of the media may account for the better success of women in political arenas as well. The appearance of politicians in other than news or election debates is supposed to profit female candidates and politicians since they are expected to be more at home in the more intimate, humane atmosphere of the talk shows, morning or entertainment programs (see Jääsaari and Martikainen 1991).

Sanctions and rewards

The level of incumbency turnover

In this chapter, the focus will be on the turnover. We start by charting the turnover figures among the MPs during 1945-1995. The second target of the study is the magnitude of turnover among the candidates during the same time period. Figure 3.1. comprises four indicators of the turnover rates in the Finnish *Eduskunta*. Newcomers include all the elected deputies without any previous experience from legislator's work, and past deputies refer to legislators who were elected before but not on the pre-election diet. Old deputies or incumbents, in turn, consist of legislators who served in the last pre-election diet.

After the 1979 election the re-election rate for incumbents has stabilized at around 60 percent, slightly below the average. Even if the findings from 1945 to 1995 are characterized by substantial stability, four deviant cases from this general pattern concerning re-election can be detected. Firstly, it was only after 1954, 1972 and 1975 that the proportion of re-elected incumbents exceeded the level of 70 percent. Secondly, the re-election figure was exceptionally low on one occasion, in 1945.

In the 1945-1995 time frame, the freshmen and freshwomen made up 34 percent of the total parliament membership, within the 18 to 50 percent range. Quite interestingly, the share of past deputies having served on some bygone diet(s) is extremely small, which may be due to several factors: the electors' antipathy towards past MPs, the unwillingness of these previous legislators to seek office or the reluctance of party selectorates to cast a vote for them in the primaries.

Finland: Formalized Procedures with Member Predominance 93

Figure 3.1 Data on parliamentary turnover in Finland 1945-1995 (%).

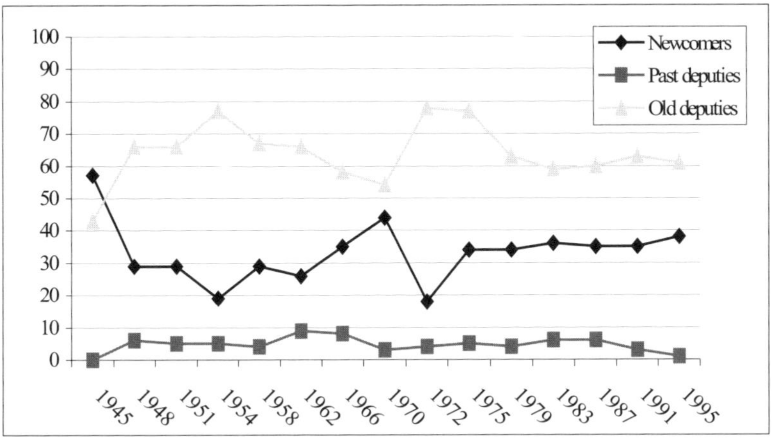

Source: Ruostetsaari (1998); Wiberg & Mattila (1997).

Turnover rates have differed quite dramatically between the parties within the same election. An instructive example of this kind of phenomenon is the 1979 election after which the Conservative Party group consisted of 50 percent newcomers in comparison with only 15 percent for the Agrarian Party. The Conservative Party differs from other major parties in respect to the average level of structural renewal of the legislators as well. The average share of newcomers for the Conservative Party has been over 30 percent during all the three time periods, namely 1940-50, 1960-70 and 1980-90, whereas in the other three major parties the equivalent proportion has in some periods declined below 30 percent. Furthermore, the variation is noticeable within the parties as well. At large, turnover fluctuates among all the parties; it has not been systematically at its highest in the newly formed, weakly organized parties.

Regarding the turnover figures for male and female deputies, the average share of newcomers is in fact identical in both genders. Since the 1975 election, however, there has on average been five percent more turnover among female than male incumbents. If the re-election rates are compared, we find that women candidates tend to be re-elected at slightly higher numbers than their male counterparts, even if the difference is not highly significant.

Reasons for turnover

Table 3.8 illustrates the effects of both the nomination and electoral systems on the level of turnover. The first column indicates the share of the incumbents who either voluntarily gave up a legislative career or was rejected as a result of candidate selection. Defeated incumbents comprise those candidates who were defeated by election results.

Two elements of turnover are apparent. On the one hand, there is a rather linear trend upward in the proportion of those deputies retiring either voluntarily or as a result of being defeated in the candidate nomination process. On the other hand, the number of defeated incumbents in general elections has been growing as well. The rate of de-election reached its highest level in the 1970 election and was at its lowest in the next election, in 1972. During the time period from 1958 to 1987, approximately 48 percent of the deputies were displaced in elections in comparison to the 31 percent dropped either as a result of their own choice or by a decision made at some stage in the nomination process.

In general, these data suggest that defeat has always exceeded retirement with the exception of the 1987 election in which the proportion of withdrawing incumbents was greater than that of defeated deputies. Since the turnover of sitting members of the legislature appears to be conditioned more by popular suffrage than by the incumbents' own choice or deselection of the nominating party, the hypothesis concerning the decisive role of elections in keeping incumbents accountable through the threat of involuntary removal appears to be confirmed. Furthermore, the hypothesis is likely to be affirmed by the fact that the trend of the average length of the legislative service has been downward, toward shorter terms (Ruostetsaari 1998).

Finland: Formalized Procedures with Member Predominance

Table 3.8 Reasons for turnover 1958-1987.

Year	Retiring incumbents	Defeated incumbents
1958	31	39
1962	28	46
1966	30	59
1970	39	59
1972	16	33
1975	30	50
1979	35	47
1983	27	58
1987	45	42
Mean	31	48

Source: Noponen 1989, 151.

By comparing the previous experience of aspirants and candidates, the effects of nominations and election on the turnover can be assessed. The incumbents' success rate in nominations was over two and a half time higher, 94, than that (36) of the freshmen without any experience from candidacy positions. When it comes to parliamentary election, the success rate was 17 times higher for incumbents than that for inexperienced candidates. Although one must bear in mind the discrepancy between procedures applied in nominations and elections, these findings are in keeping with previous results (Noponen 1989). The disadvantageous position of newcomers is not to be attributed to the selection practiced by political parties as much as to the final phase of the recruitment process in which ordinary voters elect their representatives to parliament.

Level of list turnover

In Figure 3.2 turnover of candidates is expressed by the proportions of new, past and old candidates during the time period from 1945-1995. Newcomers refer to the candidates without any previous experience from candidature. The second group, past MPs, comprises those candidates being selected before but not in the previous election. Old MPs or incumbents in turn consist of candidates who sought nomination in the last election.

As the figures of the share of newcomers demonstrate, either party selectorates have been fairly eager to endorse incumbent candidates or, alternatively, the previous candidates have retired voluntarily. Taken as a whole, the transformation of the lists has been much more voluminous than the modification among the legislators, which is natural considering the different nature of the primaries and the parliamentary elections. More interestingly, the data from 1951 to 1995 nominations show a steadily and continuously increasing trend towards expanding the proportion of newcomers, while the re-election rate for legislators has stabilized somewhat below the limit of 40 percent. Since 1975 the share of freshmen and freshwomen has remained somewhat above the average.

There is only one case, the candidate nomination carried out in 1972, where the resulting share of newcomers was less than 50 percent. This particular year was an exceptional case also regarding the turnover of legislators, since at that time as low a proportion as one fifth of the elected deputies were freshmen and freshwomen. In addition, the relatively low transformation among the elected deputies in 1954 was also reflected in the turnover rates of selected candidates, which were somewhat below the average.

What the numbers of past and old candidates suggests is that in the competition for candidate seats, the most advantaged group is that which has been nominated as candidates in the previous elections, while experience from some bygone elections is not of any help. There is only one case, the election of 1972, when the representation of past candidates on the lists exceeded the demarcation line of 10 percent, while the average has been as little as six percent for the entire period. An interesting question with reference to the topic of list turnover is whether the major changes made in the nomination institution account for the turnover figures; for example, is there any relation to be detected between the reform introduced in 1975 in which party primaries were made obligatory and the figures displaying the turnover of candidates. The rationale behind this is that compared to more unofficial procedures, party primaries may be perceived as presenting effective means to either punish or reward previous candidates as well as legislators. The data do give support to this hypothesis, since the proportion of newcomers in fact increased by 18 percent as a result of the 1975 election.

When it comes to turnover among male and female candidates, we are able to find some interesting differences. Female candidates have been more inclined than male ones to be replaced from one election to next. Consequently, the re-election rate for male candidates is somewhat higher for male (36%) than female (33%) candidates. This holds true for every election but one during 1945-1995. What is remarkable among the results is the fact that the procedural reform in the 1975 nominations actually "hit" more female than male candidates. In comparison with the turnover figures in the preceding election 1972, the turnover among female candidates increased by 20 percent, whereas the equivalent share for male candidates was 14 percent. Interesting is also the observation indicating the continuity of the candidate career. This type of career appears to be more continuous among female than male candidates. Women are not as inclined as men to seek candidature and/or to be selected after some bygone elections.

Figure 3.2 List turnover 1945-95 (%).

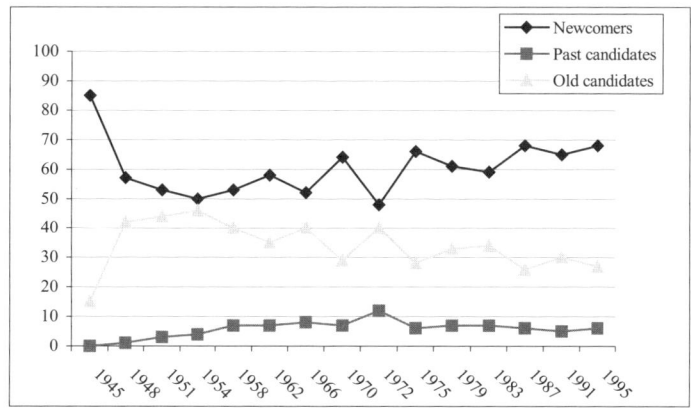

The reasons for "deselection"

The reasons for deselection of sitting MPs or previous candidates have not been systematically and exhaustively studied in Finland. Therefore we are not able to assess the relative magnitude of candidate deselection in relation to voluntary retirement as primary factors resulting in turnover. To shed some light on this topic, several interviews with party district officials were carried out.[34]

The findings drawn from the interviews did not fall short of expectations but confirmed the general picture of the victorious position of incumbents as well as of the previous candidates. Most of the respondents did not recall any such incident in which a sitting MP would have been rejected in the candidate nominations. In reality parties or, to be precise, local branches tend to enter upon nominations by charting the willingness of previous candidates and legislators in particular. Despite the fact that the highest priority is put on the recruitment of incumbents, a party organization has to take into account other considerations as well: for example, list balancing along with the demands displayed by local party members.

Along with the voluntary retirement, some turnover in candidate lists may take place as a result of internal party disputes and conflicts. As some respondents pointed out, these conflicts are an essential component of the nomination process and should not, in any event, be avoided due to the stimulating effects they will bring into the candidate selection. The demands from constituencies also affect the candidate selection process through the aims of regional representation; party constituencies are divided into smaller sub-units, each of which requires equal representation among the candidates. It is possible that some candidates, such as young people and women, are sacrificed as a result of the preference laid on regional representation, since the application of this kind of strategy presupposes both enough and not too many candidates from each relevant sub-region.

Some of the interviewees emphasized the notion of personal obligation of previous candidates and legislators as a primary motive for seeking renomination. This factor may be stressed by the party organization as well: sitting members of parliament are regarded as being responsible for testing their popularity among the entire electorate in forthcoming elections. On the other hand, considering the high amount of financial resources required in the campaigning, it is quite natural that candidates avoid testing their popularity in too many consecutive elections, and as a result of their own personal and/or party organizations' appreciation may retire after excessive unsuccessful efforts.

Even if the recruitment process is substantially and clearly functioning to the advantage of the incumbents, there may be some occasions in which incumbents and those in candidate positions are sanctioned due to severe problems in their personal life, such as bankruptcy, economic obscurities or alcoholism. It may also be the case that voters discharge their political distrust and disappointment in evicting previous legislators, and the role played by mass media is decisive in this respect particularly when it comes to negative incidences. On the other hand, there are some examples of the peculiarities of the Finnish political culture in this particular matter, since some legislators, despite their personal problems and dubious past, have been able to gather enough support to be elected to parliament. Even the sitting members of parliament are not, however, able to completely avoid being vulnerable to election results on occasions when the party gathers fewer votes in comparison with the previous election. Furthermore, as several respondents indicated, much of the turnover may be accounted for by the fact that deputies have not kept up constituency contacts in a satisfactory manner but have prioritized other pursuits instead.

The tendency towards supporting incumbents is perhaps even more strengthened with the introduction of the personal assistant system of parliamentarians after the 1995 election. As one party official noted, this reform will severely reduce the potentiality of the district organizations to intrude into, direct and govern electoral campaigning of candidates, and, what is more, undoubtedly will effect the motivational factors of non-incumbents as well. The amount of the total supply of candidates is perhaps abated and the possibilities of ordinary party members to have an influence on candidate supply and composition of lists are circumscribed. While the highly decentralized nature of the candidate selection system is recognized by several scholars in Finland and elsewhere, the results gathered in this particular study appear to highlight the relatively marginal role played by ordinary party members in bringing about the turnover even on candidate lists. On the basis of qualitative interviews and official statistics, one can reasonably argue that whether a previous candidate is reselected or not has to do more with personal assessment of her/his own success possibilities in nominations and elections rather than with the refusals of the unsatisfied (s)electorate or party organization.

Conclusions

In Finland both the institutional context for nominations, namely the reforms in electoral law and other legislative changes, and the procedures used in candidate selection have been quite profoundly transformed during the 20th century. The electoral system of Finland has evolved from a pure Scandinavian closed list system to an open list system, in which voters are able to prioritize candidates. As a consequence, the nomination practices in parliamentary elections differ quite dramatically from those of the other Nordic countries.

As far as individual voters are concerned, the development of the Finnish nomination system displays contradictory tendencies. On the one hand, the opportunities available for ordinary voters have been somewhat reduced. In the early 20th century electors were able to make use of the right to set up their own candidate lists while voting in elections and to alter the order of the candidates appearing on the lists, both of which were withdrawn in 1950s and 1960s. In addition, throughout this century voters have had the right to form their own electoral associations in order to nominate candidates. In reality these options have been quite rarely applied with the exception of the last one, which has not had, however, any substantial influence on the nominations or the results of elections in particular. On the other hand, the loss of some procedural rights has been compensated by the delegation of the power of decision over the election of MPs to the voters instead of the parties. As a consequence, voters are able to determine not only the number of seats for each party but also the ranking order of the candidates within the party lists.

These institutional reforms along with the primarily behavioral changes of the individual voters have entailed some changes in the delegation contract structuring the role of relevant actors involved in the process. Firstly, the role of individual candidates has been reinforced at the expense of the political parties: since the early 1990s voters in general, young voters and females in particular, have placed relatively more emphasis on the candidates in comparison with that of the political parties in their voting decisions (Borg 1997, 43-45). Secondly, the dominating position of political parties has been eroded by the growing discontentment with the parties, which has discharged itself in citizens' apathy, passivity and indifference both in elections and political activities in general (Pekonen 1997).

Despite these trends, the relatively firm and stable position of the political parties is reflected in the fact that outside party lists, without the parties' organizational support, it has been almost impossible to gather sufficient support to be elected to parliament. The institutional changes have reinforced the role of the parties as the primary promoters and selectors in the candidate selection process. Contrary to some assumptions, the eroding party membership has not resulted in the declining participatory rates in nominations. In general, the organizational strength along with the excessive number of members does not necessarily help parties to mobilize their members for candidate selection.

At the same time changes in electoral law have contributed both to the formalization and standardization of the Finnish nomination system. It has been gradually transformed from an informal-centralized system in the early twentieth century to a more formal-decentralized system based on relatively standardized procedures dictated, at least to a certain extent, by law. Despite the relatively few obligatory provisions of the law, this kind of regulation has presented continuity and clarity to the proceedings by spelling out the rules of the game. Especially the reforms carried out in the late 1960s and in 1975 have corroborated internal party democracy and the formalization of procedures within the political parties. Obligatory primaries have proven to be not only a useful means to test the popularity of the aspirants among party members, but a relatively accurate predictor of election results as well.

During the 20th century the locus on nominations has been gradually delegated from the national party center to party district organizations and finally from the district level to local party branches and local members. Decision making is not only assigned to local party members since the party district executive is entitled to correct certain biases on the candidate lists produced by party primaries. The picture is quite different regarding the role of national party headquarters; there are no official mechanisms available whereby the national party organization or party leaders can exercise an effect on the local-centered selection processes. This development has been contributed by the professionalization of politics with extensive support teams conducted frequently by experts and persons outside party politics (see Sundberg 1989, 56-57). The increased application of supporter teams is perceived not only as a positive phenomenon but an unfavorable one on account of a possible threat to the activity of local and municipal party branches which may bring about eroding effects on the internal party cohesion (Timonen 1975, 175).

As to the selection criteria applied in nominations, empirical evidence drawn from the 1995 candidate selections does not corroborate the relatively widely held belief that party members are to be blamed for the underrepresentation of several social and demographic groups. On the contrary, the results suggest that already at the stage at which local party members and members' associations bring aspirants forward, élitist tendencies can be detected. Considering the fact that the original array of aspirants of almost all the underrepresented groups corresponds quite accurately with the composition of the candidate lists and elected deputies, the major alterations to correct representative biases should not be aimed at changing the candidate selection practiced by party members but should try to influence the supply of women, and young and old people as well as that of non-graduates who are underrepresented in the assembly. Since the nomination processes preceding the election of deputies account for these biases to a great extent, the electorate as a principal has rather limited opportunities to affect the final composition of the candidate lists, due to the strong tendency for élitism in the nominations.

In terms of accountability and sanction mechanisms decisive in the principal-agent model, there appears to be a wide consensus on the incomparable positions of previous legislators and candidates in both nominations and elections. As the majority of the party district officials interviewed in this particular study highlighted, party selectors only utilize *ex post* sanction mechanisms when there are severe personal drawbacks, such as bankruptcies or economic obscurities, reported in the near past of the incumbent deputies. On the other hand, there are some cases to be detected showing that even these kinds of MPs with questionable pasts are able to enjoy inconceivable popularity among the electorate.

The most probable reason for the turnover of candidates, according to the majority of party district officials, is to be attributed to the voluntary retirement of candidates either due to their age, their poor success in bygone elections or as a result of their profound alteration of ambitions from political to non-political arenas. The unsatisfactory success in preceding elections may not be underlined only by the candidates themselves but also by the local party branches and district organizations, even if the possibilities for interference are severely limited for the latter. Of significance for the turnover is also the fact that previous candidates may be sacrificed as a result of such party strategies in which the highest priority is put on the regional balance. By striving for a fair regional representation of relevant sub-areas within the constituency, parties have to cope with two somewhat contradictory tendencies: to ensure the complacency of internal party groups together with the aim of not recruiting too many candidates of the risk of vote splitting.

In general, the probability of previous candidates and MPs being elected in forthcoming elections is enhanced not only through their strategic assets such as familiarity, established supporter groups and possible financial resources on offer for them, but for the legislators also by the institutionalization of the special assistant system introduced in the Finnish parliament after the 1995 parliamentary election.

Considering the relatively high turnover rates in some election years, there are some indications of the electorate asserting its power in order to hold elected representatives responsible by their involuntary removal. The turnover rate of candidates in nominations is in fact relatively impressive, with 59 percent of candidates being newcomers and 35 percent old candidates on average in comparison with that of 30 percent and 63 percent respectively, as a result of elections.

Largely, the most effective supervision mechanism, when it comes to eviction of sitting members of parliament, appears to be applied by voters instead of political parties. To put it more simply, the voluntary retirement or the defeat in party primaries accounts less for the incumbency turnover than does the behavior of a discontented or impatient electorate in almost every election from 1958 to 1987. On the basis of the empirical data analyzed in this study, it is still somewhat questionable whether the party selectorate and mass electorate are capable of holding selected candidates and officials truly accountable and, consequently, whether the recruitment process covering all the phases from aspirant supply up to elections actually ends up responding to their demands.

4

Iceland: From Party Rule to Pluralist Political Society

Svanur Kristjánsson

Introduction

This chapter deals with candidate selections in elections to the *Althingi*, the Icelandic parliament. The main focus will be on the post-1959 period when a new electoral system, dividing the country into the current eight constituencies, was introduced. When necessary, for the sake of analysis and comparison with the other Nordic countries, our data cover all of the post World War II period.

Until the 1971 parliamentary election the main political parties selected their candidates by party conventions, held at the electoral district level. Nominations were intraparty affairs, from which general voters were excluded. The 1971 election ushered in a new period, characterized by the open primary, in which participation is often open to all voters eligible in the general election. Thus Iceland became the only Western democracy with a parliamentary system of government in which the main political parties routinely employ the open primary for selecting its parliamentary candidates.

In this chapter we focus on this fundamental change in the system of nomination. First we describe the nature of the change; then we analyze the causes as well as the consequences of the alterations in the system of nominations. We pay particular attention to the relationship between party organization and the nomination method: How organization conditions the party's choice of nomination method which in turn deeply affects the future development of the party as an organized entity. [35]

Defining the actors

If MPs are viewed as agents four main principals are possible: voters, local party members or local activists, regional party leaders, and national leaders. The number of people within each category of possible principals varies considerably, notably within each category in time, between political parties and between categories.

In Iceland the electorate numbered 77,670 in 1946 with 67,896 voting, 87.4%. In the 1995 election the electorate consisted of 191,973 people, of whom 167,751 voted, or 87.4%. The four main political parties claim a total of 50,500 members. The largest party, counted in electoral support, the middle-right Independence Party (IP) claims 33,000 members; the second largest party, the center Progressive Party (PP) 7,000 members; the third largest party, the left People's Alliance (PA) 5,000 members but the fourth largest, the Social Democratic Party (SDP) claims 5,500 members (Hardarson 1999).

It is difficult to estimate precisely the total number of regional leaders for the four main parties. In addition to the factors of variability already mentioned, much depends on the definition itself. Thus many people hold official party positions at the regional level, almost without qualifying as party activists, not to mention exercising any leadership functions. The four main parties have in the post-1959 period developed very similar organizational structure. In each party nominations in parliamentary elections are formally in the hands of a party convention, one for each of the eight constituencies. The party convention selects an executive council, serving between the annual main meetings. Our estimate is that the total number of regional leaders is usually at least around 1,000 people for the four parties but not exceeding 2,000 people.

The exact number of national leaders is also difficult to identify. For one thing it depends on the position of the party leader. At times the leader is almost supreme in the party, at others he must share power with one or more of the other MPs for his party.

In conclusion, the number of participants within each category of possible principals ranges from many thousand voters to a handful of national leaders. It should also be noted that as the number decreases, "the maleness" of possible principals increases. Thus in the post-1945 period a total of 26 persons have served as leaders for the four main parties, all but one males. (The PA elected a woman MP as leader in 1995. That party is also unique in having a term-limit-eight years-for continuous holding of party office.)

In an analysis of candidate selection in parliamentary elections, MPs are the possible agents. We should, however, distinguish between each individual MP as an agent and MPs as agents through their membership in political parties. Thus, on the one hand we have the single MP, on the other the group of MPs sharing candidacies for the same party, being on the same ticket.

Defining the delegation mechanisms

The four principals can be related to the same agent(s) in individual and collective roles. This adds up to eight possible relationships between principals and agents. When coupled with the criteria of ex ante accountability and ex post accountability of the agent to the principal in each relationship, the possible instances of agent problems are up to sixteen.

Different nomination systems give rise to different "agent problems" which we must identify in our analysis of the Icelandic political system. We should be particularly alert to the questions of conflict and trade-off at three levels:

a) In the relationship between the same principal (e.g. voters) and the same agent (e.g. the individual MP). Thus the open primary might increase ex post accountability by the individual MP to voters but also be likely to decrease ex post accountability in the relationship, by introducing the need for the voters' extensive monitoring of individual MPs as increasingly free agents in their legislative capacity after the election.
b) In the relationship between the same principal (e.g. voters) and different agents, the single MPs and the collective MPs. For example, through the open primary ex ante accountability of individual MPs is decreased. The relatively easy monitoring of collective (party) MP is replaced by the need for monitoring many individual MPs.

c) In the relationship between different principals and the same agent. Consider again the open primary: Ex ante accountability by individual MPs to voters is increased while both ex ante and ex post accountability of individual MPs to party members is decreased.

The delegation-accountability conception is primarily a useful framework in studying candidate selection. By itself, it is devoid of empirical content and has hardly any intrinsic value in analyzing politics.

In the following sections we attempt to link the study of nominations to democratic theories by looking at the case of Iceland. More specifically, we pose two main questions:

1) What is the contribution of the nomination system at any one time to democracy in Iceland, defined as accountability of the MPs (the leaders) to the principal (the people)?
2) Is change in the nomination system over time linked to change in the political system as a whole, strengthening or weakening democracy?

The nomination system

Historical development

Development of the nomination system in Iceland is closely tied to evolution of the political system at large, especially the nature of party organizations and the role of political parties.

Thus, we find that the history of the political system in Iceland in the 20th century can be roughly divided into three periods. First, the pre-mass political party period, lasting basically until the early 1930s. Second, the heydays of the patronage political party with mass political party structure, playing a key role in the centralization of society (economy, culture) with the political system at the center. Last, the present system, dating back to the early 1970s, characterized by greater pluralism in society and weakening of the political parties. In important ways the current system is more alike the first period than the interregnum of party control.

At any one time three levels must be taken into account when analyzing the Icelandic political system in this century:

- The prevailing notion of democracy. Two common alternatives can be observed: a) indirect democracy or, rather parliamentary government; parties as intermediaries, articulating and aggregating, between the rulers and the ruled. b) Direct democracy or, more precisely, populism. Since direct democracy is not possible, the argument goes, then at least we can have direct links between the leaders and the people, bypassing any intermediaries. In Iceland this ideology most often boils down to some variety of "populism".
- The common conception and organization of political parties. On this score the basic categories of the cadre party versus the mass political party capture the main alternatives.
- The internal logic of the political system and its relationship to the environment (the economy, the social system). Here the actual function of parties within the political system is crucial as well as their role in the linkage between politics and society.

Taken together, these three levels form two distinct images: In one view strong political parties are vital to democracy, defined as parliamentary government. In the contending view, there is a zero-sum connection between strong parties and democracy; strong parties and democracy are inversely related. (A popular slogan in the early 1970s was: "Democracy – not rule by parties").

Now the three levels – definition of democracy, party organization, basic characteristics of the political system – do not in reality establish a political society in which the three parts nicely fit together and two pure types emerge: a) Pluralist political society, that is, direct democracy as an ideal-cadre parties-decentralized political system, or b) party rule political society. Parliamentary government-mass parties-centralized political system.

We will not enter into any general discussion of the (causal) relationships between the three levels. We do, however, claim the following:

- The distinction between the three levels is useful as is the notion that there is a strong tendency towards either pluralist political society or party rule political society.
- The study of nominations should be placed at the level of party but it is also of crucial importance to look at connections: 1) between the nomination system and the political system. 2) between the nomination system and the level of political ideas. Thus studying nomination systems becomes a part of the political scientist's main mission, analyzing "the interactions by which political societies are created, maintained and destroyed" (Lane 1996, 378).

In Iceland we can observe three rather distinct political societies in the 20th century. In this paper we are concerned with placing the nomination system in the context of two political societies: the party rule political society and its replacement, the current pluralist political society. The nomination system played an important role in this, still unfolding, transformation of the political society in Iceland, both as a dependent factor as parties responded to new circumstances and as an independent factor, inducing change in the prevailing pattern of politics.

In the discussion of the nomination systems and the electoral system, two questions are of particular importance:

1) How and why have the different nomination methods developed? More specifically, how and why did the main political parties adopt the (open) primary?
2) What are the consequences of each nomination method for the complex relationships between the possible principals (voters, local party members, regional party leaders, national leaders) and the MPs as agents?

The legal system

The legal system establishes the ground rules of politics. In the Republic of Iceland (established in 1944) these basic rules, as embodied in the Constitution, have not been fundamentally changed. The Constitution is rather unclear on many points and is based on somewhat contradictory principles: parliamentary government and semi-presidentialism. So the Constitution reflects the same tension between different ideals of political societies as, we will argue, the nomination system does. There is not, however, any direct causal link between the two systems. The legal system has remained the same while the nomination system has fundamentally changed.

The electoral system

In the period 1971-1987, forty-nine of the sixty *Althingi* members were elected in eight constituencies: thirty-seven in five- and six-member constituencies, and twelve in Reykjavík, the capital. In each constituency, seats were allotted to ranked lists, put forward by the political parties according to a simple proportional system (d'Hondt). The eleven remaining seats, the supplementary seats, were allotted to the parties that had won at least one seat in order to minimize the difference between each party's proportion of the vote and the party's proportion of seats in the *Althingi*. The supplementary seats were filled with candidates who were not elected in the constituencies but came next on their party's list. In 1987 three seats were added and new complex rules of allocation introduced, designed to better obtain the goals of exact proportional representation. As before, the voter selects one of the lists put forward by the political parties. The parties rank the candidates beforehand and the voter has little chance of altering the ranking (Hardarson 1999).

In fact through the many alterations of the electoral system in Iceland in this century the impact of the personal vote at the election level has been steadily decreasing. This has happened in two ways: a) by moving from single member and two member electoral districts in which MPs were selected by the first-past-the-post method to a multi-member PR system, b) by changing counting rules, making a voter's alterations in the ranking of candidates on the list of his choice weigh less in the allocation of seats to candidates on the same list.

Sometimes the number of such "preference votes" is high, primarily in the form of deleting unpopular candidate(s). The last time such changes affected the selection of MPs was in the election of 1946 when the popular mayor of the capital, Reykjavík, was elected but another candidate defeated although occupying a higher seat on the party list.

The electoral system change in 1959 was very extensive. The 1942-1959 system was a mixture of different methods: 1) 21 single member first-past-the-post electoral districts, 2) six two member districts with PR, 3) the capital, Reykjavík, electing eight MPs by PR, 4) eleven supplementary seats, divided between those parties receiving at least one district-elected MP.

After the 1959 electoral system change a close fit existed between the political society, characterized by the rule of parties, and the electoral system which lifted parties into a pivotal role in fielding candidates while all but abolishing the impact of the personal vote.

As it turned out this harmony did not last for a long time; one decade later the pluralist conception of political society forcefully reasserted itself-and the parties responded by changing nomination methods.

The role of the party

The section is concerned with the role of party in the system of nomination prevailing at any one time. First, we describe and analyze nomination methods in each of the four main parties. The last part contains conclusions, based on the previous parts.

Iceland has basically had a four-party system since the 1930s. The Independence Party (IP) was founded in 1929 through a merger of the Conservative Party (founded in 1924) and the Liberal Party (founded in 1926). It usually receives about 40% of the vote. The Progressive Party (PP) was established in 1916 as a farmers' party and is now located in the center of the political spectrum. Over the past 20 years the party has received around 20% of the national vote. The Social Democratic Party (SDP) was founded in 1916 as the political arm of the labor movement. It was organizationally tied to the Icelandic Federation of Labor until 1942. Since that time the SDP has usually been the smallest of the four main parties, receiving 14-16% of the vote. The People's Alliance (PA) is a descendant of the Communist Party and other breakaway groups from the SDP and normally gets around 15-18% of the vote.

Since the early 1970s one or two smaller parties have also been represented in the *Althingi*. The Women's Alliance (WA) has held seats since 1983. The WA only has women as candidates and it has never employed primaries. Its organizational structure fits neither the ideal cadre party nor the mass party type. It is therefore not included in our analysis (for a discussion of the WA, see Styrkársdóttir 1999).

In the analysis of the four main parties we focus on the relationship between party organization and the nomination method employed by each party. We start with the party most closely approximating the ideal type of the cadre party, the IP, and move to discussion of the PP, which is also essentially a cadre party but less so than the IP. Next we look at the SDP, combining features of the cadre party with mass political party formal structure. Lastly we analyze the PA, which in the post-1968 period adopted the structure and organizational practice of the mass political party.

We should also note that the organizational features of each party "fits" its ideological profile: As we move from right to left, the cadre party characteristics become less pronounced while the socialist PA is the closest to the mass political party model.

The Independence Party

Just like the Progressive Party (PP) the IP initially was a cadre party, founded by MPs without any formal organization outside the parliament, the *Althingi*. Thus no formal rules existed regarding candidate selection, who should decide upon the party's candidates.

The 1936 IP national convention adopted the first party statutes. The task of nominating candidates for elected office was entrusted to the executive committee of the local party branch. If disagreement arose "a trial election" was to be conducted in which all party voters could participate. Two methods of candidate selection had thereby been established: Either delegates (the local executive committee) or the party's voters should determine the party's candidates. In both cases party members were not assigned to direct and exclusive roles.

On the whole, however, primaries-as the trial elections came to be named-were only employed in selecting the IP's parliamentary candidates on very few occasions, until the 1971 election, which I will discuss later.

The IP's statutes basically remained the same until the 1961 national conventions. Then two main changes were adopted: the national convention now elected the party's chairman and vice chairman instead of the parliamentary group and the central committee.

Local party organizations elected delegates to one local committee; the various local committees then elected delegates to the electoral district committee, which in turn determined the party's list in parliamentary elections. Thus, two committees now separated ordinary party members from nomination decisions, and selection of the party's candidates.

Undoubtedly these organizational changes greatly strengthened local party committees. In earlier times the national party leaders sometimes could influence the selection of parliamentary candidates. They were not able to replace sitting MPs but in quite a few cases young and promising candidates entered open seats, sponsored by the national leadership: Such sponsorships were now almost impossible.

Within each of the electoral district committees various local interests contended for top seats on the party's list. Nominations were handled exclusively as local affairs.

The 1969 convention adopted a resolution urging the use of primaries to select the party's candidates in local and national elections. The party's central committee subsequently issued guidelines for primaries before the 1970 local elections, when the IP conducted primaries in many localities, including all the large ones.

Generally, primary participation was open to all: Usually no attempt was made to distinguish party members, party supporters, party voters or potential party voters.

In some cases participation of young people, from the age of 18, was encouraged; the voting age in the general election being set at 20 years. In many instances participants did not have to leave their homes to vote; ballots were distributed to all but publicly confirmed members and supporters of other parties. If requested the ballots were picked up again after voting by party workers and taken to the designated voting places.

No political party in the West has ever, at least not in the 20th century, conducted primaries as open as these. The ideology justifying the primaries also spoke to a deep-seated and popular definition of democracy in Iceland: Wide-open nomination processes means less party control, which in turn implies more democracy. Party rule and democracy are frequently considered as mutually exclusive.

Whatever the ideological message implied, results of the 1970 local elections made a strong and lasting impact on the IP's leadership. By a skillful electoral strategy of which the open primary was an integral part, they turned the electoral tables; most importantly the IP managed to keep its majority in the capital

Before the next parliamentary election, in 1971, the IP held primaries in five electoral districts.

The 1971 primaries were open, all self-declared party supporters could vote, but ballots were not distributed outside the designated voting places. The IP won a defensive victory in the parliamentary election of 1971, losing only 1.3% of the national vote and securing firmly its position as the largest political party.

The first widespread primaries before parliamentary elections demonstrated the same main features characterizing primaries in the IP ever since:

- Participation is at a high level and primary results determine top seats on the party's lists.
- The primaries became a battlefield for party factions and individual politicians but clear winners-or losers-did not emerge. Consequently intraparty conflict was not authoritatively settled.
- MP's could lose their seats in the nomination process.

On the basis of its nomination procedures we can place the IP squarely in the category of parties employing an "informal-localized process", along with parties in the United States and Canada, "the closest example of an informal-localized process ... where local party members in the Progressive Conservative Party determine most of their own rules and practices for choosing their nominee." (Norris and Lovenduski, 1995:201).

In fact the range of nomination methods employed in the IP is greater than in the Canadian party. Before one and the same general election the party might use almost as many different methods as the number of electoral districts (eight).

Conflicts on selection procedures as well as the diversity of nomination rules clearly manifest organizational decline. The IP does not operate by coordinated and standardized rules in performing a basic task of any party organization, to nominate candidates. The development of nominating methods also shows great localism within the party. This allows for great flexibility, to take account of local circumstances and reach authoritative decisions at the local level. Greater adaptability to local situations goes hand in hand with increasing danger of lingering intraparty strife and disunity.

There is a clear hierarchy within the IP, however, in the choice of a nomination rule; the primary is viewed as the most legitimate method. Confronted with challenge to sitting MPs or open top seats, the district committee must decide upon the nomination method. The probability of the primary being selected increases in direct relation to the severity of conflict. The same goes for participation level in the primaries. The greater the conflict, the higher the participation.

The IP is firmly locked into its initial justification of the primary in 1971: The primary is the most democratic method to select parliamentary candidates. It takes power from the party bosses, placing it where it belongs, with the people.

Furthermore, all IP primaries are in practice "open" primaries, regardless of the criteria of participation eligibility, to be distinguished from "closed" primaries in which only dues-paying party members can participate.

The IP does not, to start with, require party members to maintain full standing by paying membership dues. Secondly, the registration procedures maximize the number of party members; once someone enters the IP, for example in order to vote for a friend in a primary, that person will stay on the party's membership records thereafter.

This is not to deny the existence of different rules of participation in the IP primaries, which in recent elections tend towards less open primaries. The most restrictive primary rules, limiting participation to old and new party members, still do not move them out of the open primary category. Nor are less inclusive participation rules necessarily a disadvantage to challengers to the party's establishment.

In summary, the IP is bound by its past actions and its basic organizational, cadre party characteristics to maintain the open primary as an ever-present nomination option.

So far we have mainly discussed: 1) Why the IP is forced to keep the primary and 2) why the IP primaries are in effect open primaries. A political party can, however, keep the authority of party institutions while employing open primaries by one simple organizational device: The party controls entry into the primary contest: who become candidates in the primary election. In the United States, in some cases, only candidates receiving support in a party convention vote are placed on the primary ballot. In the IP – as in other parties in Iceland – such devices are non-existent. Requirements for candidacy in the IP primary are as follows:

- The candidate must be a party member and sign a declaration of intent to enter the primary.
- The candidate must be eligible to vote in the coming general election.
- The candidacy should be supported in writing by at least 20 party members.

These qualification rules are not intended to keep party control over the nomination process. In fact, one has to look very closely at the IP's history to find one case in which a man was willing to run in a primary but did not manage to obtain the necessary number of signatures.

Viewing the nomination procedures employed by the IP since 1959, the 1971 election is clearly a turning point. Before the district committees decided upon the party's lists in parliamentary elections, including and after the 1971 election, the period is characterized by the open primary as the dominant nomination method.

The Progressive Party

The PP was established in 1916 by several MPs. Then and in the next decades the party was characterized by minimal formal organizational structure; local party organizations generally did not exist. For the most part, the PP was a name for an alliance of highly independent MPs rather than a single cohesive organizational entity. Nomination of candidates was largely a local matter with MPs and other local leaders playing determining roles.

Party institutions did, however, handle nominations in the special at-large elections, with the whole country as one electoral district, selecting the minority of MPs. In 1922 and 1926 ballots were mailed to party supporters, asking for their preferences of candidates. In 1926 about 1,600 such ballots were returned, the PP receiving 3,461 votes in the election.

In both ordinary parliamentary elections and the at-large elections nominations were settled in an informal and personal fashion rather than guided by formal rules.

The early 1930s was a period of severe internal conflict within the PP, which revolved around a complex fusion of personal feuds and ideological differences. An organizational dispute was also involved. The party reformers initiated formalization of the nomination process. Local party organizations were accordingly authorized to decide on the party's candidates while needing the approval of national party institutions. "A primary" should, however, be conducted when requested by party members. Thus, the successful party insurgents intended to obtain a majority in the parliamentary group. Evidently such primaries, not confined to party members but open to party voters, were considered the most legitimate method to settle conflicts over candidates.

Before the 1933 election the PP conducted primaries. Nevertheless, the party split that year; those leaving-including the chairman-established the Farmer's Party. In the aftermath primaries were only conducted in the PP on rare occasions. The PP now had the structure of a mass political party; party institutions generally decided nominations.

Following the 1959 electoral system change, the PP established a party committee, composed of delegates from local party organizations, in each of the eight electoral districts. Nominations in parliamentary elections became the main task of these committees. Fundamental change did not, however, take place; the nomination process was simply moved from one party-elected assembly to another, larger one. Primaries were never employed at the electoral district level. The old and smaller electoral districts sometimes used primaries, involving party members, to select "their candidate" on the party's list. As in the IP, and previously noted, the new district committees in the PP further strengthened the authority of local party institutions in the nomination process. Conflict within the new district committees did not leave much room for outside candidates sponsored by the national party leadership.

In April 1969 the PP's central committee called for the district committees to conduct "open polls" before nominating candidates in coming elections, the local elections of 1970 and the next parliamentary election.

Within the PP a clear distinction was made between "an opinion poll" and "a primary". In the former, participation was limited to party members; the results were non-binding but should be noted by the selection committee before making its recommendation on the party's list. By contrast, the primary was open to all self-designated party supporters with binding results.

Before the local election in 1970, many PP local organizations conducted either opinion polls or primaries, in some cases even distributing ballots to people's homes.

The distinction between opinion polls and primaries was made explicit by statutes adopted by the PP in 1971. Both these methods were to be employed at the request of party members; a greater number was needed for having a primary conducted. As defined the opinion poll was designed so as not to undercut the authority of party institutions, which would continue to control nominations.

The PP had opinion polls taken in all eight districts before the 1971 elections. Over 11,000 people participated in these polls, more than 40% of the party's vote in the general election.

The different level of participation in the PP's polls in 1971 reflects great variations in their conduct; some district committees strictly applied the rules, limiting participation and, in some cases, not even making the results public.

Other committees in practice arranged for an open primary election, only the name was different. In still other districts the election fell somewhere in-between opinion poll and primary. Thus, the 1971 nomination practices already indicated what later elections conclusively showed; the PP organizations on the ground could not apply the official party distinction between an opinion poll and an open primary. Three main factors account for this:

- The PP is in fact not a mass political party in which payment of dues is the main defining criterion for party membership and participation in party affairs. By tradition payment of dues has never been made a precondition for active membership; a clear line does not exist between party members and party supporters. Consequently, no election can be effectively confined to "party members," since nobody knows exactly who they are.
- Some district committees did not wish to make distinctions between party members and party supporters but concentrated on maximizing participation in the nomination election.
- If a challenger to an incumbent MP succeeds in an opinion poll, it is in practice almost impossible for party institutions to refuse to follow the results. In this case the party's list can remain unaltered, only if so proposed by the challenger.

In summary, history of the nomination process in the PP since 1959 falls into three phases:

Until 1970 the traditional method was employed, i.e. the respective district committees selected the party's list.

In 1971 a new nomination method was introduced which developed into open primaries. The convention method was, however, used in all districts in two elections.

Beginning in 1983 many nomination methods are practiced by the PP. Each district committee at every election decides what method to use or it might even invent some new versions.

Party institutions still play a significant role in the PPs nomination process but their importance has diminished while individual candidates have gained more room for maneuvering. In cases of conflicts between strong candidates competing for top seats on the party's ticket, party institutions no longer possess the authority and legitimacy necessary for generally accepted settlement. The open primary is then the final arbitrator.

The Social Democratic Party

The SDP was established in 1916 as a political arm of the labor unions, joining together in a national federation. Labor unions constituted the SDP's local units, the first local political organization being founded only the following year. Later more political organizations were built but functioned mostly as weak political clubs, debating and splitting along the lines of international socialist ideologies. Thus, a communist faction operated within the SDP, until the communists formed their own party in 1930, part of the Communist International.

Labor unions remained the organizational backbone of the SDP until 1940-1942 when all organizational ties between the party and the labor unions were severed. Subsequently, the SDP adopted the formal structure of a mass political party with local party organizations as basic units.

According to the SDP's statutes the central committee had final authority concerning nominations for parliamentary elections. In the party's few strongholds local organizations did in practice control the nomination process. In most of the country, however, the SDP remained organizationally weak and the national leadership exercised considerable influence in the selection of parliamentary candidates, who-not infrequently-came from outside the respective electoral district.

After the electoral system change in 1959, the SDP employed the same nomination method as the IP and the PP at that time. Each electoral district had a party committee made up of delegates elected by local units. A special nomination subcommittee presented its recommendations to the full committee. Generally such proposals were accepted.

In 1971 the SDP conducted an open primary in one district. The traditional nomination method was employed by the SDP in 1974 as in the other parties. In 1978 the SDP held open primaries in all but two electoral districts, the 1976 SDP national convention having made that method mandatory for parliamentary elections. Candidates in the SDP primary were not required to be party members but needed the written recommendation of 25-50 party members, depending on the size of the electoral district. Participation level in the 1971 primaries was high, just over 50% of the SDP's general election vote in the six primary districts.

In 1984 the national convention changed the party statutes on nominations. An open primary was no longer required but some kind of primary was to be employed to select top candidates in parliamentary elections. Each district committee should define criteria of eligibility for voting in primaries. The convention also added new provisions to the statutes, making possible alliances between candidates in primary elections. Every candidate must declare candidacy by seats on the party's list. The candidate's name appears on the ballot according to this specification; any vote for a candidate to a seat higher than this specification is not valid. By this device candidates can avoid competing against each other, if they can reach agreement on which seats each should run for.

In 1987 three strong candidates made such a deal in Reykjavík, thereby sidestepping divisive competition in that primary. The impact on participation was clear, only 830 people voted in the primary, compared to 1,901 voters in 1983 and 2,689 in 1991 when candidate alliances were not in place.

Again, there is a trade-off involved. A political party can hardly enjoy the benefits of an open primary, notably increasing participation in the decision-making process, without also suffering the negative effects, more intraparty conflict.

Before the 1991 election the SDP only held primaries in three districts. This implied great change in the party's overall nomination process because the open primary had been the party's main nomination method since 1978. Now party committees in five districts decided on the lists, bypassing the primary altogether.

The case of the Reykjanes district is particularly instructive. Traditionally, it is the SDP stronghold, the party receiving there a higher percentage of the vote than in other districts. In the fall of 1990, the SDP district committee in Reykjanes announced selection of candidates into top seats on the parliamentary ticket, saying that national party statutes now made a primary optional and, consequently, each district committee possessed authority to nominate directly. Four other district committees followed the Reykjanes precedent.

The Reykjanes case should not be treated as abnormal. The party had gone very far in the direction of the open primary, even making it mandatory by party statutes; now party institutions had recovered. In fact the Reykjanes committee acted more authoritatively than any SDP district committee in recent memory. Apparently this development goes directly against the basic logic of the open primary, showing-contrary to our repeated argument-that party institutions can regain their authority after a long period of decline due to loss of control over nominations.

Since 1991 events in the SDP have, however, not followed a pattern of great harmony. On the contrary, the party has been torn apart by dissension. Before the 1995 election the former vice chairwoman left and formed a new political party. The SDP suffered defeat, losing 26% of its 1991 national vote, and acquired seven MPs instead of ten. The SDP was back to its situation of intraparty conflict, electoral defeat and government opposition.

Nomination conflicts in the SDP before the last election indicate clearly that local party institutions had not been permanently strengthened at all. In two electoral districts, one of them being Reykjanes, strong candidates wanted the top seats. An open primary was employed to settle these disputes; in both cases a great number of people participated while not voting for the SDP in the general election. The SDP continues to be characterized by weak party organizations and low levels of party member involvement, even by Icelandic standards. The discrepancy between the formal organizational structure and reality is also striking, the SDP having the rather elaborate formal format of a Social Democratic Party in the Scandinavian mold.

A highly institutionalized party settles disputes, for example, on nominations or leadership positions, according to formal procedures. Only a political party with a low degree of institutionalization hands authority to nominate its candidates over to non-party members and non-party voters in open primaries, as the SDP does. The party leadership also relied heavily on connecting the SDP to the state, the party having a weak societal basis. The long period of government participation in 1959-1971 functioned like a sedative, protecting temporarily against the labor and pain of party institution building, but leaving the SDP weak in dealing later with a more volatile political situation. The SDP was organizationally weakened already in the early 1940s when labor unions became independent of the party. Later government participation made concentrated efforts of party organizing seem unnecessary. In the late 1970s the SDP then opted for a short-term electoral strategy, including the open primary, rather than strengthened party institutions. Consequently, on balance, our thesis is strongly confirmed, connecting the open primary and decline of party institutions.

The People's Alliance

Two main partners established the PA in 1956: The United Socialist Party (USP) and a splinter group from the SDP. The PA was not a regular political party with its own comprehensive structure but an electoral alliance. The USP continued to exist, organized as a mass political party; the former SDP members only had their own formal organization in the capital, not in the other seven electoral districts.

Nominations were highly informal; leaders of the electoral alliance negotiated on its parliamentary candidates, maintaining a carefully constructed balance of power between the alliance partners. The USP local organizations did not have any direct role in the process, thereby preserving the elite nature of the alliance. Local PA district committees were established following the 1959 electoral system change. The nomination method was still the same.

The PA could not maintain its unity when faced with serious internal disagreement on nominations. In fact, in 1967 the PA had evolved into an organization based on contradictory principles, being both an electoral alliance and a mass political party based on newly established local party organizations. Cohesion of the electoral alliance was founded on successful negotiations at the elite level. Such a set-up simply does not allow for nominations to be handled by local party organizations. When such an institution emerged in the PA, the old structure simply cracked. The delicate power balance within the electoral alliance was not restored. The PA kept the label of "alliance" in its name but the organizational structure was fundamentally designed according to the mass political party model.

Our argument is not one of organizational determinism. We simply point out the difficulties of having an informal process solving the intrinsically delicate task of nominating parliamentary candidates, hindering-even ending-the careers of some politicians while initiating and furthering the careers of others. Then, at every election, selection must take place again.

Already in 1963 the informal elite bargaining process was placed under great stress in selecting candidates to replace those retiring. Replacement questions also came up in 1967. Agreement was not obtained; partners in the alliance seemed determined to settle old scores rather than to keep the PA together.

In 1968 the USP was dissolved while the PA adopted a formal structure similar to that of other political parties in Iceland. The PA now employed a formal nomination process. The district committees, with delegates from local party organizations, decided on the party list in parliamentary elections. Thus the PA was using basically the convention method of nominations while the two largest parties, the IP and the PP, were moving away from it towards a wide open nomination process.

In 1978 the PA experimented with a new nomination method in one electoral district. A closed primary was conducted in two rounds; in the first voters wrote in names of those they wished to become the party's top candidates in the district. In the second round voters selected from a list of those candidates receiving considerable support in the first round and willing to run. Only people with valid membership could vote in this "pre-election". (Validity of party membership depended on regular payment of party dues; simply paying their debt to the party could restore members owing more than one annual payment).

In 1979 the PA held pre-elections in two districts, sticking to the convention method in the other six, including the district introducing the pre-election. (It is worth noting that the PA organization in that district is the only one never to conduct a pre-election in the 1979-1995 period.)

The district committees in the two pre-election places both retained the final authority in deciding the party's list; the pre-election was solely designed as being helpful in preparing nomination decisions.

It so happened that in 1979 the only woman PA MP, elected in Reykjavík, retired. In the pre-election that year three men came at the top while a woman came in the fourth seat, which the PA had won in 1978 but which still remained a very marginal place. Some district committee delegates strongly wished for the woman to occupy third place on the list and called on the man coming in third in the pre-election to initiate such switching of seats. He did not do so and the committee ratified the list in accordance with the pre-election results.

In this respect the PA pre-election turned out to function similarly to primaries in the other parties; party institutions maintain the formal right to decide the list while in practice it would only be exercised in those cases where the winning candidate offers to trade places with candidates obtaining a lower seat. In the PA such an offer has never been made.

The PA seemed to employ pre-elections under two sets of circumstances: a) in cases of retirement, when new candidates had to be selected into safe or hopeful seats, b) when strong candidates were competing for top seats.

In spite of less participation in 1991, the pre-election method appeared firmly placed in the PA, being used in only one district in 1978 but in five districts in 1991. The conduct of pre-elections has not caused internal controversy in the PA, comparable to the effects of primaries in other parties. Like primaries, however, pre-elections diminish the authority of party institutions. The trend appeared to be irreversible in the PA. Pre-elections would not completely replace the convention method, which would be used only in the absence of disagreements within the party on the selection of parliamentary candidates; otherwise pre-elections would take place.

Then, in 1995 the PA turned the clock back; only two districts conducted pre-elections in which a little over three hundred people participated. In six districts the party committee decided on the list. In one of those districts a straw poll was taken among party members; the number of participants was made public (376) but not the results.

Development of the PA's nomination process clearly reveals the close linkage between nomination methods and electoral politics. The PA was initially based on mutual electoral convenience of its partners rather than common ideology. Nomination by elite negotiations was designed to build, extend and preserve an electoral alliance. The demise of the pre-election is similarly explained by the interlocking relationships of the nomination process, turnover and party electoral strategy. In the 1995 election the PA went straight back to the future. In the quest for votes it adopted the structure of electoral alliance again, the label "The PA and Independents" replacing the PA on the ballot.

Conclusions

On the basis of the overview of nomination methods presented earlier, we can draw the following conclusions:

- The 1971 parliamentary election ushered in a new period in which all the main political parties, to a various degree, have opened up the nomination process to include voters and supporters, as well as party members. Participation was often open to all eligible voters in the general election.
- Only one of these parties, the PA, has generally restricted participation in nominations to dues-paying party members.
- The main political parties now use several nomination methods. Selection rules vary between parties, electoral districts and from one election to another. One standard nomination procedure is nowhere to be found.

Tables 4.1 and 4.2 summarize two periods, 1959-1967 and the post 1970 period, with reference to the nomination methods most commonly employed by each of the four main parties.

Table 4.1 Centralization and participation in candidate selection in the major parties, 1959-1969.

Party	Effective power of center	Involvement of:	
		members	voters
IP	Very limited	Indirect convention	None
PP	Very limited	Indirect convention	None
SDP	Very limited	Indirect convention	None
PA	Very limited	Very Limited	None

Table 4.2 Centralization and participation in candidate selection in the major parties, 1970-1995.

Party	Effective power of center	Involvement of: members	voters
IP	Almost none	Occasional - indirect	High
PP	Almost none	Sometimes - indirect	Considerable
SDP	Almost none	Rare – indirect	High
PA	Almost none	Frequent – direct	Almost none

These tables show two aspects of the nomination system: 1) the level of centralization; does the central authority, leadership and/or institution, in each party make the effective decision on the party's candidates in parliamentary elections in different constituencies? 2) The openness of the nomination methods. Who can participate in the selection of candidates at the nomination stage: Party delegates, party members, or voters?

The level of centralization was rather low in the two periods covered by the tables, moving from "very limited" power of the center to "almost none" on the selection of candidates. The nomination process in Iceland is, almost, by definition, a local affair since the candidates seek to be formally nominated by the local party institutions. With few exceptions nominations are reserved for local people only. Nevertheless, being "a local person," in contrast to being "an outsider," does not carry any one fixed meaning. For one thing, the locality can officially change with electoral system change. In 1942-1959 the number of electoral districts was 28, since then it is only eight. Under both systems local ties are important, a requirement which is easier to fulfill with enlargement of constituencies. Furthermore, local residency is definitely an advantage for the prospective candidate but is not always absolutely necessary. Having local family roots can be substituted for living in the district.

"Carpetbaggers," the imposition of an outsider by the national leadership in a top seat on the list, hardly exist. In the pre-1959 electoral system promising outside candidates sometimes got their break in national politics by running for very marginal seats, at the initiative of the national party leaders. After the 1959 electoral system change, it was difficult enough for local party institutions to balance the list with regard to local representatives from the old 27 electoral districts, now combined into seven, without also having to accommodate outsiders. (Reykjavík remained one electoral district after 1959.)

On the second dimension characterizing the nomination system, the nature and level of participation, a basic change has taken place in the post-1970 period. In the case of ordinary party members the direction of change remains unclear. In the 1959-69 period ordinary party members did not participate directly in the selection of candidates as most parties employed the method of having a regional convention select the candidates. The party organization remained, however, closely tied to the respective MPs. Very rarely did the regional convention displace an MP seeking renomination. The definition of "party membership" often also remained problematic, as the parties generally did not make the payment of annual dues a prerequisite for membership (see Grímsson 1979). Nevertheless, the local party units were indirectly involved in the selection of parliamentary candidates by electing the formal selectors, the delegates to the regional party convention.

In the post-1970 period the party convention is not without importance in the nomination system. Consequently, indirect involvement of party members continues. Furthermore, in the case of one major party, the People's Alliance, ordinary party members have largely replaced party notables as gatekeepers, holding effective power of selecting candidates. Through the introduction of the open primaries Icelandic political parties have brought voters directly into the nomination process.

The primaries in Iceland have two main characteristics. First, party institutions do not screen candidates competing for top seats on the party list. The maximum requirement is that the candidate be a party member; he or she often needs the endorsement of only a low number (20-50) of party members. Secondly, the primaries are generally open primaries. As most of the political parties do not keep records based on dues-paying members, no meaningful formal distinction can be made between party members, party identifiers and other voters. Thus no restrictions on participation in primaries can be effectively applied.

The development of Icelandic political parties since the early 1970s is unique indeed: Iceland is the only democratic country in the world with a parliamentary system of government in which the main political parties routinely employ open primary elections to select parliamentary candidates. We can also observe political parties in action, being at the same time "victims" of changing circumstances and "makers" of their own destiny.

We have so far in this section concentrated on two important aspects of each nomination system, the level of centralization and the openness of participation. A third one must be added to these aspects: The standardization of the process itself. Is the process a very formal one as each party employs a standard method? Or is the selection process an informal one as the local units of the party themselves "decide on the general procedures used for selection, as well as the choice of individual candidate"? (Norris and Lovenduski, 1995:4).

Before the 1991 election, to give a recent example, the IP conducted several primaries but rules defining eligible primary voters differed greatly, ranging from the district's electorate to registered party members-including those who registered just before the primary-with various in-between rules. In one electoral district the party committee voted on contenders to the top seats (142 committee members were eligible to vote, 140 voted). In another district a survey of party members was made in the fall of 1989, to which 217 answered. Candidates were seated according to the results; in yet another district a selection committee (29 members) decided the list.

Thus, the nomination methods varied greatly, as did the number of participants, from a selection committee of 29 members to a wide-open primary with seven thousand participants. In most districts the choice of nomination procedure was a point of contention within the IP, even being determined by formal vote in the party's district committee. (In one case 43 voted for the committee to select parliamentary candidates while 41 supported open primary.)

So the alteration of the nomination system is, indeed, a fundamental one. Comparing Table 4.2 with Table 4.1 captures some of the change. The discontinuity between the two nomination systems is, however, underplayed by the tables. The current system has two new features: 1) the open primary and 2) the almost complete lack of standardization of the nomination method employed by each party.

Together these two features have produced a new nomination system radically different from the previous one. Before turning to an explanation of this change, we must first perform some groundwork;

how does one analyze the complex relationship between party organization and the nomination method? To put one crucial question, is the choice of nomination related to some general development of the political parties?

First of all, we hold on to the basic distinction between three levels of the political system: 1) the prevailing notion of democracy. 2) The common conception and organization of political parties. 3) The internal logic of the political system and its relationship to the environment.

The nomination method is an organizational property, belonging to the level of the party. The three aspects of each nomination method – centralization, participation, standardization – are all organizational attributes that are used to describe the way an organizational entity (the political party) executes one of its basic functions, recruitment of leadership. The ideal type distinction between the mass political party and the cadre party also includes a distinction between two ideal types of nomination methods. The mass party exercises an effective power of the center over nominations, restricting decision-making to dues-paying members and commonly using a formalized procedure for selection of candidates. The cadre party projects the opposite picture of decision-making, characterized by local autonomy, unclear distinction between members, party identifiers and voters: informality of the nomination process.

In the Icelandic context the fundamental question is: Why did three of the main political parties adopt the open primary while one party did not?

Table 4.2. brings out the basic differences between the People's Alliance and the other main parties. All of the four parties are highly decentralized when selecting candidates but all the parties, except the PA, involve voters in nominating candidates. The organizational features of the parties emerge as a crucial factor in explaining the original adaptation as well as the spreading of the open primary from one political party to another. In fact, in Iceland there is a perfect fit between the organization of a political party and the open primary. The IP started the open primary wave, which almost immediately spread over to the PP and, much later, to the SDP. The only mass political party, the PA, resisted the open primary, opting instead for the closed primary. Thus the PA allowed for greater participation in nominating its candidates while preserving its characteristics as a mass party, keeping nominations within the domain of dues-paying members.

The parties did not adapt because of their cadre party nature. Cadre political parties are in Iceland much older than the current practice of the open primary. Nevertheless, the choice of nomination method by each party is closely linked to the preference ranking of party goals. A cadre party values office and votes more than ideology or organizational principles. The open primary proved to work for the IP in elections, so it was copied by the PP and the SDP in their quest for office and votes. The open primary was simply added to their arsenal of electoral tactics. Furthermore, in a cadre party the open primary does not violate any basic organizational principles. In contrast, the mass party is based on a fundamental distinction between dues-paying members and non-party members. A mass party cannot adopt the open primary without breaking this organizational principle as well as its preference of ideology over votes and office.

When challenged, established parties will at first respond within the parameters set by their organizational nature and preference of goals. The open primary falls within the framework of the cadre party but outside the basic rules of the mass political party. Thus a political party seeks to reap the benefits of change and adaptation to new circumstances while avoiding the cost of drastic organizational restructuring.

So the study of nominations should be placed at the level of party but we must also look at connections: 1) between the nomination system and the political system, notably the electoral system and 2) between the nomination system and the level of political ideas.

The decline of the party hypothesis provides a useful context for discussing the organizational development of parties as well as the connections between political parties, society at large and development of political ideas.

Nevertheless, the move from hypothesis to theory necessitates the specification of causation, sorting out changing organizational attributes of parties from the linkages connecting party to society or party to popular political ideas. Thus organizational change does not by itself indicate any "decline of party," in the sense of political parties becoming less important in shaping the development of society.

After reviewing the history of the nomination systems in Iceland in the light of theories of party development and change, one is left with three basic findings:

1) The development of the nomination system is closely linked to the organization of political parties. As the party organization of the major parties strengthened in the early 1960s, the nomination system became formalized across parties and electoral districts. The parties were firmly in control of nominations, not allowing for any involvement of voters at the nomination stage. The parties remained, however, as cadre parties tend to be, very pragmatic and flexible parties, intensely seeking office and votes. When challenged in the early 1970s, the Icelandic political parties adopted the open primary. This nomination method implies less party control of the recruitment of candidates. This in turn leads to more party disunity and decreased autonomy of the party organization from local circumstances and pressures.
2) The idea and language of causation are extremely useful in analyzing nomination systems. In 1959 the electoral system change in Iceland introduced a uniform PR system in eight multi-member electoral districts. This "pushed" towards considerable uniformity of party organization and then standardization of the method of candidate selection. The organizations of all parties were faced with the same task: The composition of party lists for electoral competition in multi-member districts.

    Similarly the nomination method must clearly be classified as a dependable variable in the beginning of the political upheavals of the last three decades. The parties chose to bring back the personal vote by way of the open primary instead of engaging, yet again, in the complicated and difficult task of redesigning the electoral system. The new nomination system then gained far-reaching momentum, as the logic of the open primary became a crucial factor in a fundamental shift from a party rule political society to a political society characterized by personal politics.
3) The development of the parties in Iceland goes in a circle but not in some linear direction from party rule to continuous weakening of

party. In this context, at least, the decline of party hypothesis is rather misplaced. It is more to the point to ask: What explains the unique and relatively short period of the party rule political society?

The contours of twentieth century Icelandic political history cannot be traced by following the rise and decline of the mass political party, which never really took hold on Icelandic soil, but rather by analyzing the building and then the recent retreat – but not the end- of patronage politics.

By adopting the open primary the established political parties attempted to preserve their electoral standing and patronage nature in the face of widespread public dissatisfaction. In this effort these parties have partly succeeded. In fact the personal vote of the open primary fits neatly into a patronage political system (see Kristinsson 1996). Still the parties have undoubtedly become less important in shaping the future course of society. In summary, the nomination system has helped the parties to survive as electoral groups but at the cost of organizational autonomy and the capacity for governance.

The role of the media

The mass media function very differently in the present pluralist political society compared to the time of the political society ruled by parties. In the latter system, the media played no independent role in the process of candidate selection. The press was party-controlled as every newspaper belonged to one of the four political blocs, always edited by trusted party people. The monopoly state radio (starting in 1930) and the monopoly state television (from 1967) were both placed under control of the four parties.

With the introduction of the open primary in the early 1970s the role of the media began to change. The impact of the media is of an indirect rather than a direct nature. Thus the media rarely select, endorse or oppose particular candidates seeking nomination.

By its very nature the open primary pits one candidate against other(s) wanting the same prize: placement in a safe or, at least, hoped for seat. In this contest it is the personal vote that counts. Under these circumstances the media play a role as the candidates attempt to reach prospective primary voters. Name recognition is crucial, as the unknown candidate does not stand a chance. Skillful use of the mass media for personal benefit often separates the successful from the seekers. Sometimes mass media people become candidates themselves, other candidates adapt by learning marketing skills or take a short-cut: they buy media advice and access by advertising.

The open primary can be viewed as a new kind of threshold, particularly for new candidates. The mass media are often important in influencing a) who attempts to cross the threshold and b) who gets over and who stumbles, or even falls flat on his face.

The new media environment is characterized by increased professionalism and media competition for readers, viewers and advertisement revenues. The individual candidate is not merely at the mercy of the media admitting or denying access and exposure. The candidate can also use the new situation to his advantage as the various media outlets compete for public attention by finding "hot" materials.

Thus the media system interacts with the nomination system, affecting the process and outcome of the candidate selection. Nevertheless, the new ground rules for competition in the nomination process differ considerably, depending on several factors.

In all electoral districts, except the capital, local ties of candidates can be the decisive factor in the nomination outcome, more important than positive media image and professional promotion of individual candidates. The wise candidate does not, however, engage in an experiment, measuring the importance of the media relative to local ties in determining his nomination fate; he simply cultivates both.

Sanctions and rewards

We have now described and analyzed the system of nomination. The next step is to consider the consequences of the method of nomination employed. Specifically we ask: Did the shift from the convention method to the open primary affect the recruitment of MPs?

We begin this section by mapping in some detail the basic characteristics of turnover of MPs, paying particular attention to retirement and defeat of MPs at two stages: at the nomination stage and in the general election. Then we move to the question of causation. Specifically, did changes in nomination methods in the four main parties produce changes in turnover of MPs and/or MPs with different background and career characteristics? The section ends by examining the issue of women's under-representation in national parliaments in the light of the Icelandic case. There we find the system of nomination to be a crucial explanatory factor.

Turnover of MPs: Overview

On average, newcomers constituted nearly 30% of MPs in the 1959-1995 period. Turnover was lowest in 1963 but highest in the 1991 election.

Table 4.3 Turnover of MPs. Overview 1946-1995.

MPs	Elections	Reelected		Newcomers		Not renominated		Defeated	
		N	%	N	%	N	%	N	%
52	1946	41	79	11	21	8	15	3	6
52	1949	37	71	15	29	12	23	3	6
52	1953	41	79	11	21	5	10	6	12
52	1956	38	73	14	27	5	10	6	12
52	1959 (June)	36	69	16	31	6	12	10	19
60	1959 (Oct)	43	72	17	28	4	7	5	8
60	1963	51	85	9	15	7	12	2	3
60	1967	46	77	14	23	12	20	2	3
60	1971	41	68	19	32	14	23	5	8
60	1974	45	75	15	25	13	22	2	3
60	1978	39	65	21	35	10	17	11	18
60	1979	42	70	18	30	13	22	5	8
60	1983	46	77	14	23	6	10	8	13
63	1987	41	65	22	35	14	22	5	8
63	1991	35	55	28	45	20	32	8	13
63	1995	42	67	21	33	14	22	7	11
Average		42	72	17	28	10	17	6	10

Besides these two "abnormal" elections, turnovers tend to revolve around the mean number. (In 1959 the number of MPs increased from 52 to 60. Thus the percentage of newcomers was relatively high while both retirement and electoral defeat of MPs was low.) A slight increase in turnover has clearly taken place since 1959, although the trend is not a strong one. The first three elections are below the mean but turnovers in the last three are above the 30% figure.

A positive relationship exists between electoral volatility and turnover. Nevertheless, the pattern is not overwhelming. This is largely explained by the fact that retirement of MPs does not correspond to fluctuations in the popular vote in the same fashion as electoral defeat of MPs. In the low volatility election of 1967, to name one clear example, two more MPs retired than in the "earthquake" election of 1978. Only two MPs were defeated in 1967 while a record number bit the dust in 1978. Overall, turnover in 1967 was slightly below the mean, in 1978 slightly above.

Generally speaking, turnover of MPs is determined by two stages of recruitment gatekeeping, separating the mere seekers from the successful candidates. One is the nomination stage, the other is the election itself. We now move to an overall description of these stages in the recruitment of Icelandic MPs. Further analysis is properly conducted at the level of political parties which are involved in both stages, nominating candidates and entering lists for competition in general elections.

M.Ps are not re-elected for two main reasons: They have retired, not gone through the gate of party nomination, or have been defeated, so that the election gate closed on them.

Table 4.4 contains information on 138 retiring MPs. We have looked at each and every retirement and recorded the main reason for retirement.

Table 4.4 Not renominated: Reasons. Overview 1959-1995.

Elections	(1) Age, sickness Death	(2) High public office	(3) Internal Conflict	(4) Other Reasons	(5) Total
1959	4				4
1963	1	2	2	2	7
1967	7	4	1		12
1971	7	4	5	1	17
1974	9	2	3		14
1978	7		4		11
1979	7	1	4	2	14
1983	2		5	1	8
1987	4	2	7	3	16
1991	9	4	4	3	20
1995	4	4	4	3	15
Total	61	23	39	15	138

In almost all cases the chief cause of retirement is straightforward. The reason "internal party conflict" is very carefully defined to include only those in which the respective MP has publicly given such conflict as the reason for not seeking re-election and/or the MP has been denied renomination. "Old age" is viewed as a reason for retirement, even in cases where pressure has been put on MPs, at least over 60 years old, to retire. There might also be more than one reason for retirement but only one is recorded. When, for example, internal party conflict has been manifested but later the MP involved quits because of appointment to public office, that retirement goes into column (2) in Table 4.4. Column (4) basically consists of two groups of MPs: Those leaving to pursue private careers and MPs for the Women's Alliance, who have left the *Althingi* because of a party term-limit rule for its elected representatives. Internal party conflict might be involved in those cases but classification into column (3) is never based on such "inside" information. Thus, subjective judgment of retirement reasons is avoided.

The most frequent cause for MPs retirement is a "natural" one: old age, sickness or death. (Column (1) mostly contains old age since "retirement" due to sickness and death is only involved in a handful of cases.) We should note that this reason accounts for less than half of the retirements. Together the categories of "high public office" and "internal party conflict" account for as many cases.

Putting our information together, an overall picture emerges in which basically only MPs from three parties are involved in public office appointments. At first, appointment of MPs was restricted to government MPs; several types of public office were available to those MPs. Then after a period of few retirements in this category, ten MPs retired because of appointment to public office in only six years 1987-1993. Furthermore, such appointments are no longer confined to government MPs but are instead regulated by an informal but effective "quota system," giving three parties – the IP, the SDP and the PP – access to directorships of state banks. Appointments of MPs as ambassadors are more dependent on particular circumstances. (For example, no MP from the largest party, the IP, has been appointed ambassador since 1971.)

We return to the topic of the MPs' employment in later chapters; there we attempt to place the information concerning MPs and public office employment in the context of our general analysis of political recruitment in Iceland. The basis argument is that cadre-parties "need" access to top public offices to facilitate turnovers, enabling old-timers to leave as MPs to make room for new leaders.

The second topic we deal with now is development of retirement due to internal party conflict. This is the second most frequent cause of retirement. Either MPs are denied renomination by their party and/or they run on a new list. Before the 1971 election, such retirement was extremely rare; in fact the three pre-1971 cases all took place in the same electoral district, due to special circumstances. (The IP had four sitting MPs in 1959 but only two safe seats). The 1971 election proved to be a turning point in this respect. In 1971-1987 almost 30 MPs retired because of internal party strife, in the same period 36 MPs retired for natural reasons, old age, sickness or death. In fact in both the 1983 and the 1987 elections, internal party conflict was the most frequent cause of retirement.

In 1959-1995 a total number of 138 MPs retired while 56 MPs were defeated. Thus the nomination stage explains far more retirement cases than electoral volatility as such. This general rule does not, however, hold for all elections. In 1978 and 1987 the same number of MPs was defeated as retired.

Furthermore, all defeats of MPs are not caused directly by electoral swings.

Table 4.5 Defeated: Reasons. Overview 1959-1995.

Election	(1) Voting Change	(2) Lower/Different Seat	(3) New Party Nomination	(4) Total
1959			-	-
1963	2			2
1967	2			2
1971	3	1	1	5
1974	1		1	2
1978	9	1	1	11
1979	2	2	1	5
1983	3	4	1	8
1987	2	2	1	5
1991	7	2	-	9
1995	4	2	1	7
Total	35	14	7	56

Table 4.5 brings out this fact, which shows that only 35 defeats can be attributed to electoral losses while 14 MPs were defeated subsequently to being moved down the party list-in almost all cases in accordance with results of open primary elections. Such degrading of MPs occurred for the first time in the 1971 election. Since then one or more MPs have also switched parties, becoming candidates for another party, on every election. Some have been re-elected others defeated.

With only two major exceptions (1963, 1991) the overall turnover rate in the *Althingi* was remarkably steady in the 1959-1995 period, around 30%. The previous discussion shows, however, that the MPs' occupational security has decreased greatly in the post-1970 period. The number of re-elected MPs has not significantly decreased but great uncertainty has developed concerning who will be re-elected, who will retire or who will be defeated in the general election. MPs are not assured of renomination or re-election. Intraparty conflict over nomination has increased along with greater volatility in the vote. The political careers of many MPs are now ended against their will-either at the nomination stage or by the voters.

Our analysis also shows that electoral volatility only explains a limited number of MPs' turnovers. In 1959-1995 a total of 199 MPs either retired or were defeated; only 35 of them were defeated directly because of changes in the vote. In this category we should add seven MPs who switched party and were defeated (see Table 4.5).

Therefore, 21% of MPs' turnover was caused by electoral volatility. Most turnovers had been determined before the general election at the nomination stage, at the level of political parties. The next four chapters treat political recruitment in Iceland's four main political parties.

Turnover of MPs: The four parties
The Independence Party

Tables 4.6 and 4.7 show the basic turnover features of IP MPs.

Table 4.6 MPs – The Independence Party. Turnover.

MPs	Elections	Reelected N	%	Newcomers N	%
60-24	1959	16	80	7	29
60-24	1963	19	79	5	21
60-23	1967	17	71	6	26
60-22	1971	13	57	9	41
60-25	1974	19	86	6	24
60-20	1978	16	80	6	27
60-21	1979	16	80	6	27
60-23	1983	17	85	7	26
63-18	1987	16	70	2	11
63-25	1991	11	61	15	58
63-25	1995	20	77	5	20
Average		16.4	74	6.5	28

Table 4.7 MPs – The Independence Party 1959-1995: Reasons for retirement and defeat.

	Retirement				Defeat		Total
Year	(1)	(2)	(3)	(4)	(5)	(6)	
1959	1						1
1963		1	2	2			5
1967	3	3	1				7
1971	4	3	2			1	10
1974	2	1					3
1978	5				3	1	9
1979	1		2				3
1983	2		1			2	5
1987		1	2	1	1	2	7
1991	3	2	1			1	7
1995	3	3					6
Total	24	14	11	3	4	7	63

For Tables 4.7., 4.9., 4.11. and 4.13: Retirement reasons:
Column (1): Age, sickness, death.
Column (2): Appointment to high public office.
Column (3): Internal party conflict.
Column (4): Other reasons. Defeat reasons: Column (5): Change in electoral party support.
Column (6): Lower/different seat on party list; new party nomination.

A total of 63 MPs were not re-elected in eleven parliamentary elections 1959-1995; 52 MPs retired while 11 were defeated in the general election. The turnover rate differed greatly by elections but the absence of a straight relationship between changes in the IP's share of parliamentary seats and its turnover should be noted. Electoral victories (1974, 1991) and defeats (1978, 1987) are indeed associated with high turnover but so are elections with minimal change in seats, notably the 1971 election. Once again, we observe the importance of the party factor. Political parties put up the lists; the nomination process figures prominently in turnovers, much more than electoral volatility.

The turnover rate has been rather steady but the division between MPs retirements and incumbency defeats differs by periods. In 1959-1974 the nomination stage functions as the main gatekeeper; during the time of the Restoration Government (1959-1971) turnover of IP MPs is highly regulated. The national party leadership appears to possess both the determination and the means necessary for orderly turnovers. This is clearly shown by the 1971 election when nine of 23 MPs were not up for re-election. The introduction of primaries did have an impact, mostly by deterring MPs from seeking re-election, but the IP also used state power to appoint its MPs to public office, thus facilitating their retirement. In 1959-1971 seven IP MPs retired for that reason alone.

Table 4.7 brings out the reasons for retirement of IP MPs. Fourteen MPs quit because of internal party conflict. Before 1971 not a single MP retired for that reason – with the exception of three MPs in one and the same electoral district where special circumstances prevailed within the party. In fact, since 1979 as many MPs (9) have retired because of party conflict as for the "natural" cause of old age.

Before 1971 an IP MP was not defeated in parliamentary election because he occupied a seat below the one in the earlier election. Starting in 1971 this has been the fate of nine IP MPs. Yet again we observe the same turnover pattern: The 1971 election marks the turning point.

The Progressive Party

Tables 4.8 and 4.9 contain basic information on MPs' turnover in the PP. A total of 44 MPs in the PP were not re-elected: 30 retired and 14 were defeated in the general election. The nomination stage is the gatekeeper to continuing careers more often than election results.

Table 4.8 MPs – The Progressive Party. Turnover.

MPs	Elections	Reelected N	%	Newcomers N	%
60-17	1959	14	74	3	18
60-19	1963	17	94	3	16
60-18	1967	15	79	3	17
60-17	1971	16	89	1	6
60-17	1974	10	59	7	41
60-12	1978	11	65	1	8
60-17	1979	9	75	8	47
60-14	1983	14	82	0	0
63-13	1987	8	57	5	38
63-13	1991	10	77	3	23
63-15	1995	9	69	6	40
		12.1	75	3.6	23

Table 4.9 The Progressive Party 1959-1995: Reasons for retirement and defeat.

Year	Retirement (1)	(2)	(3)	(4)	Defeat (5)	(6)	Total
1959	2						2
1963	1						1
1967	3				1		4
1971	2						2
1974	6	1					7
1978	1				4	1	6
1979	2	1					3
1983			2		1		3
1987	3	1	1		1		6
1991	1		1		1		3
1995	1	1				1	3
Total	22	4	4		8	2	40

The overall turnover is low in the 1959-1974 period; the party's electoral support is also very steady, at the 25-28% level. Natural retirement-old age, death-was just about the only cause of MPs' retirement. In fact until 1978 only one PP MP was really defeated in the general election.

All but two of the ten newcomers had been seated in the *Althingi* before as alternate or elected members. The PP was outside the national government in 1959-1971. No PP MP retired after being appointed to high public office; none quit or was forced to retire because of internal party conflict.

Beginning in the 1974 election, overall turnover rate in the PP has varied greatly between elections. Turnover was high in four elections (1974, 1979, 1987, 1991), but almost none in two (1979, 1983). Only in the 1991 election has the turnover been close to the PP's average for the period.

There is a clear tendency for turnover to be high when the party is victorious (1979, 1995) and low in times of defeat (1978, 1983) but two stable elections (1974, 1987) produced high turnover of MPs. We should also note that most of the turnover still takes place at the nomination level. Defeat because of votes lost in a general election is a fate basically only suffered by PP MPs in one election (1978).

Looking at retirement reasons (Table 4.5) we observe the same pattern continuing until 1991 but only two PP MPs leave after being appointed to high public office.

Starting in 1983 the PP has suffered splits in all four national elections. In three of these elections new lists have been established, headed by former PP MPs. In 1983-1995 11 MPs were retired, "only" five because of old age or death. In all cases disagreements over selection of candidates was the main factor causing party strife; ideological differences were only voiced after the splits had taken place, if invoked at all.

In half a century (1934-1983) only one PP MP retired. Thus, the pattern of turnover in the PP in the post-1983 period is quite unique for the party, more characterized by strife but without the ideological content marking the early 1930s intraparty disputes and split.

The Social Democratic Party

Our discussion of turnover in the SDP is divided into two related subjects: first, the overall pattern of turnover (see Table 4.10). Secondly, we look at reasons for retirement (see Table 4.11).

Table 4.10 MPs – The Social Democratic Party. Turnover.

		Reelected		Newcomers	
MPs	Elections	N	%	N	%
60-9	1959	5	83	4	44
60-8	1963	8	89	0	0
60-9	1967	7	88	2	22
60-6	1971	4	44	2	33
60-5	1974	4	67	1	20
60-14	1978	2	40	12	86
60-10	1979	9	64	1	10
60-6	1983	5	50	1	17
63-10	1987	6	100	4	40
63-10	1991	6	60	4	40
63-7	1995	4	40	3	43
Average		5.5	66	3.1	32

Table 4.11 The Social Democratic Party 1959-1995: Reasons for retirement and defeat.

Year	Retirement				Defeat		Total
	(1)	(2)	(3)	(4)	(5)	(6)	
1959			1				1
1963					1		1
1967		1					1
1971	1	1		1	2		5
1974			1		1		2
1978			3				3
1979	1		2	1	1		5
1983		1	1		2	1	5
1987							
1991	1	1			1	1	4
1995		3	1		2		6
total	3	7	9	2	10	2	33

The SDP enjoyed stability of voting support during the three elections while participating in the Restoration Government (1959-1971). In 1967 the SDP had the same number (9) of MPs as in 1959. All but two of the SDP MPs as in 1959 were elected yet again eight years later; only one

MP had been defeated in a general election; another had retired as MP- and foreign minister-to become ambassador to the United Kingdom.

Starting in 1971, a pattern of turnover instability has characterized the SDP. Partly, this is explained by fluctuations in the party's share of the national vote, the SDP suffering repeated losses and gaining one splendid victory in 1978 but only once satisfactory results in two elections in a row (1987-1991). The proportion of new MPs relative to re-elected MPs goes from the low of 10% to the astonishing figure of 86%, which must be a record for an established political party in Western Europe.

Trends of retirement reasons also indicate turnover instability. Nineteen SDP MPs retired in the 1971-1995 period; one MP retired because of old age, two others because of illness. In fact, the most frequent reason for retirement of SDP MPs is being appointed to public office, closely followed by internal conflict as a reason. The overall number of retired MPs is just about the same in the SDP as in the PA. The contrast in retirement reasons could, however, not be clearer. The most frequent reason in the PA was old age and illness while only one PA MP left for high public office.

In four elections in 1959-1971 only one SDP MP retired because of internal conflict, when an MP elected in the summer of 1959 was in the fall election rejected in favor of a local candidate. Starting in 1974 six SDP MPs have retired because of internal conflict, two leaving to establish new political parties (1983, 1995). To this list of internal conflict leavers, we might add two more MPs defeated in the general election, having occupied new seats while candidates in their old seats were elected.

The People's Alliance

Our discussion of turnover in the PA is divided into two related parts. First, we describe the basic pattern of turnover in the 1959-1995 period (see Table 4.12). Secondly, we analyze reasons for retirement (see Table 4.13).

Table 4.12 MPs – The People's Alliance. Turnover.

MPs	Elections	Reelected N	%	Newcomers N	%
60-10	1959	7	100	3	30
60-9	1963	7	70	2	22
60-10	1967	6	67	4	40
60-10	1971	6	60	4	40
60-11	1974	10	100	1	9
60-14	1978	10	91	4	29
60-11	1979	8	57	3	27
60-10	1983	9	82	1	10
63-8	1987	7	70	1	13
63-9	1991	6	75	3	33
63-9	1995	7	78	2	22
		7.6	77	2.6	25

Table 4.13 The People's Alliance 1959-1995: Reasons for retirement and defeat.

Year	Retirement (1)	(2)	(3)	(4)	Defeat (5)	(6)	Total
1959							
1963	1	1			1		3
1967	2				1		3
1971			3		1		4
1974							
1978	1						1
1979	3			2	1		6
1983				1		1	2
1987			2	1			3
1991	2						2
1995					1	1	2
total	9	1	5	4	5	2	26

In the PA turnover occurs at the nomination stage rather than in general elections. In eleven elections (1959-1995), only seven MPs were defeated, including two who had been moved down the list but would have been re-elected in the old seats. Consequently electoral loss only directly caused the defeat of five MPs.

The most obvious explanation for low turnover of MPs through electoral defeat simply might be stability of the party's vote. This explanation does not generally apply to the PA; in 1978-1987 its parliamentary group was almost cut in half while only one incumbent MP was defeated (in 1979).

So we are once again back to the nomination stage. Table 4.11. shows the reasons for MPs' retirement. At first retirements took place for "natural" reasons. Three MPs quit because of old age, the fourth left to keep on with his job as state bank director. New MPs came from the ranks of people previously serving in the *Althingi*, either as elected MPs or alternates.

Then came the split; in 1967 the PA entered two rival lists in Reykjavík after disagreement on new candidates, replacing those leaving top seats. In 1971 three former PA MPs were candidates for other parties.

In 1971 the PA did manage to re-establish a pattern of peaceful turnovers at the nomination stage, now under control of a party committee in each of the eight electoral districts. The PA also pursued a strategy of strengthening its foundation by offering hopeful parliamentary seats to people from outside the party. Some of the new MPs came by this route.

Beginning in 1979 the turnover pattern changed yet again, now characterized at the same time by involuntary retirement and defeats of MPs, due to internal conflict, *and* internal recruitment of MPs. In fact *all* new PA MPs in the 1979-1991 period had moved up the party list, starting in lower seats but then moving to top seats by victories in pre-elections. The recruitment of outsiders stopped completely. The involuntary turnovers did not, however, result in party splits. Nearly all those MPs stayed in the PA, none became a member of some other party.

In 1995 the PA obtained the same number of MPs (9); two MPs were defeated in the election, one of them had been moved down the list. One of the new MPs is not a member of the party. Other "independents" were also candidates for "the PA and Independents" list, one being elected as an alternate MP.

Conclusions

In all the parties the turnover of the MPs has fundamentally changed. Retirement due to old age has declined while retirement for other reasons, notably because of internal party conflict, has increased. Defeat of incumbents has also become more frequent. Turnover change did not, however, take place in the same fashion in all parties or at the same time:

- In the IP some alteration in turnover pattern happened in 1971. The stable turnover of I.P. MPs at the 1974 election turned out to be caused by special circumstances; thereafter turnover patterns have drastically changed.
- In the PP the 1978 election was a turning point. Previously, regular and peaceful turnover of MPs characterized the party. Starting in 1978 public conflict has become common in the nomination process, including forceful retirement of MPs and, in some cases, ex-PP members becoming MPs for other parties.
- One SDP MP was forced to retire in 1974. Since 1978 two main reasons account for almost all SDP MPs not re-elected: Forced retirement and electoral defeat.
- The pattern of the MPs turnover in the PA has not changed in a linear fashion. Turnover predominantly occurs at the nomination stage rather than in the general election. The party's closed primary is clearly associated with internal recruitment while the convention method is likely to produce candidates recruited from outside the party.

Nomination method, turnover and main characteristics of MPs: The question of causation

We have described developments of the nomination method, the turnover and the main characteristics of MPs in the 1959-1995 period. We have emphasized the timing and party-specific nature of each factor studied. Given this information we can turn to the question of overall causation. Specifically, did changes in nomination methods in the four main parties produce changes in turnover of MPs and/or MPs with different backgrounds and career characteristics?

The Independence Party

The new nomination method, the open primary, which the party started in 1970, is clearly associated with increasing public conflict concerning selections of parliamentary candidates. Turnover of MPs has become highly unpredictable, the number of involuntary retirements and defeats of MPs has grown. The direction of causation is, however, quite complex. The open primary is best viewed as standing in dynamic interaction with party institutions. Adoption of the open primary shows declining authority of the party in settling selection disputes. The open primary in turn has its own logic of altering the structure of opportunities in political recruitments, placing a premium on the personal vote, encouraging and maintaining factionalism in the IP. Career patterns of MPs changed considerably in the 1960s, before the open primary. The process of professionalization does not seem directly related to changes in nomination methods.

Here the overall politics-society linkage is of particular importance: More demands were placed on MPs, their salaries were raised and pension rights secured. Professionalization and specialization of work becomes more common, decreasing the possibility of MPs keeping other jobs in the public or private sector.

The nomination method employed has not directly affected the number of women MPs in the IP. Two female MPs remained the maximum for two decades after basic alterations in the nomination process. The open primary has, however, profoundly affected the status of women in the party. To start with, by the open primary the IP as an organization does not shoulder any responsibility for placing more women in safe and hopeful seats. Secondly, women MPs in the IP are very vulnerable; they occupy marginal seats and are likely to be defeated in the nomination process. Four women MPs in the IP have not been re-elected in the 1959-1995 period, only one retired because of old age. Thirdly, women MPs are not induced to retire by appointment to high public office.

The Progressive Party

The nomination process opened up in 1971 but turnover of MPs continued as before, predominantly by voluntary retirement. Since 1978 new nomination methods, particularly the open primary, have gone hand in hand with public intraparty conflicts in selecting candidates.

Professionalization of MPs' careers increased in the 1960s and does not seem to be directly tied to changing nomination methods and/or turnover patterns.

As pointed out earlier, the PP has three women MPs. Before 1987 the party had one female MP, who was defeated in the 1953 general election after one term. The current women MPs have been re-elected: one twice, another once. With such few cases it is difficult to assess the connection, if any, between nomination methods and the number and status of women MPs in the PP. It seems, nevertheless, safe to emphasize the importance of active and forceful women's association within the party in securing some place for women in the PP's internal power structure. None of the three MPs occupy marginal seats; one is a cabinet-minister and another is head of the parliamentary party.

The Social Democratic Party

The change was uniquely abrupt. In 1978 a new parliamentary group was created, very different from older ones. The open primary was introduced; involuntary retirement and defeat of MPs characterized MPs' turnover; intraparty conflict was endemic; the MPs became full-time politicians. The party received 14 MPs in 1978, only two of whom were re-elected MPs. Such a transformation has not occurred in other parties.

The SDP now only has one woman MP One other female was elected MP in 1978 but left the party in 1994 because of internal conflict. Again, the case of SDP supports the conclusion that open primaries are disadvantageous to women's representation. In such personal contests women usually lose and there is nobody visible to blame either; the faceless primary participants have decided. The will of party institutions in the SDP to secure women's status is indicated by the fact that the only woman MP is head of the parliamentary party and the 1996 national convention selected women into three of four top party leadership positions.

The People's Alliance

Changes in nomination methods are not related to public intraparty conflict. In the quest for party democracy a new nomination method, the closed primary, was introduced; it contributed directly to closed recruitment, candidates being selected from the party ranks. Neither professionalization of MPs nor decrease of trade union leaders as PA MPs are directly associated with nomination methods.

The PA currently has two women MPs. Two have not been re-elected. One retired voluntarily, the other was moved down the list by party convention and subsequently defeated. The impact of nomination method on the number of PA female representatives and the place of women in the party is hard to trace, given such few cases. However, the convention method appears to secure some share of top seats for women, not guaranteed by the closed primary. The PA has instituted a 40% minimum quota for each sex in elections of delegates to party institutions. Party conventions normally place women in the second or third seat on parliamentary lists. Thus the majority of PA's alternate MPs are women. When one PA MP resigned in 1996 (he was elected Iceland's president), a woman took his seat, bringing the number of PA female MPs up to three (33%).

Our general conclusion concerning nomination methods, turnover, background characteristics and MPs' careers is the following: Changes in nomination methods and turnover pattern of MPs are closely linked. Thus, the open primary leads to loss of party control over the outcome of political recruitment. In 1959-1970 the four parties primarily used the convention in selecting parliamentary candidates.

Turnover of MPs was party controlled and highly predictable. Involuntary turnover and defeat of M.Ps only rarely occurred. The open primary changed all of this. New recruitment processes created new patterns of recruitment outcome.

Again the organizational factor is important. The three cadre parties (the IP, the PP and the SDP) adopted the open primary, which all but ended the effective control of the political recruitment and turnover by party institutions. This, in turn, created great uncertainty in turnovers of MPs, forcing political leaders to build and maintain personal political bases, thereby strengthening the character of their respective party as a coalition of strongly independent politicians.

Similar influence of the organizational factor, working through the mechanism of political recruitment, can also be observed in the only mass party, the PA. The new nomination method, the closed primary, effectively underlined the control of recruitment by party members. Turnover of MPs became highly predictable as party members selected top candidates from their own ranks. Thus, service to the party was emphasized, strongly reinforcing the organizational features of the PA as a membership political party.

Changes in background characteristics and career patterns are not directly associated with the nomination methods selected. Timing of the professionalization process differs considerably between the four parties, indicating the importance of party-specific factors, notably the degree of party organization autonomy and the party's government status. Thus, the relatively autonomous PA, predominantly then an opposition party, had professional MPs very early while the SDP, a less autonomous government party, did not have a full-time parliamentary group until the very late 1970's

Considerable research has been done on conditions affecting the share of women in legislatures at the national and sub-national level. Here we find the only cumulative studies on the connection between the process and outcome of political recruitment. The two major findings can be summarized as follows:

"It is well established that multimember district electoral systems, especially party list proportional representation systems, tend to have substantially higher percentages of women legislators than single member district systems." (Matland and Studlar 1996, 707.)

Iceland: From Party Rule to Pluralist Political Society

"If no party actively promotes women's representation, there would be no innovation to be diffused across the other parties. It might be that those countries with proportional representation systems that are leaders in female representation have experienced contagion while those countries with PR systems which lag behind are those where no contagion has occurred." (Matland and Studlar 1996, 729.)

On the whole, the case of Iceland does not contradict these conclusions. The overall percentage of women in the *Althingi* in 1995, 25%, was near that of the top countries, considerably higher than the highest single member, first-past-the-post country (New Zealand, 16%) but 8-15% below the other Nordic countries (Norris and Lovenduski 1995, 187. In the election of 1999, the percentage of women in the *Althingi* rose to a record high of 34%, however). The share of women MPs for the traditional four parties in Iceland also remained minimal until the challenge presented by the Women's Alliance, entering lists in national elections for the first time in 1983. Nevertheless, the share of women MPs in the traditional political parties was far below their Nordic counterparts. The highest percentage among the Icelandic four parties, 22% in the PA, was below the lowest Swedish party, *Moderata Samlingspartiet* with 26% in 1994. The women's share in the traditional parties in Iceland (18% in 1995) was less than half the percentage of women MPs in the traditional five parties in Sweden (41%).

On the basis of our research on Icelandic politics, we are able to add one more piece in solving the puzzle of women's underrepresentation: the nature of political parties or, more specifically, the basic logic of the party system. An established party system characterized by the absence of party domination over recruitment neither will nor can respond to women's challenge by fundamentally changing the outcome of political recruitment by nominating many women in safe and hopeful seats. Instead the traditional parties will mainly resort to symbolic politics, emphasizing issues important to women in party declarations and electoral campaigns. Such parties will also increase women's representation in party institutions. Thus, as the party organizations decline the share of women in party positions goes up. Symbolic politics are produced as substitutes for concrete actions in raising women's representation in national decision-making bodies.

Thus, women's share of MPs is highest when three factors converge:
1) Proportionel Representation electoral system
2) Challenge to traditional parties from some party or parties nominating more women candidates in safe and hopeful seats.
3) The nomination process in traditional parties is party controlled, making it possible to institute formal or informal quotas for women on the parties' lists.

This constellation seems to be the necessary one for achieving the Scandinavian level of women's representation in the national legislature. Iceland shares with the other Nordic countries the first two preconditions but the third one is missing. Hence, Iceland lags far behind in changing the male dominated outcome of political recruitment.

We have discussed the impact of electoral systems and nomination methods on women's representation. The PR system clearly facilitates women's representation but what about systemic differences between PR countries?

Matland and Studlar (1996, 729-730) write:

"Another factor that needs to be investigated is whether micro contagion depends more on party magnitude, i.e. the number of seats the party expects to win, or on the nomination system. It seems likely that in proportional representation systems with low district magnitudes, for example Ireland or Iceland, that a party trying to decide how to react to the promotion of greater female representation might face a dilemma similar to the one faced by parties in single member districts."

First of all, district magnitude in Iceland is not very low. The country is divided into eight districts, electing 5-18 MPs, the average magnitude being 7.9. In Norway 4-15 seats are allocated to 19 districts, 8.7 average. In Sweden comparable figures are 2-37 seats in 28 districts, the average is 12.5 seats.

The largest Icelandic party, the IP, has two MPs in six districts, five and eight MPs in the Reykjanes and Reykjavík districts. The second largest party, the PP, has two MPs in all districts except one MP in one district.

In the 1959-1995 period eight women were elected MPs for the IP, four in Reykjavík, two in Reykjanes and two in the other six districts. The complete absence of women MPs for the IP from four electoral districts correlates clearly with the low number of MPs the party receives in these districts.

In general there is a close connection between district magnitude and female representation in the traditional parties. The six districts with a lower number of MPs have in 1959-1995 elected a total of five women MPs for these parties while the two larger districts have elected twelve women MPs.

Nevertheless district magnitude, or the expected size of the party's delegation from each district, does not provide any explanation for the very limited share of women MPs in Iceland. Thus, in a different context parties with extremely low district magnitude can have high female representation. In Sweden two small traditional parties, the Left Party and the Center Party, have thinly spread parliamentary groups. In the 1994 election the Left Party received 22 MPs in 19 districts, for "maximum" of two MPs in these districts. Ten (45%) of the party's MPs are women. The case of the Center Party is particularly telling. In 1991 the party received 31 MPs in 28 districts, ten women MPs (32%). In 1994 the Center lost four seats, getting one MP in 23 districts and two MPs in each of two districts. The number of female MPs is ten (37%).

Left and Center are both traditional parties in Swedish politics, facing challenges to increase the number of female MPs with minimum representation from each electoral district. Both parties have done so. In fact in the Center Party the position of female candidates is less insecure than that of male MPs; the party lost four seats in 1994 while the number of women MPs remained the same.

The election of female MPs in *some* parties – like the IP – is related to the size of the party delegation in each district. The practice of increasing female representation does not, however, depend necessarily in any way on the size of the party delegation within the electoral system of proportional representation. So the answer to the question posed by Matland and Studlar (1996) is clear: The nomination system employed is *the* crucial factor explaining the share of women MPs. Significant increase in female representation is explained by fundamental change in the nomination process, instituting formal or informal quotas for women of the party's safe and hopeful seats.

None of the traditional parties in Iceland have adopted quotas for female candidates in parliamentary elections. The pressure on the parties to increase female representation came exclusively from small outside parties that, with the exception of the Women's Alliance, also proved to be only a temporary threat to the old parties. With their present systems of nomination, the traditional parties have neither the will nor the means necessary to significantly increase female representation in the parliamentary group. The contagion theory proposed by Matland and Studlar (1996) presupposes linkage between party strategy, nomination process and nomination outcome (women's representation). We find this to be a fruitful way of theorizing. The theory has limited value, however, when the party does not control the nomination process. In Iceland the traditional parties have largely abdicated this responsibility. The contagion effect never really started, whereby established parties respond to quotas for women in competing parties by adopting similar change in their system of nomination. Consequently the marginalization of women by men continues in the four parties.

Conclusions

This section is divided into two main parts. First, we deal with the nomination system in the period of the party rule political society. We focus on two aspects: a) The function of the nomination system in the relationships between the four possible principals: voters, party members, regional party leaders, national leaders-and MPs as agents on two levels, individual MPs and party MPs. b) The function of the nomination system in maintaining, strengthening or weakening the political institutions at the core of democratic government, those institutions fostering accountability of the rulers to the ruled.

In the second part we discuss the nomination system in the current pluralist political society, analyzing the same two aspects as in the first part; first the actors in the nomination system, then that system in the context of the overall system of exchange characterizing any political society.

The party rule of political society

On the surface of things voters seemed to be without any importance in the nomination process. The voters certainly did not have a direct role in selecting candidates for any party; the personal vote did not count in the selection process or in the general election. Indirectly, however, the voters served as principals to MPs through the nomination system. Thus, the prospective MPs usually had to prove their electoral appeal at the local level prior to nomination for a top seat on the party ticket in parliamentary elections. Only in Reykjavík was there a fit between the boundaries of one local government and one electoral district. The rest of the country was divided into over two hundred local communities-and local governments-but only seven electoral districts. So would-be MPs had strong incentives and ample opportunities to enter local politics, establishing connections with local voters.

Undoubtedly the regional party leaders formed the most significant principal to the MPs. They were instrumental in inducing MPs, both as individual MPs and party MPs, to ex ante and ex post accountability. The party list was decided by the regional convention, composed of representatives selected by local party members. In reality very few regional party leaders existed but rather local party leaders, serving as local delegates in a representative institution. The regional convention had final institutional authority in the selection process. At this level local leaders engaged in negotiations and compromise, balancing the ticket with reference to various, mostly local, interests. The individual MP could generally count on the loyalty and support of party members in exchange for deliverance of goods and services to the district in general and party members in particular. The MP was also expected to follow national party discipline.

The party members did not participate directly in the nomination process. They did, however, elect representatives to the regional convention. In cases of competition between prospective MPs for the support of delegates from the same local community, party members became directly involved in choosing between candidates running for membership in the regional convention. When an incumbent MP retired, such contests sometimes did take place but a sitting MP only rarely lost his seat through local "palace-revolt".

As explained earlier in this chapter, the 1959 electoral system change all but ended the limited influence exercised by the national party leaders in nomination decisions. The national leaders did, nevertheless, cultivate and maintain personal relationships with local leaders in all electoral districts. Consequently both aspiring candidates and sitting MPs generally stayed clear of conflicts with national leaders provided that vital local interests were not a bone of contention.

From the point of view of the responsible party school, the nomination system greatly facilitated accountability of the rulers to the ruled. Thus, the political party played a key role in political recruitment, training political leaders and-through the nomination system-selecting them as candidates. Later the party served as the main keeper of their fate, rewarding the faithful by renomination and punishing the (few) errant ones.

The party convention method places one possible principal, the local party leaders, at the center of the process of political recruitment. At the same time it pushes the other possible principals: voters, party members, national leaders-to the sidelines but not completely off the nomination stage. This nomination clearly strengthens party organization and party leadership at the local level.

Furthermore, party control of nominations fits closely with the notion of democracy as party government and the dominant role of the political system against other fields of society (economy, culture). Indeed, the party rule political society forms one coherent entity!

The question of democracy remains. Is the party rule political society the incarnation of the democratic society, providing the people with the ways and means of making the rulers accountable? Instead of answering the question with a simple "yes" or "no" let us, for a while, side-step it and move on to treatment of a different political society in Iceland, the pluralist one.

At the very end we return to the larger issue: the linkage between nomination methods and democratic government.

The pluralist political society

After the introduction of the open primary as a frequently used nomination device, a new system of candidate selection has gradually been firmly established. In terms of delegation and accountability between the four possible principals and the two agents, the strongest single relationship is now that between the voters and individual MPs. The increase in ex ante accountability of individual MPs to voters by the open primary is rather clear: The average voter can participate in an open primary-sometimes even in more than one open primary since such participation is not legally prohibited – and decide on the party's nominees.

The voter also retains his right to vote in the general election, irrespective of primary voting, under the circumstances in which the parties eagerly seek to convince the marginal voters, thereby increasing the MPs' ex post accountability through elections. The ex post accountability of individual MPs to voters through the open primary is more problematic. The cost of monitoring goes up, since the individual MP becomes more of a free agent, more independent of party in his actions. At the same time, the voters' possibility of control of individual MPs increases; in the open primary voters can deny sitting MPs' renomination. The main trend is unmistakable; the open primary is conducive to stronger ties between voters and MPs than existed with the regional party convention in control of nominations.

The relationship between voters and party MPs becomes quite complicated because of the open primary. It becomes more difficult for the voters to impose ex post accountability on the representatives of a political party, who frequently do not behave collectively in politics, while paradoxically the open primary gives voters an additional opportunity to punish and reward sitting MPs.

Two possible principals, party activists and national leaders, lose considerably as a result of the open primary. Party members elect delegates to the regional party convention from their ranks. Consequently, in the nomination process dominated by party delegates all non-party members are excluded. The open primary greatly blurs the distinction between party members and outsiders. A familiar collective action problem asserts itself. Why incur the cost of party membership when you can enjoy all the benefits for free? In an open primary the vote of "the free loader" counts the same as that of the party member. Both ex ante and ex post accountability of individual MPs and party MPs to party members has decreased.

The situation of national leaders in the new nomination system is quite complex. In fact they must be viewed as being in the double role of a principal and an agent. The open primary can place more limits on their power as national party leaders. This is what might occur under the new nomination rule: The national convention selects a party leader, conferring upon him the role of principal, since formally all of the party's MPs are agents of the national party. This same party leader is also, as an MP, an agent with several possible principals. With the open primary the party leader, in his role as an MP, becomes vulnerable to the whims of the primary voters and to intraparty nomination competition and challenge from his fellow party members with strong personal following. (In fact the political career of the IP chairman was in 1983 ended when he fell in an open primary from first to seventh place on the party's list. He was not re-elected as a MP and soon after decided not to seek another term as party chairman.) Under the present rules of the nominations, it takes very special circumstances for any national party leader to exercise influence on the selection of his party's nominees outside his own electoral district.

The current nomination system weakens the relationships of regional party leaders as principals to the individual MPs and the party MPs. Nevertheless, under some circumstances these two weak links combine in a relatively strong linkage, making MPs more accountable to regional party leaders than to any other principal, including the voters. First of all, before each parliamentary election the regional party convention decides upon the nomination method to be used. Secondly, the regional party convention retains the final authority for composition of the party's list. Generally the convention makes its decisions on both counts under great constraints. When strong candidates are competing for nomination to the same seats the pressure for the open primary is usually overwhelming. After all, the party has in the past proclaimed the open primary as "democracy in action" in sharp contrast to "the non-democratic party control of nominations." Similarly the party convention is more or less forced to honor the open primary and place candidates in top seats in accordance with the results.

Nevertheless, the regional party convention has some role in the screening process, since few nomination contenders emerge successful without at least some support from delegates to the regional party convention. Likewise, the MPs regularly consult with regional party leaders, most often establishing and maintaining personal relationships with them.

From one point the nomination system is a dependent factor. The open primary was a concerted response of the parties to changing circumstances: an attempt to build new party-society connections, and grow new roots. In short, the parties were trying to survive by finding new ways of life while still maintaining their patronage nature.

From the point of view of the main parties their efforts have been basically successful. The four party format has been preserved. From our theoretical vantage point a complex chain of events has transformed the Icelandic political parties as well as the logic of the political system as a whole. The development leading from the weakening of party institutions to accountable political parties can be analyzed as a four-step process (Sjöblom 1986) Step 1: loss of party domination over recruitment leads to less party cohesion. Step 2: decreased party cohesion makes it more difficult to formulate policy within the party. Step 3: the less party policies are formulated, the more difficult it becomes for parties to achieve authority in government decision-making. And step 4: people therefore find it more difficult to hold parties accountable, thereby decreasing democracy (Kristjánsson 1998 a): 178).

So we are faced with a paradox: the conscious attempt to increase democracy has indeed decreased accountability of the political parties. The solution to this riddle, our constant argument remains, lies in placing analysis of the nomination system firmly at the level of party and then viewing the way the system is embedded in a particular political culture and a pattern of political governance.

Thus the change in the nomination system in Iceland resulted from widespread dissatisfaction and protest against the culture and praxis of patronage with the established political parties at the helm. The public demanded democracy; the parties gave the people the open primary.

A new pluralist political society has gradually emerged with organized political parties in a declining role. Attempts to ensure more accountability of the rulers to the ruled are not primarily channeled through the established political parties but by other means: new political parties, interest groups, single issue groups, the mass media, the domestic legal system, a greater role for the *Althingi* in overseeing and controlling the executive. Furthermore, the quest for more accountability is not confined to the domestic field. Thus the subjects have increasingly the will and the means to redress grievances against the domestic institutions outside the nation-state, often by emphasizing their rights as established by Iceland's membership in European and international organizations and institutions. The increasing concern for citizen rights is also evident in the 1995 constitutional change, adding 15 new clauses covering the full range of human rights (Kristjánsson 1998 b): 24).

In comparing delegation and accountability of political leaders to the people in the old party rule political society, much depends on the theoretical framework employed. A political scientist adhering to the classical pluralist conception of democracy views the change predominantly in positive terms, the trend towards decentralization of power and increased accountability being unmistakable. In contrast, someone from the responsible party school or the critical pluralist school (e.g. Dahl 1990) maintains that the open primary contributes to development towards "pseudo-democracy", a political society which looks very democratic but in reality the people face greater difficulties in making leaders accountable and, thereby, exercising sovereignty. From this perspective, the change in the nomination system in Iceland has in the name of democracy decreased the possibility of truly democratic governance.

5

Norway: Party Dominance and Decentralized Decision-Making[36]

Henry Valen, Hanne Marthe Narud and Audun Skare

Introduction

Nominations for elections to parliament *Storting* in Norway are characterized by four distinctive features:

- The formal procedures are regulated by law.
- Decision-making is limited to the extra-parliamentary party organization.
- The system is highly decentralized.
- The selection of candidates reflects numerous group interests relevant for the electoral basis of the respective parties.

The study of nominations requires a distinction to be made between, on the one hand, the procedures relating to the main electoral system and, on the other, the organizational process of selection. Of course, these two stages are interrelated in the sense that the procedural part forms a framework for decision-making.

Consistently with this distinction, the subsequent analysis will be organized in six parts: After the first introductory part, which gives an account of the historical development, the second part describes the nomination system (i.e. the formal procedures). The organizational process is the theme of the third part, whereas part four deals with the selection of candidates and its outcome. We then proceed to the question of elite turnover. The final empirical part discusses the reactions of the electorate towards candidate selection. The latter stage has been included because in the representative chain the voters constitute the ultimate principal, although they are not directly involved in the decision-making.

Before turning to the analysis a brief account is warranted about the origins of the current system.

Research background

A first attempt to study nominations in Norway was initiated in 1950 by a political science seminar at the University of Oslo.[37] The study focused upon decision-making within political parties: Who decides the composition of electoral lists of a given party; the national party leadership or the grass-root organizations in the various constituencies? This general problem was pursued in a number of subsequent publications (Greve, 1953; Valen, 1956, 1958, 1966, 1988; Wyller, 1959; Christensen, 1976). Later, other pertinent questions emerged as well: How and to what extent does the nomination process reflect competition between social groups and political factions within the parties? Which personal and social characteristics are relevant in the recruitment of candidates? To what extent do the selected candidates represent an average of the electorate regarding social and demographic background variables? In addition, two recent studies should be observed. The first one was a content analysis by Narud (1988, 1991, 1994) of newspaper coverage of the nominations in 1965 and 1985. Her main concern was the changing role of the mass media in the process of candidate selection. Secondly, in connection with the nominations at the 1993 *Storting* election Skare (1994, 1996) investigated the role of ideology and political controversies in the selection of candidates.

In the present chapter an attempt is made to study nominations in a perspective of representative democracy. In so doing, we will lean on the basic arguments from the principal-agent theory outlined in chapter one. Pursuing previous research we are concerned with decision-making inside the political parties: Who makes the crucial decisions: party members, local leaders, or national leaders? Secondly, we are interested in the role of the electorate: To what extent has the average voter an opportunity to influence the selection of candidates? Finally, we are concerned with the outcome of the selection process: What kind of candidates are produced by the current system? And what are the long-term trends in the recruitment process? Our data sources are: a leadership study of 1957 (Valen and Katz, 1964);[38] a study of nominations from 1985 (Matthews and Valen, 1999)[39] and 1993 (Skare, 1996).[40] We are preoccupied with the mechanisms governing the process of delegation, and how these mechanisms influence the principal-agent relationship. We start this chapter by describing the historical development of the Norwegian nomination system, and discuss the various legal and institutional devices providing the 'contract' between the principal and his agent(s). This first section also pays attention to the role of the political parties in the process of candidate selection and discusses the ways in which they condition the delegation of authority from the voters to the political elites.

Antecedents of the system – historical development

The present nomination system in Norway dates back to the Nomination Act of 1920. Briefly speaking, this law prescribed that nominations at *Storting* elections should be decided by constituency conventions consisting of delegates from local units (communes) of the respective parties. The Nomination Act coincided with the introduction of a system of proportional representation (PR), and the procedures of candidate selection may be seen as a part of the electoral system. As far as Norway is concerned, no systematic analysis is available regarding the interrelationship between these two institutions, but historical accounts from several local communities suggest that certain standard nomination procedures gradually emerged during the early stages of party development (Danielsen, 1964; Mjeldheim, 1978, 1984).

The representative form of government introduced in 1814 prescribed a system of indirect elections. The selection of representatives was made by electoral colleges (*valgmannsting*) arranged in the separate constituencies. The ordinary voter was only permitted to vote for delegates to the electoral college. In the latter half of the century the activities of the emerging liberal reform movement led to political competition regarding the choice of electors (*valgmenn*) as well as of representatives. Some prominent newspapers and local organizations announced their support for specific candidates (Danielsen, 1964:61-79). At the election of 1882, which was the first straight partisan election in this country, the selection of both *valgmenn* and representatives was totally dominated by the two competing parties, *Venstre* (the Left) and *Høire* (the Right) (Mjeldheim, 1984:285). Some of the subsequent elections were somewhat less politicized, but the parties kept their grip on the nomination process, particularly in urban constituencies. In a way the *valgmannsting* constituted a nominating assembly.

In an electoral reform of 1905 the indirect elections were replaced by a system of majority elections in single-member constituencies, modeled on the continental European systems with run-off elections. If no single candidate in a given constituency obtained a majority in the first election, new elections were arranged in which the candidate obtaining a plurality of the votes won the seat. The system permitted all parties to run candidates in both elections. They were even permitted to shift candidates from the first to the second election.

The new electoral system provided an entirely new institutional framework for candidate selection. As long as voting rights were restricted under the indirect electoral system, most of the voters may have been able to recognize candidates running for electoral colleges as well as for the final election. However, with the introduction of universal suffrage (for men) at the end of the 19th Century, the choice of representatives must have become more remote for ordinary citizens. The introduction of majority elections implied that the voters of a given constituency were faced with several competing candidates running for specific parties. In fact, the desire for a more direct link between voters and MPs seems to have been the main reason why a majority election system was preferred (Kristvik and Rokkan, 1966).

The effects of the institutional change were equally important at the level of the political parties. The first election might be seen as a test of the popularity of the competing candidates. According to Mjeldheim there was a tendency for the parties, particularly the Liberals, to allow several candidates to run in the first election and then to choose the most popular one for the second round (Mjeldheim, 1978:135-141; Helland and Saglie, 1997:8). But this approach could only be applied in constituencies in which the party held a strong position. A more common procedure was to arrange 'test' elections (primaries) among the party's members and voters in the respective constituencies to measure the popularity of aspiring candidates.

The period from 1905 to 1918, in which the majority election system was applied, was a time for experiments. In the public debate on nominations two main considerations were emphasized (Mjeldheim, 1978:82-83). On the one hand there was a call for *democratization* of the process of candidate selection. A main criticism of the old indirect system was that it had been elitist and oligarchic in relation to the electorate. Now the time had come to transfer power to the voters and let them have a say in the selection of representatives. On the other hand, forceful arguments were put forward for maintaining *party unity* and cooperation among divergent interests inside the respective parties. These two considerations, democratization and party unity, were to some extent contradictory to one another. The debate turned on the question of how to organize the nomination process in order to meet these demands.

Two main procedures emerged (Mjeldheim, 1978:83-120): (1) *'Test' elections* (primaries), which were the answer to the call for democratic legitimacy; (2) district meetings which were representative bodies for the constituency party. This second method was supposed to be conducive to cooperation and interest aggregation within the party. One can easily see the resemblance between the district meeting and the electoral college (*valgmannsting*) of the old system. Mjeldheim (1978) has indicated that combinations of these two approaches were applied in a number of constituencies as a compromise between the demand for an open democratic process, on the one hand, and the call for party unity and cooperation, on the other. It has not been documented to what extent the various methods were applied, but Mjeldheim (1978:120) suggests that the long-term trend was in favor of the convention method (district meetings) which apparently was the dominating form at the 1918 election.

Mjeldheim's study focuses on the development of the Liberal Party. There is no similar study of the two main competitors at that time, the Conservatives and Labor. However, Mjeldheim (1978:84-85) suggests that the Liberals and the Conservatives tended to apply similar procedures within individual constituencies.

One interesting aspect should be observed in these early stages of party development: the role of social organizations in the election process. By promoting their interests in relation to nominations, various organizations were in a strong bargaining position vis-à-vis the political parties. Under the system of indirect elections several groups were involved in the selection of electors, e.g. occupational and cultural groups (Danielsen, 1964:67-76). During the majority election system (1905-1919) various groups could operate inside as well as outside the political parties. Moreover, they could demonstrate their strength by running separate candidates in the first election, and then negotiate with specific parties in relation to the run-off election. Most notably, this was the strategy of the farmer's organization (*Landmandsforbundet*), which ran separate candidates in the elections of 1912, 1915 and 1918. As will be discussed below, the introduction of a PR-system with list elections provided organized groups with entirely new opportunities to affect the selection of candidates.

The new system

The introduction of proportional representation, which was the major purpose of the 1919 electoral reform, was bound to affect the selection of candidates. The PR-system entailed multi-member constituencies, and each constituency in this sparsely populated country would cover relatively large areas. As a result of multi-member constituencies a territorial component was added to the competition for nominations. Territorial conflicts might also be anticipated at the level of the electorate, in the sense that from 1919 onwards the voters would be faced with lists of candidates and not with a few single candidates as under the majority system. Hence, it was decided that law should regulate procedures for candidate selection.

The parliamentary commission, which worked out the new electoral system, was also asked to draw up nomination procedures.[41] Obviously, the commission relied upon past experiences from the two previous electoral systems. At the same time they were expected to collect information about nominations in other countries. The latter task was not an easy one since information on this matter was scarce. The United States, however, was a notable exception, and here the commission was able to find relevant literature as well as a substantial body of legislation (Ranney, 1981:97-99). In both the US and Norway competing patterns were evident, primary elections versus a convention model. However, the two countries differed in the sense that the long-term trend in the US was in favor of primary elections, while in Norway the convention model gained ground. The latter model was adopted in the Norwegian Nomination Act of 1920.[42]

The basic idea was that a nomination meeting consisting of delegates from all local units (communes) in the constituency should select the candidates and decide their ranking on the list, and the decisions made by this convention should be final, i.e. it could not be overruled by public authorities or national party leaders. Only dues-paying party members of voting age are permitted to participate in the conventions and in the local meetings that choose delegates for the conventions. The report of the Electoral Commission refers to the old *valgmannsting* as a model for the new system. Nonetheless, the demand for democratic control was recognized in the Nomination Act, which permitted the conventions to submit the list to a referendum among party members. In that case the result of the referendum was to be conclusive. However, such a referendum has never been held. Another concession to the grassroots materialized through the composition of the convention. The number of delegates from each commune is determined by the number of votes for the respective parties in the preceding *Storting* election, although the small communes are slightly overrepresented (Valen, 1988:212).

The legal framework

The electoral law requires that the parties present lists of candidates, and the candidates on each list are ranked in the order in which the party wishes to see them elected. The prescribed rules are mandatory, and the parties must abide by the law if they wish to have their expenses covered by public funding. If not, they may choose to ignore the Nomination Act. This requirement may seem odd. It should be noted, however, that in 1920 when the law was passed, the travel costs for the delegates were a burden for the parties. The territorial extension of the constituencies necessitated by the PR-system added greatly to the expenses. In practice, the parties tended to follow the law, with a notable exception for the city of Oslo, where distances are so small that expenses for arranging nomination meetings are negligible. Anyhow, the parties generally accepted the procedures prescribed by the Nomination Act, even though by current standards the economic benefits from abiding by the law may seem marginal. According to the national party headquarters the parties apply the convention model throughout the country, even when the law is not formally observed. By an amendment in 1985 the procedures for nominations were incorporated into the general election law, but the legal status of these rules remained unchanged.

There are 19 constituencies in the country, one for each of the 18 provinces (*fylker*) and one for the city of Oslo. The number of seats varies with the size of the electorate from 4 to 15.[43] The number of candidates on a given list must equal the prescribed number of seats for that constituency. In addition, the parties may nominate six 'reserve' candidates. Thus, if a constituency has ten seats, each party may nominate 16 candidates. Obviously, only a few of the candidates at the top of the list have a chance of being elected, either as a representative or as an alternate representative.[44] List position is indeed important in the selection of candidates and has a major impact on the demands set forward by the gatekeepers. But also the lower places on the list have an important symbolic weight in the parties' attempt to balance the ticket with a variety of group interests. We shall return to these points later when the criteria for candidate selection are discussed.

Finally, it should be added that the only option for Norwegian voters is the choice among competing party lists. The voters are permitted to change the list by crossing out the name of one or more candidates. However, in practice such deletions by individual voters do not affect the final result since an overwhelming part of the electorate must make the same change in order to overrule the rankings made by the party.[45] According to the legal rules, nominations at *Storting* elections occur in a decentralized fashion in the sense that the composition of electoral lists is decided in the respective constituencies, without interference by the national party leaders. However, it may be questioned whether the actual decision-making is consistent with the formal procedures. In order to evaluate the system a closer look at the organizational process within the parties is required.

The organizational process

Preparations for nominations start about one year before the election, when the provincial branch of the party appoints a nomination committee, which is entrusted with the task of presenting a proposal for a list to the nomination convention. The committee reflects the interests of major sub-groups within the constituency party, e.g. representatives of various geographical areas and of different occupational and demographic groups. No fixed rules exist about the role of the executive board of the constituency party. In some cases the nominating committee is identical with the board, but more often the executive seems to be represented in the committee by one or more members.

The nominating conventions, which are normally held six to nine months before the election, are composed of delegates from local party organizations in all communes in the constituency.[46] In each locality the delegates are elected at meetings in which all dues-paying party members of voting age are permitted to participate. The delegates are elected by a majority vote.

In all parties it is common that the nomination committee starts by asking candidates from the party's list at the preceding election if they are available for renomination. Responses to this question are then circulated to the local organizations. However, as will be discussed later, renomination of former candidates does not come automatically, even if the persons involved are ardently available. When local units have had time to discuss the nominations, the committee drafts a list on the basis of local proposals. Normally, this draft is sent out for a further round of discussion. After receiving local reactions the committee submits a recommendation to the nominating convention. In some cases, mainly in minor parties, the procedure seems to include only one stage: candidate proposals are sent from local organizations to the nomination committee, which then drafts a list proposal and submits it directly to the convention.

Normally, local organizations discuss the ranking of the top candidates and try to promote local aspirants. All parties report that local organizations carry great weight when the committees draw up their lists. Frequently, the proposed rank ordering of candidates is determined by the number of votes cast in favor of the competing persons at local meetings. The wishes of the local party are also expressed in the vote of the delegates, although delegates are not mandated to vote in accordance with local decisions. Obviously, list proposals by the nomination committees structure the debate at the convention. Yet, all parties report that committee proposals are rarely adopted in their entirety. In the convention the decision on each candidate is reached by a majority vote.

A decentralized process

As noted above, the law does not recognize intervention by national party leaders in nomination proceedings in individual constituencies.[47] The constituencies of Oslo and Akershus (the province surrounding the capital) are exceptions. Since the parties have their national headquarters in the capital, the top leaders are inclined to be involved in the extra-parliamentary party branches of those constituencies, and many of them are nominated for elections here. Party branches in other constituencies, however, seem to be zealous defenders of their autonomy (Valen, 1956).

In the introductory section a distinction was made between on the one hand the formal procedures as prescribed by the law, and on the other the organizational process. It may be questioned whether national party leaders are able to affect the selection of candidates indirectly via their control of the party organization.[48] For one thing, leaders can appoint prospective candidates to positions of high prestige and visibility. By bringing a person to public attention, they may increase his/her chances of being nominated provided he is otherwise acceptable to his constituency. This method is particularly applicable to parties holding governmental power. Moreover, national leaders have the possibility of influencing the constituency level by working through informal networks inside their respective parties. Since the nomination committee holds a key position in the proceedings of the convention, the best means for leaders to influence decisions would seem to be through the committee, although (officially at least) national party headquarters are not informed about the composition of the nomination committee in the various constituencies.[49] How do national leaders fit into the internal channels of communications as reported by members of the nomination committees? The data have been presented in Table 5.1.

Table 5.1 Groups reported to have contacted members of nomination committees 1985, by party.[1]

Party	Aspirants	Members of the *Storting*	National party leaders	Mayors, local politicians	Provincial and local parties	Groups outside the party	Number of respondents
Socialist Left	17	4	15	16	83	17	76
Labor	28	22	1	53	84	33	109
Liberal	15	2	15	35	83	19	52
Christian	17	16	10	34	77	18	95
Center	10	7	4	41	74	10	68
Conservative	43	38	10	55	90	22	103
Progress	64	11	20	24	93	9	45
Total	27	17	9	39	83	20	548

Source: Valen, 1988:216.

1 Entries indicate percentage responding affirmatively.

The table confirms that there is indeed little contact between national leaders and committee members. The respondents were asked: 'Which of the following groups contacted you about the selection of candidates?' Only one out of ten reported that national leaders had contacted them. A slightly higher proportion indicated contact with members of the *Storting*. Potential candidates contacted nearly three out of ten. The main message conveyed by Table 5.1 is that most of the discussions were with local politicians as well as with leaders of local party organizations. Finally, 20 percent of the respondents reported having been contacted by leaders of organizations outside the parties.

A closer look at Table 5.1 reveals some interesting variations among the parties. Without entering into a detailed analysis, a few tendencies deserve mentioning. Although contacts with local and provincial leaders appear to be equally important in all parties, local politicians were mentioned least frequently in the Socialist Left and in the Progress Party. The obvious explanation is that these small parties (in 1985) have relatively few representatives in local office. A similar explanation may be applied when small parties report correspondingly low contacts with members of the *Storting*. However, the fairly large number of Conservatives mentioning the latter kind of contact suggests that it is not only the number of seats that counts. After all, the Labor Party has a larger parliamentary group than the Conservatives. According to long tradition, the parliamentary group constitutes the most important center of power in the Conservative Party (Sejersted, 1984:198-200). The fact that the Conservative respondents were most inclined to mention contacts with parliamentarians may well reflect the power structure of the party. In the Labor Party, by comparison, the extra-parliamentary party organization tends to wield relatively more power (Valen and Katz, 1964:63-95).

Respondents of the three smallest parties, the Socialist Left, the Liberals and the Progress Party, were most inclined to mention contact with national leaders. This may simply mean that parties with only a handful of representatives in parliament feel more need than larger parties to choose candidates who can perform certain roles in parliamentary work. It is not surprising that few respondents report having been contacted by aspiring candidates. In Norwegian political culture it is not considered good manners to advocate one's own political career, with an exception for persons who have already been representatives to the *Storting*. Table 5.1 indicates a striking difference between, on the one hand, the two parties of the right, the Conservatives and the Progress Party, and, on the other hand, all other parties, with the former parties reporting greater contact with aspirants. Finally, Labor respondents most frequently mentioned contacts with groups outside the parties. This trend probably reflects the close ties between Labor and the trade union movement. However, outside contacts were also mentioned in other parties, most notably in the Conservative Party, which has close links to the business community.

Data concerning the political process support the notion of a decentralized nomination system. However, this does not exclude the possibility that national leaders might occasionally exert influence although they tend to deny doing so. Public debate in recent years suggests that the Progress Party deviates somewhat from other parties in this respect. The national leader of the Progress Party, Mr. Carl I. Hagen, has been accused by the mass media and even by his own party activists of intervening in the nomination process at the constituency level.[50] The Progress Party, which was formed in 1973 by the charismatic and right-wing populist leader Anders Lange, differs from the older parties of the system. Mr. Lange's – and later Mr. Hagen's – style of leadership has endowed them with a unique and unusually dominating position within their own party.[51] On several occasions factional activities have been manifest, in which some of the party's MPs as well as other activists have challenged Mr. Hagen's position.[52] At the 2001 *Storting* election great factional turbulence coincided with the nomination process. Some former MP's were either expelled or suspended from the party.[53] No doubt, Mr. Hagen must have played an active role in the selection of Progress Party candidates before the 2001 general elections. In a TV program on October 4 he admitted that in a few cases it had been necessary to advise the constituencies about the list composition.

So far, it has not been substantiated whether the practice observed in 2001 is a normal pattern for candidate selection in the Progress Party, although it has been asserted in public debate at previous elections that the central party leadership has been involved in the process – at least in some constituencies. Interestingly, a couple of tendencies observed in Table 5.1 would be consistent with the assumption of a deviating pattern for the Progress Party. The proportion of respondents indicating that they have contacted aspirants for nomination is considerably higher for the Progress Party than for other parties. Moreover, the proportion mentioning contacts with national party leaders is highest in the Progress Party.

As mentioned, there is no evidence of direct interference by central leaders in other parties. However, they may exert influence indirectly by contacting local and provincial leaders and asking them to support specific candidates. Moreover, there is the role of the media to consider. The media are not only an important source of information for the public; several studies indicate that the media have an impact on electoral campaigning generally and the selection of candidates more specifically, particularly in the American political system where primaries are applied (Ranney, 1983). Although the selection of candidates in Norway is a prerogative of the political parties, they have to take into account reactions of the public. Hence, a relevant question is: How do the mass media present the various candidates and their involvement in current issues?

The media

In an attempt to measure the impact of the mass media on the selection of candidates Narud (1988, 1991, 1994) examined the local newspaper coverage of nominations in three provinces at the *Storting* elections of 1965 and 1985.[54] A sample of newspapers with different party affiliations was selected. A major hypothesis was that the party press would be biased in favor of its own party when commenting upon the selection of candidates. Hence, it would attempt to water down conflicts when writing about the nominations of its own party, and to do exactly the opposite (i.e. stress conflicts) when covering the selection of candidates in competing parties. The hypothesis was based upon the assumption that parties act strategically. Party unity is an important prerequisite for electoral gains, and the party press will utilize internal party strife in its propaganda against political competitors.

The analysis supported the hypothesis that the local party press would be biased in favor of its own party when internal party strife was in focus. Hence, there was a clear tendency towards stressing problems in competing parties, whereas the process of screening and selection in own party was presented as less conflictual (Narud, 1994). Moreover, there was a striking contrast between the media coverage in 1985 and 1965. First of all, the attention given to nominations was much more limited in 1965 than it was in 1985. This was not surprising, of course, given the fact that the nomination conventions were not opened to the media until the late 1960s. And secondly, the newspapers in 1965 were almost exclusively preoccupied with their own parties' nominations and gave little or no information about nominations in competing parties. Consequently, negative propaganda against other parties was almost absent in 1965. No references were made to ideological splits, for instance, or policy controversies between competing candidates (Narud, 1991).

The analysis revealed that interesting changes had taken place in media focus between the two points in time. In 1965 the newspapers pointed to the candidates' group affiliation and their political platform, and they were seldom or never preoccupied with the personal qualities of the aspirants. By contrast, in 1985 considerable attention was given to the professional competence of the aspiring candidates, as well as to their affiliation to social and demographic groups. In addition, in 1985 the newspapers centered their attention on the personal characteristics of the candidates as well as on certain aspects of their private lives. The overall conclusion is that Norwegian media have become important actors during the process of candidate selection by actively taking part in the screening of candidates.

Candidate selection

We now turn to the basic question of how electoral lists are composed. Which criteria are applied in the selection of candidates? Students of leadership have attempted, rather unsuccessfully, to identify some general traits that make some individuals leaders and others followers. It has been firmly demonstrated, however, that common leadership characteristics do not exist, except that leaders are more active than other citizens (Katz, 1973; Burns, 1978; Blondel, 1980). The qualities that make a person a leader differ from one group to the next, and from one situation to another. A crucial question is therefore how a leader relates to his environments and to the demands and structural settings of his group. Hence, as to the selection of candidates we may expect variations in personality evaluations from one party to another. The main question is: How is a given person expected to perform in his role as a representative? This role entails activities in several arenas, in national politics, in his/her party, in relation to the constituency, and even to specific parts of the constituency. Considering the variety of crossing interests and demands within political parties, it is not surprising that the selection of candidates may sometimes create considerable turbulence.

We shall approach candidate selection in Norway by applying Seligman's distinction between two stages in the nomination process: Certification (of possible candidates) and nomination (the actual selection).

The local vs. the provincial level

In the Norwegian system the certification as well as the selection of individual candidates takes place within the realm of the party organization. However, two different levels of the party organization are responsible for each stage. The certification of aspirants is basically the responsibility of the local party organization, although the media may also play a major role in articulating cultural norms and political considerations relevant for candidate evaluations. The nomination of candidates, on the other hand, takes place at the provincial level. In practice, however, the provincial level serves as a meeting place for local activists, because the nomination of candidates is a result of the vote of an aggregate of local party delegates at the nomination convention.

Certification criteria

How do the parties choose from the pool of possible candidates? Norms for eligibility are rarely spelled out in party statutes. Rather, the process of screening and evaluation is based upon norms and values that are part of the political culture of a given society or a given party. In an attempt to investigate the question of 'certification' in the late 1950s, political leaders were asked to evaluate the personal characteristics of aspirants whom they would like to see nominated (Valen and Katz, 1964).[55] The local leaders emphasized political and professional competence as the most important criteria. Next came ethical qualities like honesty, reliability and fair-mindedness, whereas in the third and fourth place came party loyalties and platform abilities (Valen, 1966:124). The term 'platform abilities' includes qualities such as charisma, eloquence, being a communicator, and above all the ability to perform in the mass media and to do electoral campaigning.

In addition, the party leaders were asked if there were some qualities they would consider unfortunate for a candidate.[56] On this question three out of four mentioned some moral weaknesses: Dishonesty, irresponsibility, undependability, drunkenness, 'over-striving.' One fourth of the respondents mentioned failure of the candidate to maintain rapport with voters. But surprisingly few leaders mentioned as negative qualities lack of competence, for instance, or lack of party loyalty and lack of support from specific social groups (Valen, 1966:124).

Differences between parties were marginal, with one notable exception: Labor leaders were far more inclined than other leaders to emphasize party loyalty and firmness of conviction as important standards for selection (Valen, 1966:124-125). This trend was interpreted as an expression of differences in party structure and party philosophy. Labor was seen as closer to the Party Democracy type of party, and the non-socialist parties more as examples of Rational-Efficient parties (cf. Wright, 1971a, 1971b).[57]

The question of candidate evaluation was also included in a study of the party nominations for the 1985 general election.[58] When comparing the results from the latter study to those from the 1957 study, Valen (1988) observed a remarkable stability in demands for personal characteristics by the parties. Again, political and professional competence were strongly emphasized as requirements for nomination, while moral qualities as well as party loyalty were mentioned less frequently than in 1957. The most striking difference, however, was the number of respondents mentioning platform abilities in 1985 compared to almost 30 years earlier (Valen, 1988:220). The significant increase in demands for platform abilities runs parallel to the growing attention of the media to the process of candidate selection (Narud, 1991), and this is likely to reflect a trend towards greater visibility of political leaders in Norwegian politics.

When one compares the two nomination studies (i.e. 1957 vs. 1985), the parties seemed to have become much more similar in terms of desired qualities (Valen, 1988). In contrast to the 1957 results, emphasis on party loyalty in 1985 was no stronger in Labor than in other parties. Hence, the non-socialist parties may have moved in direction of the Party Democracy type, or more likely: the Labor Party has lost some of its original character, as norms of loyalty and service to the organization have weakened.

Top versus lower candidates

In the process of screening and selecting among aspirants, the objective of all parties is to obtain a 'strong' list of candidates. However, a distinction should be made between top candidates, i.e. candidates who may have some chance of being elected to parliament, and those lower down on the list. Requirements for personal and professional skills are likely to differ somewhat between the two groups of candidates, since the lower group of candidates has practically no electoral chance. Hence, the upper strata on the list are likely to face stricter demands from the convention. The 1985 nomination study as well as the study from 1993 both included questions designed to ascertain whether requirements for nomination differ for the two groups. Table 5.2 demonstrates the results for the 1985 study.

Table 5.2 Characteristics considered most important for being certified 1985 (percentages).[1]

	Platform abilities	Enjoys confidence in own party	Experience of public office	Enjoys support in important organization	Active in party work	Represents some group interest	Independent in relation to group	No answer	Total (N)
Top[2] candidates	31	50	9	2	4	1	3	0	100 (584)
Lower candidates	27	36	5	6	10	14	1	1	100 (584)

Source: Valen 1988:221.

1 Respondents were asked to mention the three most important characteristics for each group. The table only includes the first characteristics mentioned. The pattern is identical when the second and third characteristics are also considered.
2 The number of top candidates is not fixed. It varies with the size of the party or rather with electoral support in the respective constituencies.

The table demonstrates that the differences between top and lower candidates are not great. Top candidates first and foremost need to enjoy confidence in their own party, to be good campaigners and to be politically experienced. Confidence in their own party and platform abilities are the two most important requirements also vis-à-vis the lower candidates, although to a lesser degree than for the top ones. On the other hand, representation of group interests, involvement in organizations outside the parties, and active participation in party work are mentioned more frequently for lower than for top candidates. Differences in these responses by members of different parties and from different types of constituencies were small and seemingly random (Valen, 1988:221; Matthews and Valen, 1999:xx).

Turning to the 1993 nomination study, the results confirm that the parties put strong emphasis on political and professional competence. The data for 1985 and 1993 are not directly comparable.[59] Nevertheless, more than 80 percent of the delegates mention knowledge of politics and current issues as one of the most important qualities for being certified, and an average of 60 percent mention platform abilities. The Liberals are particularly prone to underline this quality, whereas the party is less concerned about 'political courage' than the other parties. As demonstrated in Table 5.3, apart from the observed deviations concerning the Liberals, differences between the parties are marginal.

Table 5.3 Qualities desired in top candidates 1993. Percentage of the delegates on the convention who have mentioned the desired quality as one of the three most important.

Top layer - Criteria for certification	Soc. Left	Labour	Center	Chr.	Liberal	Cons.	Progr.	Average
Good knowledge of politics/issues	91	79	77	81	76	80	86	81
Platform abilities, communication	59	43	69	63	73	57	55	60
Political courage (the ability to take unpopular stand)	45	50	47	53	35	56	54	49
Experience from local politics	28	32	39	41	33	23	15	30
Active in party-organizational work	36	40	20	14	12	18	24	23
Independent in relation to group	11	21	12	9	38	30	38	23
Well thought of in local community	13	15	15	17	24	19	11	16
Experience from parliamentary work	14	19	20	15	6	14	16	15
Position in economic interest organization	2	1	1	2	1	2	1	2
Position in religious/ cultural organization	0	0	0	4	1	1	1	1
N	277	524	185	147	189	400	162	

The picture is somewhat different when one looks at the fourth most important criterion. The parties of the center, the Christian People's Party and the Center Party, are inclined to mention experience from local politics as important, whereas the two parties in the socialist bloc, Labor and the Socialist Left, emphasize the importance of being active in party organization work. The parties of the right, on the other hand, the Conservatives and the Progress Party as well as the Liberals, stress 'independence in relation to groups' as an important demand for possible candidates. The differences between the parties are likely to reflect variations in historical background and ideology as well as differences in their concern for electoral appeal.

When assessing the lower layer of aspirants, pretty much the same pattern as in Table 5.3 is evident; good knowledge of politics, current issues and platform abilities are considered important prerequisites. In general, the difference between top and lower candidates is similar across party lines. Most of the discussion in the nomination convention, however, concerns competition for the 'promising' places on the list, i.e. places where the candidates will have some chance of being elected. It is easier to fill the lower places, but even these selections are important because lower candidates help shape the political and social profile of the list.

Group representation and 'ticket balancing'

In composing a list with the proper number of candidates, as prescribed by the electoral law, the nominating convention is bound to choose among persons proposed by local party organizations and/or promoted by the nomination committee. Conceivably, the number of 'aspiring' candidates considered eligible for nomination may be much higher than the number of available list positions. Hence, the selection of candidates may involve difficult decision-making.

As a point of departure, let us consider some strategic challenges facing the competing parties of a given system. In general, political parties have to cope with two seemingly contradictory sets of demands: On the one hand a call for diversity, on the other a call for unity. The importance of ticket balancing lies first and foremost in the electoral connection: through ticket balancing the parties are able to appeal directly to the voters (Valen, 1988; Matthews and Valen, 1999). But two additional arguments may be introduced as well: By nominating candidates who belong to several different organizations, the parties present an image of concern with a variety of social interests. Indeed, aggregation of interests is one of the major functions of political parties, as opposed to that of the interest organizations (Almond and Coleman, 1960), and ticket balancing, therefore, constitutes a link between parties and organizations in the community. In addition, ticket balancing fulfills important intraparty considerations, as certain groups within the party, including geographical areas, are given recognition, and are thus encouraged to render the party their active and loyal support (Valen, 1988).

The integrative function of ticket balancing is indeed important in party systems like the Norwegian one, in which various groups and organizations outside the parties advance their interests directly through the political parties. However, group activities are sometimes disintegrative to the party in the sense that they may threaten party unity and weaken the party's position among the voters. One of the most intricate problems facing a party seems to be how to build up or preserve the image of a united group with relatively consistent policies, and at the same time allow factional activity to develop, thereby giving the impression of a democratic organization during the process of candidate selection. In the subsequent pages we will focus upon some criteria that are more or less valid in all parties.

Territorial representation

Attachment to local interests is an important requirement in the selection of nominees, and the commune of residence for each candidate is almost always indicated on the electoral list. First of all, it is common practice that candidates should be residents of the constituency in which they seek nomination. In fact, until 1952 there was a residency rule (*bostadsbånd*) stipulated in the Constitution, which made an exception only for present and previous cabinet ministers. The residency rule was abolished by a constitutional amendment of 1952, but the demand for constituency ties has always remained strong during the process of candidate selection. In 1957 only one percent of the nominees were residents of some other constituency than the one in which they were nominated (Valen, 1966:151). Thirty years later the pattern is exactly the same; the number of non-residents nominated in 1985 was 1.2 percent, and in 1993 it had decreased to .5 percent.[60] However, even these 'alien' candidates tend to belong to their constituencies through work or kinship, with the notable exception of a handful of 'aliens' in Oslo and Akershus (Valen, 1988:224).[61]

Moreover, local interests are expressed through territorial representation on the list. The geographical balancing concerns not only the number of candidates; it also affects the rank ordering of the list. Except for some of the largest cities, two candidates ranked next to each other rarely come from the same commune or even from neighboring communes. District representation is linked to the local political interests of the constituency, for example industrial activities, the construction of roads and location of public institutions. Geography, therefore, is an important criterion for ticket balancing, and is, with the exception of Oslo, greatly emphasized in the local media during the nomination process (Narud, 1994:308).

The local interests are also expressed in the political experience of the nominees. The local party leadership plays a dominant role in the nomination process, and a great majority of the nominees hold local or provincial office. We therefore find strong local identifications among Norwegian parliamentarians. In his analysis of Norwegian parliamentarians in the 1990s, Knut Heidar (1997:104) points out that close to one fourth of the legislators considered it 'very important' to 'argue the interests and opinions of their own region/electoral district.' Moreover, Norwegian parliamentarians list constituency initiatives as the reason for many of the contacts they have with bureaucracy and ministers (Hernes and Nergaard, 1989:201-209).

Representation of women

In recent years the representation of women has taken on great importance. Representation of women is largely promoted through the women's organizations of the various parties. Traditionally, the parties nominated only a few female candidates in each constituency, mostly among the lower candidates. In the early 1980s, however, the parties of the left introduced women's quotas and tended to nominate men and women alternately from top to bottom of the list. Recently, therefore, we have witnessed a considerable increase in the number of women elected to parliament. The election of 1985 constituted a major breakthrough, as the quota system assured a high proportion of women not only among the total number of candidates nominated, but also among the top candidates (Valen, 1986). In recent years the parties of the center and right, if not in the party statutes have adopted the principle of women's quotas also, at least as a norm for ticket balancing. Only the Progress Party has consistently refused to implement a gender quota system, but even in this party the number of female candidates has been increasing.

The reform, however, was not introduced without turbulence. In 1985, in the province of Sogn og Fjordane (on the West Coast), the demands for women's representation came into conflict with the balancing of district interests, which are seen as extremely important in this territorially divided fjord province. The Labor Party's national convention had introduced the quota system in 1984, and the party branches generally accepted the rule. However, in Sogn og Fjordane, in which Labor could hope to obtain two seats at most, the two incumbents, both men representing different parts of the constituency, were renominated and given the two top positions on the ballot. This led to an outcry in the Labor women's movement, which appealed to the central party leadership to cancel the nominations and place a woman in one of the two top positions. Both the executive committee and the national committee recommended that the party in Sogn og Fjordane reconsider the nomination. But the constituency party refused to obey, referring to the rule in the Nomination Act stating that decisions made by the nomination conventions are final. The local media followed the conflict closely, and several party activists as well as media commentators were involved in the debate arguing against 'central party tyranny,' as they put it. One rather illuminating remark is to be found in one of the local newspapers (Narud, 1994:302-303):

The fact that the women at the national level are engaged in the 'abuse' of their colleagues in Sogn og Fjordane is no more than we must expect, but when also the central branch of the party's youth organization demands a new meeting, you may wonder: Do they know where Sogn og Fjordane is?
(Sogn Dagblad, December 13, 1984)

In order to avoid serious party splits, the central party leaders had no choice but to accept the constituency decision. It is important to note, however, that territorial conflicts are less predominant in some of the central constituencies, and that in the absence of these conflicts other group considerations develop correspondingly more in importance.

Other selection criteria

Other types of group representation on the lists include youth, occupation and certain social and political organizations. The representation of youth, which is promoted by the parties' youth organizations, secures the renewal of leadership within the respective parties and is a common demand in all parties. The representation of certain occupations and organizations, on the other hand, tends to be party specific and is related to the parties' electoral expectations. In order to be promoted a candidate needs the support of some specific section of the selectorate, and aspirant's chances of being selected are higher the more groups he/she appeals to.

Political views

From what has previously been said, we should expect that the local and provincial leaders will prefer candidates who are likely to conform to the party's platform, particularly with regard to principled issues, i.e. issues that parties consider to be important for some of the major policies, and which are more or less closely related to the respective parties' ideology. Hence, the question is: How important are the political views of the aspirants in the screening and selection of candidates?

Having very few previous studies to lean on, Skare (1996) made an attempt to analyze this question empirically in connection with the nominations for the 1993 *Storting* elections. In his survey to party delegates he included a question about the importance of candidates agreeing with (a) the party line or (b) the delegates' own views on important issues. For the purpose of analyzing factional activity, the 1993 nominations fitted quite neatly. The EU-membership question was on the political agenda, and conflicts between as well as within political parties reached an all time high. In this situation it would seem particularly important for the local leaders to reflect on the candidates' political views.

The analysis suggested that the political views of individual candidates mattered in the selection process. In addition, Skare detected an interesting difference between 'new' parties and 'old' or traditional parties in the level of issue agreement (Skare, 1996:333).[62] On 'new' political issues, for instance issues that have to do with the environment vs. standard of living and economic growth, the delegates from the traditional parties appeared to be more split than the delegates from the 'new' parties. Possibly, these kinds of issues are not anchored in party ideology to the same extent as other and more conventional types of issues. However, when singling out the upper candidates on the lists, issue agreement increased substantially also concerning the 'new' types of issues. Skare concludes that the parties, even in politically turbulent times, are capable of putting together an ideologically homogeneous group of top candidates. These results support the notion that the parties are very sensitive towards ideological factions and therefore put much emphasis on presenting a united list of top politicians (Skare, 1996:348).

The outcome of nominations

The preceding discussion suggests that a great variety of criteria are at work in the selection process. Territorial components, service in local and provincial government, gender, as well as political views are important credentials for Norwegian parliamentarians. Through the process of screening and selection Norwegian parties therefore attain a relatively high degree of social representativeness, reflected traditionally in a comparatively high proportion of working-class parliamentarians and more recently women (see e.g. Valen, 1966; Hellevik, 1969; Raaum, 1995; Skjeie 1997; Matthews and Valen, 1999). In a long-term perspective the predominant trend has been the replacement of farmers and blue-collar workers with career politicians (Eliassen and Pedersen, 1978; Heidar, 1988; Matthews and Valen, 1999; Narud, 1999).

This trend is clearly reflected in Table 5.4, which describes the occupational background of MPs since 1945.

Table 5.4 Occupational background of Norwegian MPs 1945-2001.

Election year Occupation	1945	1949	1953	1957	1961	1965	1969	1973
Blue-collar	12	11	11	9	7	5	5	8
White-collar	35	35	35	33	30	33	35	31
Teacher	9	9	4	5	9	11	15	21
Farm/fish[1]	23	26	28	27	25	20	14	13
Lawyer	5	2	5	5	3	3	3	2
Journalist	5	7	7	5	7	7	9	8
Party work[2]	3	3	4	5	4	5	4	6
Other[3]	8	6	7	11	15	16	15	12
N	150	150	150	150	150	150	150	155

Election year Occupation	1977	1981	1985	1989	1993	1997	2001	Average
Blue-collar	6	4	1	2	5	7	5	6,5
White-collar	34	34	41	38	35	31	32	34
Teacher	19	17	17	15	12	13	9	12
Farm/fish[1]	12	14	9	7	7	3	3	15,5
Lawyer	1	2	1	-	-	-	1	2
Journalist	7	5	5	2	1	2	2	5
Party work	5	4	7	16	21	29	31	10
Other[2]	16	20	18	19	19	15	17	14
N	155	155	157	165	165	165	165	-

1 Includes also those MPs who combine farming with other types of work.
2 Includes MPs employed in the party organization or with full-time positions at the local or provincial level (e.g. mayors), as well as ministers and state secretaries.
3 Includes students, housewives, self-employed, organizational workers and other liberal professions.

The proportion of working-class MPs has declined over time together with representatives recruited from the primary sector (farming and fishing). The number of teachers, on the other hand, has increased, whereas the number of white-collar employees has remained quite stable over time. In contrast to many other countries, the number of lawyers has never been extensive in the Norwegian or in any of the other Scandinavian legislatures (Pedersen, 1972).[63] The most remarkable change observed from the table, however, has to do with the increase in the number of MPs whose occupational background lies in *party or party-related work* in the 1980s and 1990s (as opposed to the more general category of 'political experience'). Matthews and Valen (1999) notice the same tendency in their analysis based on data from the 1985 nomination study. They conclude that a new generation has appeared on the political scene, whose experience is largely derived from public office or from party office. When checked for sectoral background, the figures confirm that the number of MPs recruited from the public sector has increased, whereas a steady decline has taken place in the number of people recruited from the private sector. One important reason is probably the increased number of female representatives in the *Storting*, as indicated in Figure 5.1.

Figure 5.1 The proportion of MPs employed in the public sector by Gender, 1965-2001.

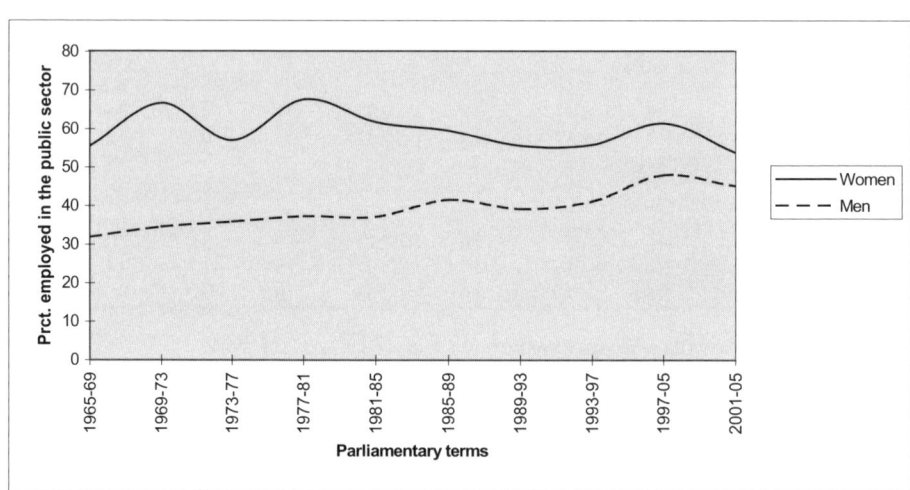

Figure 5.1. demonstrates that the proportion employed in the public sector is consistently higher for women than for men and, consequently, women are systematically underrepresented in the private sector. The high proportion of women in the public sector correlates with the growth of this sector throughout the post-war period (Hernes and Martinussen, 1980).

Hence, what we see from these data is a considerable transformation of the political elites in terms of professional background, occupation and sector. In addition, an intellectual professionalization of the legislature has taken place, expressed through the increased level of education among the representatives. In the period from 1945 to

1961, 34 percent of the MPs had a higher education, whereas this percentage had increased to 46 percent between 1961 and 1985 (Eliassen, 1985:120). In 1996 the number of MPs with a higher education had reached 63 percent as compared to only 23 percent of the electorate. Table 5.5 demonstrates the social and demographic backgrounds of the party representatives compared to that of the voters.[64]

Table 5.5 Social and demographic representativeness of the Norwegian Storting. 1996.

Socio-economic group	Elites	Voters	Difference
Gender	(N=165)		
male	62	50	+12
Female	38	50	-12
Age group	(N=165)		
18-35	11	38	-27
36-44	17	21	-4
45-54	45	17	+28
55+	27	24	+3
Sector[1]	(N=129)		
Public	47	39	+8
Private	53	61	-8
Education[2]	(N=163)		
Low	1	23	-22
Middle	36	53	-17
High	63	24	+39
Occupation[3]			
blue-collar	10	33	-23
white-collar	76	59	+17
self-employed	9	4	+5
farmer-fisherman	5	4	+1

Source: Narud and Valen, 2000.

1. The sectoral classifications of the representatives refer to what was relevant for them when they first were elected to parliament.
2. The classification of educational level is based on the following *country specific categories:*
   »low« (barneskole, ungdomsskole)
   »middle« (gymnas 1 (yrkesskole), gymnas 2 (eksamen artium), and
   »high« (universitet 1, universitet 2, universitet 3, forsker).
   This classification implies that the 'middle' category is everything between compulsory education (low) and all types of started university education (high).
3. The occupational classifications of the representatives refer to what applied when they first were elected to parliament.

Highly educated, middle-aged men with a white-collar background dominate the *Storting*. Even though the number of MPs recruited from the public sector has increased for the last couple of decades, the private sector is still overrepresented, and women are underrepresented compared to men. However, compared to most other Western legislatures, a level of 40 percent female MPs is high (see e.g. Skjeie, 1992; Norris, 1996). During the last few decades the recruitment of women has changed from a narrow group representation to almost gender parity on electoral lists. Indeed, this development constitutes the most remarkable change in political representation in Norway since the introduction of the PR electoral system. The political parties accepted this transition by adapting to the demands from a rapidly growing women's liberation movement. The interesting question is: Why did this mobilization occur? What motivated women's increased activity?

Feminist mobilization

Students of feminist research have given great attention to the question of female representation and participation (see e.g. Skjeie, 1992; 1997; Raaum, 1995; Norris and Lovenduski, 1995; Skjeie and Hernes, 1997). Explanations for the high level of inclusion of women in the Nordic countries have been sought in institutional factors (e.g. the electoral systems), in an egalitarian 'political culture,' as well as in the comparatively strong position of the women's movement (see e.g. Skjeie, 1997:290). For the purpose of this chapter, we will focus upon two major and probably interrelated structural trends that seem to be particularly important. The first concerns the mobilization of women in the labor force, while the second relates to the educational revolution.

In Norway the proportion of women (15-74 years of age) in active employment increased from 45 percent in 1972 to 64 percent in 1995 (Historisk Statistikk, 1994, Table 9.7). By belonging to working places outside the family and through membership in occupational/professional organizations, an overwhelming number of women obtained access to relevant political networks. The educational explosion after 1960 included both men and women, but relatively speaking the women profited most. While the level of education had traditionally been higher for men, the women now obtained parity and, in fact, at the end of the 1980s they surpassed the men. This trend is clearly reflected also at the level of the political elites. Figure 5.2 gives an overview of MPs with a university education in the period from 1965 to 2001.

Figure 5.2 The proportion of MPs with higher education by gender. 1965-2001.

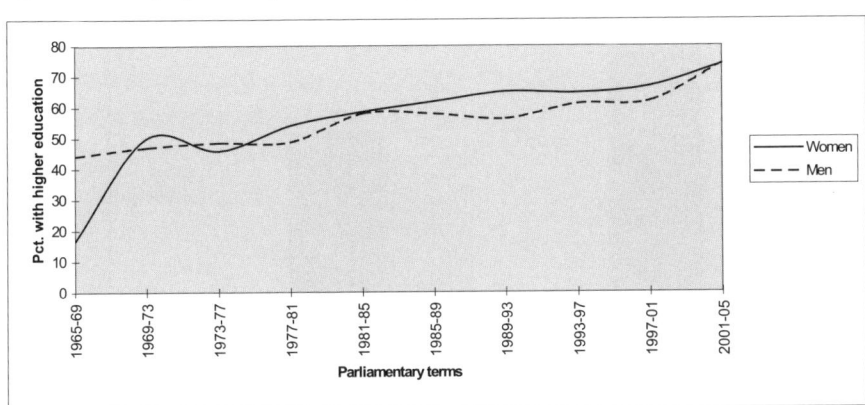

As we shall see, education directly affected the level of *political consciousness* of women.

Gender, education and conflict avoidance

The election study of 1957 included a battery of questions, which were designed for measuring 'conflict avoidance,' and which was expected to explain the underrepresentation of women in politics.[65] The hypothesis was that women are more inclined than men to avoid conflicts and public confrontations.[66] The hypothesis mainly applied to activities in which actors are expected to face competition and confrontations. Since confrontations are likely to occur more frequently with increasing position in the political system, women were expected to be more reluctant than men to seek top positions.

The data from 1957 indeed supported this hypothesis, but when the same battery of questions was included in a study of the 1981 election, the differences between men and women had almost disappeared. The tendencies for the two elections have been described in Figure 5.3.

Figure 5.3 Variations in conflict avoidance between male and female voters in 1957 and 1981. Percent.

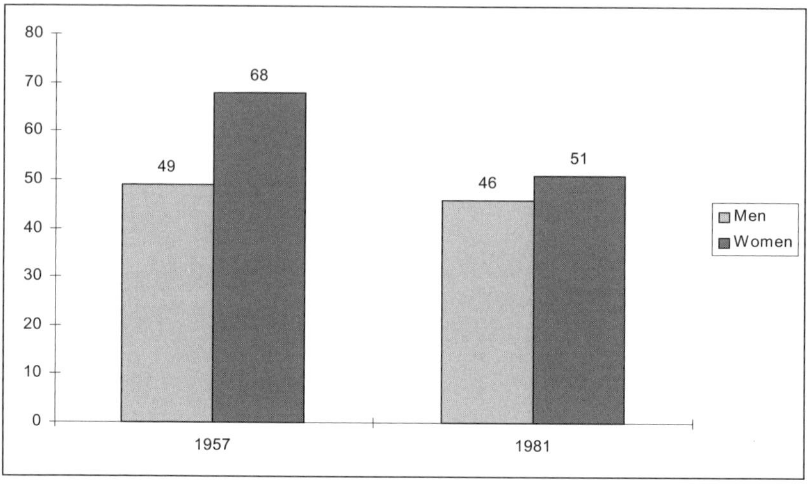

Year	Men	Women
1957	49	68
1981	46	51

Source: Valen, 1989:100.

In 1957 the tendency is consistent for all age groups, although the gender difference is greatest among young voters (18-30 years). In 1981 there is no difference between men and women for young and middle-aged people, while there is still a sizable discrepancy for people above 50 years of age.

However, our main concern is variation according to educational level. The data have been presented in Figure 5.4.

Figure 5.4 Conflict avoidance by gender and education in 1981. Percent.

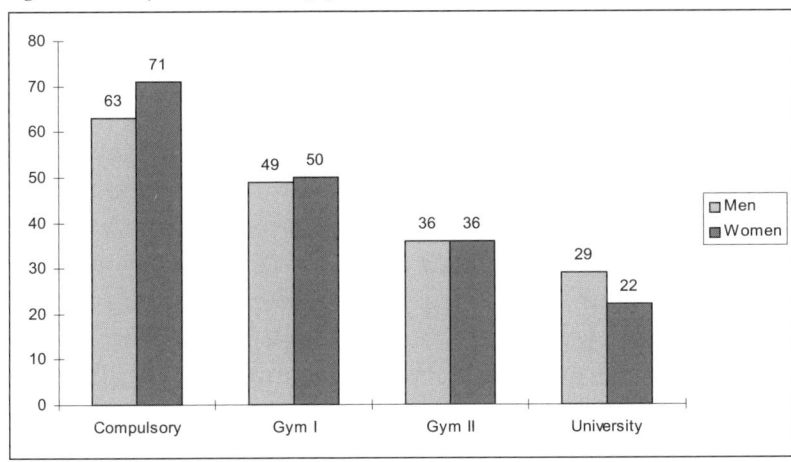

Source: Valen, 1989:105

Because education has been classified in different ways, we are not in a position to make direct comparisons between the two elections. But Figure 4 indicates a clear tendency for 1981. For voters with only elementary education, women are more inclined than men to indicate conflict avoidance. With increasing education responses of avoidance tend to decline, and the differences between men and women disappear. For people with a university education men are, in fact, more inclined than women to indicate conflict avoidance.

In general, the data reveal that the notion of conflict avoidance has changed entirely in character during the quarter of the century that has elapsed between 1957 and 1981. At the latter date women do not seek to avoid political confrontations. On the contrary, they are ready to challenge the men in competition for political office, and the increased level of education has contributed towards this development. The extent to which women are able to compete successfully when seeking re-election will be dealt with in the subsequent pages.

Sanctions and rewards

Criteria for the selection of candidates reflect demands and expectations by the activists of the extra-parliamentary party organization. The extent to which candidates are able to meet these demands is an important prerequisite for successful delegation of authority. How do we know that delegation works? One indicator is the decision of the party to renominate their candidates, another the willingness of the electorate to re-elect the MPs. The first question that ought to be considered, therefore, concerns the concept of 'incumbency,' i.e. the possible reselection of former candidates. To what extent do they still enjoy the confidence of the selectorate? And under which circumstances are they deselected?

Incumbency turnover

The importance of 'incumbency' relates to an almost universal tendency for reselection of incumbent representatives/candidates. Ranney (1981:98-99) observes that: (...) 'the greatest advantage an aspirant for a candidacy can have is to hold the office already.' The reasons given were first of all that incumbents are better known than non-incumbents by both the voters and the selectorate of the constituency. Moreover, Ranney emphasizes the advantages of seniority, in particular the knowledge and experience acquired from holding office and contacts established in hierarchies of power. By dropping the incumbent in favor of a newcomer, the constituency may lose benefits that might possibly be obtained by reselection. These mechanisms seem to be at work in any society.

Before an election Norwegian parties tend to ask their incumbent candidates if they are interested in renominations. Those who react affirmatively will be considered as aspirants, and consistently with Ranney's argument they are likely to benefit from their seniority (Ranney, 1981). However, for reselection some kind of support is needed from specific groups or active networks inside the party. Reselection cannot be taken for granted, even if the incumbent so wishes. This point was clearly elucidated in a limited study before the 1997 *Storting* election, when a student interviewed at length nine representatives about their political basis both in the constituency and on the national level. He also inquired about their outlook for renomination.[67] One of the respondents had decided to withdraw from the *Storting*, while the remaining eight were running for renomination. These candidates were strongly concerned with their position in the constituency, and five of them were worried about their chances of being reselected. The respondents tended to see national involvement as a threat against their position in relation to the constituency.[68] Examples from the 1997 nominations demonstrated that their concerns were not entirely unfounded. In the run-ups to the September 1997 elections several leading parliamentarians, including the parliamentary leader of the Conservative Party, were either deselected or given less favorable ballot placement than they had previously enjoyed. Several commentators interpreted these incidents as a sign of decreasing confidence in the candidates due to their involvement in national issues at the expense of constituency interests.[69] We do not have the data to follow up these matters at any length. In the subsequent pages we shall only briefly consider some main tendencies in the turnover of candidates.

Turnover and continuity on the lists

We will start by examining the magnitude of turnover from one election to the next. Although recent elections constitute our major concern, we will extend the time perspective by starting prior to the war. Our first target is to look at all *list* candidates. Control counting indicates that tendencies over time are similar throughout the country. Hence, we have limited this survey to three large constituencies: Akershus, Hordaland and Nordland.[70] Turnover on the list from one election to the next has been presented in Figure 5.5.

Figure 5.5 Turnover on electoral lists from 1933-1997 for three Norwegian provinces, Akershus, Hordaland and Nordland. Percent of candidates who were not renominated.

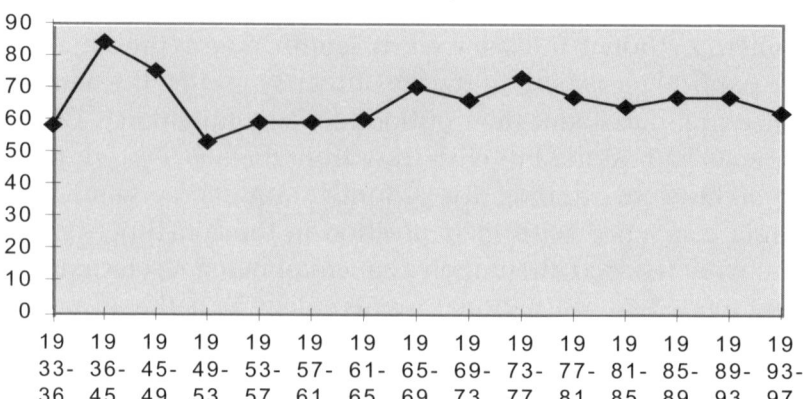

In the period before World War II, nearly half of the former list candidates tended to be renominated at each election, but in 1945 the turnover was enormous. Nine years had passed since the last prewar election. Equally important was the fact that during the years from 1940-45, when the country was occupied, all parties were banned. Thus, in 1945 the party organizations had to be re-established; consequently, the traditional recruitment of party leadership was interrupted. In 1945 the criteria for candidate selection deviated entirely from the 'normal' pattern. A major concern was the war experiences of aspiring candidates.[71] Hence, a great number of the candidates nominated in 1945 did not come up to the traditional standards for political recruitment and, as Figure 5.1 indicates, turnover was way above average also in 1949.

However, at this point a new post-war generation emerged, which dominated Norwegian politics until the end of the 1960s. Since 1969 the rate of turnover has remained slightly above average. Although variations between the parties tend to be small, it is worth mentioning that the average turnover is greatest in the new parties, the Socialist Left and the Progress Party, and it is lowest in the Labor Party. This tendency suggests that the strength and complexity of party organization tends to stabilize leadership recruitment. Moreover, the observed differences may indicate that in any party it takes time to develop a stable core of leaders. The latter point can also be deduced from a comparison of male and female candidates. When considering men and women separately since 1969, we find that turnover tends to be highest for women. The relatively lower stability in the recruitment of women may suggest that women originally were in minority in the core of party activists. In the subsequent period of expansion there was simply a low supply of female aspirants.

Some interesting variations are evident among the parties. In the parties of the left, in which the mobilization of women started, turnover tends to be lower for women than for men. The tendency is reversed for the Progress Party, which has never accepted the idea of gender quotas in candidate recruitment. In this party the turnover is much higher for women than for men. In the other parties there is more similarity between the genders in the rate of turnover. The data presented so far include all list candidates in the three constituencies. We may assume, however, that persons who have already served in the *Storting* are more able than candidates with a lower ranking on the list to profit from their political and professional experiences. Hence, our candidates have been classified in two groups: Top candidates, i.e. those who may have some chance of being elected either as representatives, or as alternate representatives, versus the rest.[72] When considering list turnover at elections from 1945 to 1997, the average figure was 43 percent for top candidates and 72 percent for the rest. Thus, the benefit from incumbency basically applies for those with parliamentary experience. As demonstrated in Figure 5.6, this tendency has been consistent at all elections since 1945.

Figure 5.6 Turnover of top and lower candidates on lists 1945-1997. Percent.

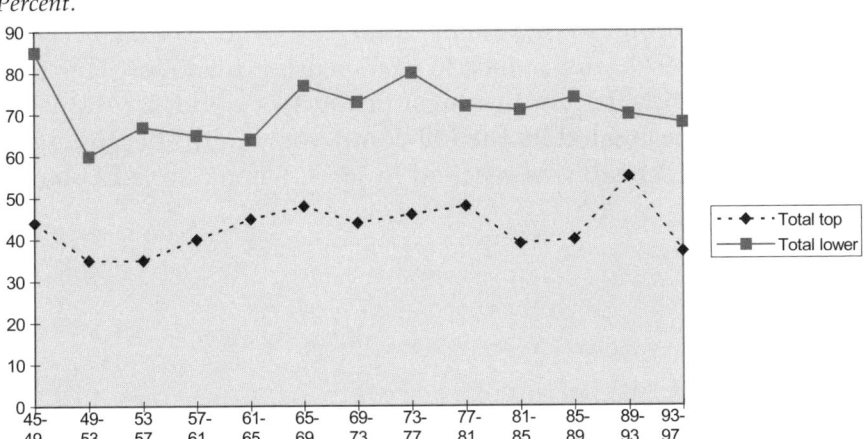

Turnover and continuity in the legislature

We now turn to our main target group, the elected representatives to the *Storting*. In Figure 5.7 we have described the average rate of turnover for all MPs from one election to the next from 1949 to 2001.

Figure 5.7 Legislative turnover at the Storting 1949-2001. Includes all members of the Storting. Percent.

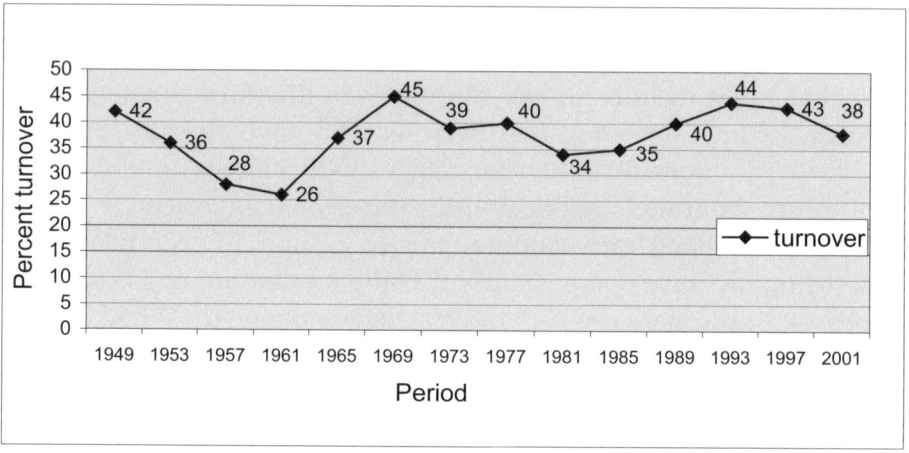

Average turnover in the post war period has been 38 per cent, but the curve indicates enormous variations over time. Three peaks are evident in this material. The first one occurred in 1949, when the political system was returning to normalcy after the war. The next peak occurred around 1970 after a decade of increasing turnover. This tendency coincides with the youth unrest of the 1960s and, a little later, with the turbulence created by the EU-controversy in the beginning of the 1970s. The third peak was reached in 1993, when a new EU-battle was going on.

Reasons for turnover

Our next question concerns the reasons for turnover. Lacking the relevant data, we are unable to answer this complicated question in a satisfactory way. However, some obvious reasons may easily be detected. For one thing, MPs may lose their position because of electoral decline for their respective parties. Figure 5.3 indicates that elections with a high turnover tend to coincide with periods of high electoral volatility and corresponding changes in vote distributions among the parties. Notable examples are the elections from 1969-77 and 1989-93 in which electoral changes were unusually high because of the very divisive EU-debate (Valen and Urwin, 1985; Aardal and Valen, 1995).

Secondly, candidates may disappear from the lists for natural reasons, such as death, illness or aging. As to the latter category, it seems to be a general expectation in most parties, although exceptions may be found, that top candidates who will turn 70 during the subsequent electoral period should not seek renomination. In general, death and aging reflect generational shifts in candidate selection.

Table 5.6 Reasons for turnover at Storting elections 1949-2001.
Includes all elected representatives. Percent.

Year	1949	1953	1957	1961	1965	1969	1973	1977	1981	1985	1989	1993	1997	2001
Re-selected	59	64	72	74	64	55	61	60	66	64	60	56	57	62
Natural reasons*)	9	13	17	11	17	16	15	4	6	5	4	4	2	1
Election result	16	10	5	6	4	6	13	18	12	5	8	14	17	12
Removed for other reasons	16	13	6	9	15	23	11	18	16	26	28	26	24	25
Total %	100	100	100	100	100	100	100	100	100	100	100	100	100	100
N	150	150	150	150	150	150	155	155	155	157	165	165	165	165

* death, aging, illness.

Table 5.6 presents four categories of incumbents: (1) those who are reselected, (2) those who have lost their seats as a result of the election, (3) those who have fallen out for 'natural' reasons (i.e. death, illness or aging), and (4) the rest, those who have been removed for other reasons. The proportion of reselected incumbents is consistently high, but it reached a top level at the very stable elections of 1957 and 1961. More variations are evident for the categories reflecting turnover. The effects of electoral changes are relatively low, except for the 1977 and the 1997 elections, which both occurred after an EU referendum. Shifts caused by death and aging are far less numerous, but the peaks reached in 1957 and in the 1960s reflect the end of the first postwar generation. From 1977 onwards death and aging have been consistently less important causes of legislative turnover. These tendencies coincide with a decline in the average age of the representatives during the last three decades.

Variations over time are greatest for those who have been removed for other reasons. Their number was highest in 1969 and at all elections since 1985. From the point of view of delegation and accountability, the two most interesting categories are those who have been removed as 'a result of the election' and 'for other reasons.' In the first case the voters have rejected them, in the second they have been removed by the selectorate. However, removed for 'other reasons' may cover a number of circumstances, e.g. that the incumbent has been challenged by new aspirants, that he/she is not considered strong enough, or has lost backing among his/her former supporters. In addition, the category includes candidates who have withdrawn voluntarily, which may in some cases mean that the nomination committee has hinted that he/she is likely to be defeated. 'Voluntary withdrawal' is then seen as a face-saving mechanism.

Incumbency and gender

The final point to be considered is the possible difference between men and women in the level of turnover. The results are presented in Figure 5.8.

Figure 5.8 Legislative turnover at the Storting elections by gender. 1949-2001. Includes all members of the Storting. Percent.

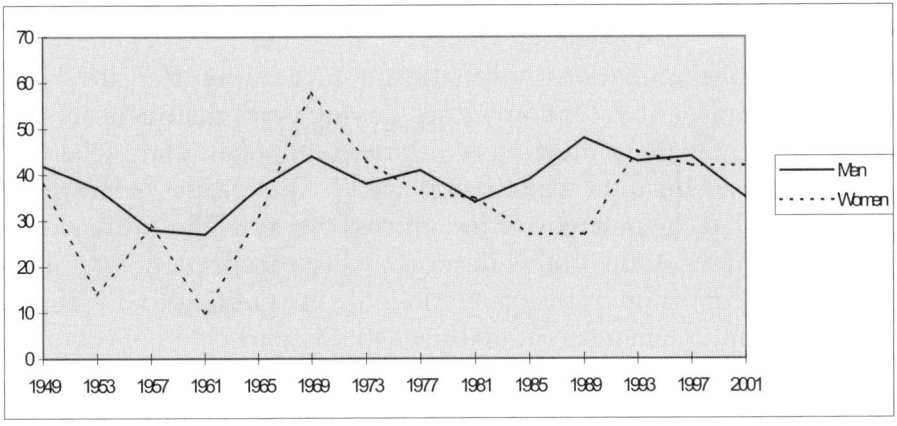

No consistent pattern is evident from Figure 8. The main message from this figure is that female MPs reveal a much more unstable pattern than men, as turnover varies considerably from one electoral period to the next. For women turnover reaches an all time high in 1969, whereas it is extremely low in 1953 and 1961. Observe, however, that N is very low in the latter two cases, since so few women were elected to parliament in those years. In the total post-war period the average level of turnover has been slightly less for women than for men, 33.4 versus 38.6 percent respectively. When reasons for turnover are checked, no differences appear between female and male MPs.

In a long-term perspective the level of legislative turnover has been quite favorable from the point of view of Norwegian parliamentarians. Most parties have allowed their incumbents to accumulate up to three or four terms of seniority, and their major obstacle seems to have been getting their party's nod. Recent development, however, e.g. the increased level of voter volatility, indicates that incumbent politicians are facing a more demanding and competitive set of principals. As the final part of the analysis, therefore, let us examine the voters' involvement in and reaction towards candidate selection.

Nominations and the electorate

An analysis of nominations will naturally focus upon the elite level, since the law prescribes that only dues-paying party members are permitted to participate in meetings concerned with candidate selection, and this rule seems to be strictly observed by the parties.[73] However, considering that the outcome of the process concerns the entire electorate, the reactions of the voters deserve a closer inspection. First, how large is the proportion of the electorate who are entitled to direct participation? And to what extent do they actually participate? Second, to what extent does the average voter recognize the candidates on the electoral lists? Finally, we shall look at the concept of group representation in relation to voter reactions.

The questions of participation have been dealt with in Table 5.7, which is based on data from the 1985 *Storting* election.

Table 5.7 Selectorate and number of delegates at nomination conventions, 1985, by party.

Party	Party members in % of votes	Participated in nomination process: % of voters[a]	Number of delegates in nomination conventions[b]	Delegates as % of voters	Delegates as % of members
Socialist Left	11	9	1,433	1.1	9.2
Labor	15	4	2,806	0.3	1.8
Liberal	21	7	710	0.7	4.2
Christian	29	8	1,260	0.6	2.0
Center	26	5	988	0.6	2.2
Conservative	16	3	2,787	0.4	2.2
Progress	8	8	703	0.6	9.2
Total	15	5	10,687	0.6	4.5

Source: Valen, 1988:214.

a Figures from 1985 election survey.
b Estimated on the basis of 1981 election statistics.
  Figures for Oslo were obtained directly from the parties.

Aspiring candidates are recruited from the ranks of party activists. In 1985 about 15 percent of the voters were dues-paying party members. This proportion had been relatively stable over three decades (Svåsand, 1985:49-53), but since the end of the 1980s the proportion declined to about 10 percent, a figure that remained stable at the three subsequent elections (1989, 1993 and 1997).[74] There has also been a decline in the proportion indicating participation either in the nominating conventions or in local meetings discussing candidates or electing delegates to the conventions. In 1985 this proportion was nearly five percent of the electorate (Matthews and Valen, 1999), whereas the 1997 election study indicates that the corresponding figure was only two percent. In proportion to dues-paying party members, activists constituted one out of three in 1985 as compared to one out of six in 1997. Indeed, the data confirm that participation in the process of nominations is limited to a tiny number of party activists, and in recent years the few have become even fewer.

Awareness of nominations

In the selection of candidates the parties seem to be basically concerned with expected reactions of the electorate. Persons with a background in specific groups are nominated because they will presumably appeal to corresponding categories of voters. Thus, concern for the voters serves as an ultimate legitimization in the process of selection. A pertinent question is: To what extent do the voters know about the electoral list? In the 1985 election study the voters were asked: 'Can you name one or more candidates on the lists of any party at the election of 1985 in your constituency?' Two out of three voters were able to identify one or more candidates. On average the respondents identified two candidates.

The results confirmed that the knowledge is considerably higher for party members (the selectorate) than for the rest of the voters. The question of candidate knowledge was included also in the 1997 election study, and the voters were asked to indicate up to three names.[75] The level of candidate knowledge in 1997 is very similar to that of

1985: only about two thirds of the voters are able to mention one or more candidates on the party lists. The average knowledge in 1997 is almost identical to that of 1985. As was the case then, knowledge in 1997 is considerably higher for party members than for the ordinary voters.[76] However, considering the great number of candidates the figures from both surveys indicate a rather low level of voter knowledge.

Voter reactions towards group representation

In the 1985 election study the respondents were presented with the idea of group representation in the *Storting*. They were then asked whether they thought that certain groups were under-represented, e.g. women: 'Do you think there should be more or fewer female MPs in the *Storting*, is the present number about right, or does it not matter to you?' The results are presented in Table 5.8.

Table 5.8 Attitudes towards representation of women, by gender. 1985 election study.

	More women needed	About right as it is	Fewer women	Indifferent	Total (N=100%)
Women	47	27	2	24	1012
Men	37	30	2	31	1094

A large proportion of both genders are in favor of a strong representation for women, but the demand for more female MPs in the *Storting* is significantly higher among women than among men. The percentage indicating indifference towards this question is much higher among men than among women.

Another relevant demographic group at nominations is the young people (i.e. voters under the age of 30). When asked about this group, more than half of the respondents was in favor of more young candidates. As demonstrated in Table 5.9, young people are particularly alert about own interests.

Table 5.9 Attitudes towards representation of people under 30 years old. 1985 study.

Age	More young candidates	About right as it is	Fewer	Indifferent	Total (N=100%)
30 years or less	71	15	1	13	529
Over 30	47	32	7	14	1501

Seven out of ten young respondents wanted to strengthen the representation of youth, while less than half of the older ones held a similar view.

When asked about the representation of the temperance movement, variations are enormous between respondents indicating a temperance position and the non-temperance people: 61 percent in the first group as compared to only six percent in the second would like to see more temperance people in the *Storting*. An interesting aspect of this demand is the great proportion indicating indifference. For active temperance people the figure is 19 percent, as compared to 43 percent for temperance people with low involvement in the issue, and 56 percent for non-temperance people.

Finally, the respondents were asked about the representation of three specific occupational groups: workers, farmers and independents in business. The results are presented in Table 5.10.

Table 5.10 Attitudes towards representation of occupational groups. 1985 study.

	Workers		Farmers		Independents	
	Workers	Other occupations	Farmers	Other occupations	Independents	Other occupations
More representatives	58	44	50	21	32	19
About right	21	29	30	46	43	47
Fewer	1	2	1	6	5	10
Indifferent	20	25	19	27	20	24
Total (N=100%)	652	1252	105	1734	187	1640

The demand for an increased group representation is strongest for the workers, with farmers in the second place, and independents in business in the third. However, for each of the groups the expressed attitude is significantly higher for respondents belonging to the respective occupation than for people in other occupations. For all the groups mentioned, the data support the assumption held by parties that the electorate is concerned with the political representation of their own interests. It is a paradox, however, that in spite of the expressed group demands the voters are not much aware of the composition of the electoral lists. Moreover, it is surprising that group representation is rarely debated before the election, with a notable exception for female representation. The explanation may simply be that the concern for group interests is perceived as part of the party platform. Through the mass media the voters are more or less informed about the current system of ticket balancing. The situation might change dramatically if some party happened to ignore some important group interests in the selection of candidates. In that case competing parties would most likely bring this fact to the attention of the electorate.

Conclusions

In Norway nomination procedures are formalized in a specific law that forms a part of the electoral system. Nominations are made by representative conventions organized by the constituency branches of the extra-parliamentary party organizations. The electoral lists drawn up by the conventions are final and cannot be changed by the central party leaders. It may be questioned, however, whether the national leaders are able to affect the decisions indirectly by intervening in the organizational process leading up to the convention. The data presented in this chapter suggest that the selectorate is predominantly concerned with constituency interests in their nomination. In general, the material supports the notion of a highly decentralized nomination process. However, the Progress Party seems to be a notable exception. Data from the 2001 *Storting* election suggests that the party's national leader played an active role during the nomination process in several constituencies. As to the other parties we should also observe a couple of exceptions. For one thing, central leaders have easier access to (and hence, more possible influence on) the nominations in Oslo (the Capital) and the surrounding province of Akershus than in the rest of the country. Moreover, in these two constituencies local interests are to some extent overshadowed by the concern for national interests. Secondly, contacts concerning candidate selection between national and provincial leaders are reported to be closer in minor than in larger parties.

Ticket balancing and group representation are important elements for candidate selection in all parties. Most notable is territorial representation, which is materialized partly by the nomination of candidates attached to a given constituency, partly by the selection of candidates from different regions within the province. The purpose of ticket balancing is obviously to strengthen the party appeal to significant groups of the electorate. The parties tend to legitimize their selection by referring to anticipated voter reactions. However, the voters' knowledge of candidates is surprisingly low. On the other hand, the voter reactions towards group representation tend to be consistent with the parties' assumptions. Thus, the ticket balancing applied by the parties may serve as a safety valve against potential protest reactions by the electorate.

As a result of group representation the recruitment of candidates is not one-sidedly biased in favor of some specific social stratum. On the contrary, candidates are selected from a great variety of social groups, although with a tendency in favor of an elite within the separate groups. Three long-term trends are evident in candidate recruitment, a professionalization of politicians, a strong increase in the number of representatives with a background in the public sector, and a strong increase in the number of female MPs.

Only dues-paying party members are permitted to participate in the nomination process. The ordinary voter has only a choice between competing electoral lists, but no direct possibility of affecting the candidate selection of the parties.

Consequently, the elected representatives are only accountable to their respective parties, while the ability of the electorate to claim accountability is limited to their choice of party.

6

Conclusions

HANNE MARTHE NARUD, MOGENS N. PEDERSEN
AND HENRY VALEN

Our main concern with this book has been to evaluate nominations as instruments of democracy. Nominations are mechanisms for the selection of political leaders, and they are devices for citizens' control of the elected representatives. Hence, we have compared the institutions, procedures and norms shaping the nominations in four countries in Northern Europe: Denmark, Finland, Iceland and Norway. The political systems of these four countries are similar in many respects. Most notably, they all apply proportional election systems, in which the competing parties run separate lists in multimember constituencies. Yet, despite great institutional similarities considerable variations are evident regarding nominations and candidate recruitment. In referring to the research questions specified in the introductory chapter, a brief summary of the findings may elucidate comparative perspectives in current development.

The institutional setting

Changes in nomination procedures tend to be closely linked to the electoral reforms in the respective countries. In recent decades changes have occurred most frequently in Finland and Iceland, whereas Denmark and Norway have remained more stable. We should note two tendencies in the long-term development. First, decision-making in the nomination process has gradually become more decentralized. The power of the central party leadership has declined while the local and regional branches of the party organization have gained a dominating position. The second main tendency has to do with increasing inclusiveness in the selection of candidates. The right of dues-paying party members to participate in the process seems to have been generally recognized, but more important is the demand for more democratization, in the sense that also ordinary voters should have a direct say in the selection process.

How are nominations organized?

There is no simple or straightforward answer to the above question, since in most countries nomination procedures are not specified in the electoral law. Two of our countries, Finland and Norway, constitute exceptions in this respect. Both have introduced specific legislation concerning nominations, but in both cases the rules are not mandatory, except for parties that claim public financing of their expenses in relation to nominations.

The existing procedural rules in Finland and Norway specify a convention model for nominations. Electoral lists are decided in the respective constituencies by separate conventions consisting of delegates from all local communities. The number of delegates from each local unit is roughly proportional to the number of votes obtained by the respective parties at the previous election. Participation in the process is limited to the political parties. Rank and file party members are invited to participate in local meetings and to propose candidates and/or delegates to the nomination conventions. In Finland local primaries are arranged for the purpose of discussing and voting for proposed candidates. In Norway the corresponding activities take place within ordinary party meetings. The parties have generally adopted the procedures, which are prescribed by the legal rules, even in cases when they do not apply the law. According to this model the procedures are decentralized: Nominations are determined in the separate constituencies without intervention by national party leaders.

In Denmark and Iceland there are no legal regulations governing the nominations. In both these countries practices vary from one party to the next. Danish parties apply a version of the convention model, rather similar to that of Finland and Norway. The decision-making in the nomination process takes place in the constituency party organizations. However, in Denmark as well as is Norway there is one notable exception to the general party norms. In both countries the national leaders of the right-wing populist parties seem to play a dominant role in the selection of candidates. Interestingly, these parties were formed in the beginning of the 1970s. The tendency observed may suggest that they are less inclined than the older parties to accept the well-established organizational structure of the latter.

The report on Iceland indicates that the parties used to apply a convention model there too. However, in the beginning of the 1970s Icelandic parties introduced primaries as the dominant pattern of candidate selection. Some of the parties use closed primaries, i.e. primaries restricted to the party members. Others use entirely open primaries. The introduction of primaries implies a broadening of the electoral process and a great increase in the influence of the individual voter. Consequently, the Icelandic chapter suggests a sharp decline in the power of the political parties.

The procedures described present the organizational context of the nomination process, but for evaluating the power structure of a given party, it is necessary to make a distinction between the organization and the informal networks in the party. Even if central leaders are not legally permitted to intervene in the nomination process in individual constituencies, they might conceivably be able to influence decisions through contacts with local or regional leaders.

What are the mechanisms for screening?

When asked about required qualities of prospective candidates, previous studies have demonstrated that party leaders are inclined to emphasize personal competence (Valen and Katz, 1964; Valen, 1966; 1988). However, a further inquiry reveals that there is no consensus in the political community concerning the evaluation of personal skills. Moreover, personality variables seem to be more or less overshadowed by a number of social and political considerations that serve as screening mechanisms in the actual choice of candidates. In fact, these two types of characteristics correspond roughly to the distinction made by Seligman (1967) between two stages in the process of nominations, certification and selection. In this project relevant data are not available for evaluating personality characteristics (save for the Norwegian chapter). However, since presumably the character of political leadership reflects major ideologies and the political culture of a given society, we may assume that there will be only minor variations between our four Nordic countries in this respect. Hence, our main concern will be various types of "group representation" applied as screening mechanisms in the selection process. Assuming that the composition of the list has a direct effect upon the preferences of the voters, the parties are inclined to choose candidates who appeal to various subsets of the electorate. Since the electoral bases of the competing parties vary, the character of group representation also tends to vary from one party to another. Yet, some tendencies seem to prevail in all parties. Most general is the demand for geographical representation. This demand is of particular importance in Norway, Finland and Iceland. Each constituency in these three sparsely populated countries tends to cover a sizable area. Hence, parties select candidates from all over the territory. In fact, it seems to be a normal pattern – at least in Finland and Norway – that each constituency is divided into territorial subunits that compete for nominations within the respective parties. Almost without exception it does not occur that more than one candidate from a given local community is nominated to a safe spot on the same list.

Moreover, the concern for geographical background is reflected in a demand that prospective candidates should be linked to the constituency in which they are nominated, either by family ties or by long-lasting residence. The attachment of candidates to the constituency is a well-established norm in three of the countries, Finland, Iceland and Norway, but it is not required by law. Geographical background seems to be less of a requirement at nominations in Denmark, which is the most densely populated and the smallest country in terms of territory. Another major mechanism for selection is gender. Until around 1970, women were one of several competing groups to be represented with a couple of candidates on each list. In most cases they were not located in a safe spot, but quite a few female candidates were granted a pivotal place on the list, obviously in order to appeal to the large number of female voters. The number of female candidates has increased considerably over the last three decades. Equality of representation for men and women has become a general demand in nearly all parties. Some have explained this characteristic by the existence of a fairly egalitarian political culture. Others have pointed to institutional and structural factors, such as multimember PR systems, women's notable proportion of the labor force connected to a strong and active women's movement (see e.g. Skard and Haavio-Mannila, 1986; Matland and Studlar, 1996).

Most list candidates are in the age bracket of 35-55 years. There has always been a demand for increased representation of the younger voters. Of course, youth organizations support this demand, which provides a continuous renewal of parliamentary representation.

In their search for candidates political parties pay considerable attention to occupational background. For one thing, the parliamentary caucus of the respective parties requires some candidates with specific skills. But equally important is the appeal to occupational groups in which given parties may expect to maintain or increase their vote, e.g. organized labor, farmers, fisheries, or specified middle-class occupations. Thus, each electoral list in these countries covers a wide scale of occupational positions. In this respect Nordic parties deviate from a general pattern in most countries of nominating professionals, and most notably lawyers (Putnam, 1976). Nonetheless, the nominated candidates in our four countries belong to the upper strata of their respective occupational groups.

Finally, we should observe that group representation might also include other groups than the four categories mentioned above, e.g. candidates from ethnic minorities or religious congregations. Moreover, factions reflecting controversial positions on current issues may occasionally try to affect the list composition. A recent example is the struggle in Norway about EU membership.

What is the outcome of the screening process?

We have defined the "outcome" of the screening process as the social and demographic outlook of the selected candidates (cf. chapter 1). To what extent do the legislators reflect the society from which they are drawn in terms of various types of background characteristics? We have already indicated the answer in the previous section. One of the most dominating features of the Nordic legislatures has been the increased level of higher education, a development pattern that our four countries share with virtually all other European legislatures (see e.g. Best and Cotta, 2000). Another striking feature, as we have seen, has been the growing number of women elected for public office. For the purpose of this chapter, we have focused on the impact of the various stages of the recruitment process. Is the outcome of the process primarily due to the nomination procedures, or is it caused by the preferences of the individual voters?

The Icelandic chapter demonstrates that the nomination method applied does not necessarily affect the number of women MPs in the various parties. The system of open primaries, however, has profoundly affected the status of women, as it does not assume any responsibility for placing more women in safe seats. While the convention method appears to secure some share of top seats for women, Kristjánsson's analysis indicates that open primaries have been disadvantageous to women's representation in Iceland. The use of primaries, therefore, may account for the relatively fewer women in the *Althingi* compared to the numbers in the other three parliaments. In making a distinction between aspirants, candidates and legislators, Kuitunen finds significant effects of all stages in the recruitment process in Finland. Here, the voters accentuate the élitist bias of the candidate supply, since voters are more inclined than the party selectorates to vote for highly educated and middle-aged urban residents. On the other hand, the electorate has rather limited opportunities to affect the final composition of the list. The analyses from Denmark, Iceland and Finland, which are all systems with elements of preference voting, indicate that electoral and nomination effects are very complex and difficult to disentangle. In addition, one must consider that more women participate in elections

Conclusions 223

and politics than before, and that there are indications of a more positive attitude towards female candidates. By contrast, the increase in the number of female representatives in Norway, which has no preferential voting system, is best understood in the light of the party norms governing the nomination procedures. The rule of female "quotas" has been adopted by most parties, and among the criteria for group representation, women have the highest priority, particularly in the parties of the left.

What is the level of parliamentary turnover?

Representative democracy means delegation, and delegation triggers the need for control. The indicator for control that we have applied in this book is the level of parliamentary turnover. Two questions have been analyzed: What is the overall rate of turnover? And what are the main reasons for turnover?

The data concerning turnover rates for MPs in our four countries reveal that the voters do exercise control through general elections. The average rate of turnover is about 30 per cent for all four countries taken together. This runs parallel to the results for a number of other West-European legislatures (Best and Cotta, 2000:504-505). Moreover, in a long-term perspective, the chances for incumbents to be re-elected have been quite favorable in all four countries. A substantial proportion of MPs remain in office for more than two terms, thereby gaining substantial parliamentary experience. Indeed, this fact together with the relatively high socio-economic background status of MPs compared to that of the electorate means that interest representation is taken care of by some highly professional agents.

The Icelandic chapter, which has the most detailed data on turnover, indicates that it has fundamentally changed in all the parties since primaries were introduced in the 1970s. Retirement due to old age has declined while retirement for other reasons, notably because of internal party conflict, has increased. Defeat of incumbents has also become more frequent. Consequently, changes in nomination methods and turnover pattern of MPs are closely linked. Overall, the open primary system has led to a loss of party control over the outcome of political recruitment. Interestingly, the Finnish chapter demonstrates that, considering the relatively high turnover rates in some elections, the turnover rates of candidates at nominations are quite impressive. There are about twice as many newcomers as a result of the nominations as there are as a result of elections.

In all countries high turnover rates tend to coincide with periods of high electoral volatility and corresponding changes in vote distribution. Notable examples are the elections in Norway and Denmark in the 1970s, in which electoral volatility was unusually high. In addition, a generation shift took place in many parties during the late 1960s. Pedersen (1984) has demonstrated that a close statistical relationship exists between electoral volatility, turnover and seniority distributions (see also Pedersen, 1994). Hence, the trends of parliamentary turnover are a result of electoral fluctuations as well as of changes in the generational cohorts The overall pattern of increased electoral volatility in the Nordic countries nevertheless indicates that incumbent politicians are facing a more demanding and competitive set of principals today than was the case a few decades ago. This fact confirms the decisive role of elections in keeping incumbents accountable through the threat of involuntary removal.

The multi-leveled network of principals and agents

In a parliamentary system, defining the principal-agent relationships is a complex matter. In this book we have combined the more traditional approach to nomination studies with that of agency theory. The principal-agent approach is first and foremost an approach for understanding authority relationships. In its most simplistic form this relationship exists between individuals. However, in the types of systems we deal with here, the political party forms the basis for political representation as well as for recruitment. Parties structure the first step in the chain of delegation by offering programs and candidates committed to these programs. Parties therefore serve as a kind of a "proximate principal" aiming to exercise control over their MPs (Mitchell, 2000). The extent to which there is a direct link between voters and MPs is then conditioned upon the existence of effective preferential voting or open primaries.

Since we are preoccupied with parliamentary nominations, we must consider networks of party-related principal-agent relationships, which are conditioned by a variety of institutions and existing norms for delegation. The country-based chapters of this book clearly illustrate the multitude of nomination practices and the richness of ideas displayed by the parties. In every country there are a number of formal and informal procedures for nominations generating some complex sets of principal-agent relationships. Two aspects stand out as more crucial for understanding which groups or individuals act as principals in relation to the party representatives: the rate and broadness of *participation* in the nominations, and the level of *centralization* of the process.

These two dimensions generate a system in which elected representatives are accountable partly to the voters, partly to local leaders and partly to the central party leadership. The degree of centralization of the nomination procedures is important from several perspectives. First of all, it generates a multifaceted system of "national principals" versus "local principals", which complicates the question of agent accountability. Decentralized nominations would put forward local agents and affect the focus of incumbent candidates seeking reselection. By contrast, centralized nominations would promote national policy "servants" with incentives for pursuing a parliamentary career. In decentralized systems, like the Nordic ones, the party MPs face demands from the central party leadership as well as from the local party leadership. Since the local party controls reselection, the representatives must devote sufficient time to specific problems of the constituency. Incumbent candidates may therefore be well advised to keep up constituency contacts in a satisfactory manner rather than to give priority to other tasks. On the other hand, elected representatives meet demands from the central leadership for party discipline and cohesion in parliamentary behavior. Thus, individual candidates may face the problem of conflicting demands from the two sets of principals.

Citizen control over candidate selection

The inclusion of the electorate in the selection of candidates has gained ground for the last couple of decades in many West-European parties (Bille, 2001; Pennings and Hazan, 2001). Among our four Nordic countries, this tendency has been most pronounced in the Icelandic parties. The idea of party democracy and citizen inclusiveness was the main reason why several of them adopted primary elections in the 1970s. Although the other Nordic countries have not followed the Icelanders, they have been concerned with the rights of the voters in the choice of candidates. For this purpose, Denmark and Finland have incorporated different forms of preference voting. Finland has changed its electoral system so that each voter has to choose not only a partisan list, but also some specific candidate on that list. Hence, the Finnish model is a compromise between the convention method on the one hand, and primary elections on the other. Denmark, as early as 1920, introduced a similar method, although it is not fully as open as the Finnish system. Norway, on the other hand, has maintained the "closed" system under which the selection of candidates has been restricted to the local party branches. Indications exists, however, that demands may be put forward also in Norway for a democratization of the process, most likely by introducing some kind of preferential voting system.

The observed tendency towards inclusion of the electorate in the process of candidate selection has important consequences for the functioning of representative democracy. First of all, the various institutional mechanisms provide the voters with different means to control their representatives. While nominations in Norway lean heavily on ex ante control mechanisms through the screening that takes place during the nomination procedures, Denmark, Finland and Iceland have introduced ex post control through a stronger inclusion of the voters. These differences have implications for the accountability of

Conclusions

individual candidates. The accountability of elected representatives in closed list system is low vis-à-vis individual voters, since they may be protected from voter sanctions by "secure" positions on the list. Hence, potential agency losses (i.e. unwanted behavior from MPs) are more likely in these types of systems than they are in systems where the career of a politician depends on the preferences of the voters. By contrast, democratization of the process promotes incentives to seek a personal vote, thereby reducing the risks for agency losses in the voter-MP relationship. Furthermore, the opening up of the nomination process gives other actors, most importantly the mass media, potential influence on the question of candidate selection. Even though nominations in the Nordic countries are still far from the media-driven ones in the US (Ranney, 1983), the country-based chapters indicate that the media play a much more active role than they did before in the parliamentary systems discussed in this volume. On the one hand, this development enhances voter monitoring, as it gives information about party discussions and priorities during the nomination process. On the other hand, it might increase the importance of the candidates' personal appeal and populist behavior. Modern media have a tendency to focus on personal abilities and the political "game" rather than organizational and political screening mechanisms. This might in fact reduce the value of the information presented to the public. It remains to be seen if the media development will gradually diminish the dominance of the party organizations in the selection of candidates.

Notes, References, Contributors

Notes

1. We are grateful to Torbjörn Bergman, Magnus Blomgren, and Wolfgang C. Müller for critical comments on this chapter. In addition, we would like to thank the participants of the politics seminar at the Institute for Social Research in Oslo for valuable suggestions.
2. In several countries, e.g. the United States and Great Britain, a distinction is made between nominations and the selection of candidates. In the Nordic countries the two terms are normally used interchangeably, as will also be the norm in this book.
3. See Katz and Mair (1992) for detailed descriptions of the rules for party candidate selection in Western Democracies.
4. For a thorough discussion on the problems of delegation and accountability in multi-level parliamentary systems, see e.g. Strøm, 1999, 2000; Bergman, Müller and Strøm, 2000; Lupia and McCubbins, 2000.
5. Technically, there are two necessary conditions for agency losses, divergent preferences on the one hand, and asymmetric information, on the other (Strøm, 2000).
6. Consider for example a system with fixed term limits, in which MPs can serve only one term. Here, it is not meaningful to talk about *electoral* accountability, even though the elected representative may be accountable to some other party in other respects (e.g. to the Court). Under these circumstances elections serve as mechanisms for choosing political representatives rather than as devices for control. See Fearon (1999) for a principled discussion about electoral accountability and the control of politicians.
7. See Müller (2000) for a theoretical account of the intermediate role of the party in the system of delegation.
8. Dilemmas like these may occur in several circumstances and at several levels of the party. The local gatekeepers, i.e. the local members and party activists are well aware of their power to deselect. An interesting example is to be found from Norwegian politics, where the lack of responsiveness from the central party leadership in the Labor Party triggered uproar among local party activists in November 1999. Here, a meeting was held in the capital, Oslo, to discuss suggested rules on taxation of electric power. The tax proposal was unpopular among the local party branches, because it was seen to jeopardize local incomes to the communes. The central party leadership was invited to the meeting, but none of them showed up. Infuriated with their leaders, a number of delegates accused the party leadership of "insensitiveness" and "lack of credibility" One newspaper wrote: "Several mayors pointed to the forthcoming parliamentary nominations, and that they indeed looked forward to replacing people that are not trustworthy. – 'When the nominations begin, we are in charge, and this is a question of raw power,' one delegate said" (*Aftenposten*, November 12, 1999).
9. Several scholars have pointed out the difficulty of the task of identifying the key selectorate, since several groups may in fact influence different stages of the recruitment process, and since practices may vary between different parties in different countries. In addition, formal constitutional powers may disguise de facto control (see e.g. Norris, 1996). The right of the party organization to veto, for instance, or in some way alter the choice of party members, frustrates our ability

to connect a candidate with a specific selectorate. Nevertheless, identifying the key selectorates is important, since their composition and nature presumably shape the activity of incumbent candidates. Here, the principal-agent analogy for the selector-candidate relationship offers the possibility of a "nested" set of principals and agents, in which candidates (the agents) must adhere to the selectors' (principals') preferences in order to win and maintain their job. Since the selectorates constitute the effective constituency to which the elite member will be accountable, selectorates, or rather the anticipated reactions of the selectorates, affect the behavior of candidates post hoc.

10 Many Danish historians have told the story. A good account is given by Skovmand (1964: 275-77), who also renders the poem by Emil Aarestrup.
11 A brief description of the major phases in the development of the Danish party system can be found in Pedersen, 1993. The major sources for nominations during the 19th century are Hatting & Winding, 1950; Dybdahl, 1969; and Elklit, 1988.
12 Of these six new members one had already been serving as a member for several years since she had replaced another MP, who had been appointed member of the EU Commission in 1994.
13 The nomination district of Otterup had for many years been the "home" of the top politician, Ritt Bjerregaard, and the new, young, and female candidate was widely seen as a genuine political successor of Mrs. Bjerregaard.
14 A compilation of legal texts plus a contemporary one can be found in Brockmeyer et al. 1983. This text is, however, no longer totally valid. For a brief and succinct description in English, see Ministry of the Interior, 1996.
15 The internal guidelines of the Danish Public Service Radio & Television Channel do, however, regulate parts of the campaign by stipulating equal access and free access. Advertisements by political parties on national as well as regional radio and television channels are not permitted.
16 See further Ministry of the Interior, 1996. For an analysis of the entire issue of financial support for Danish parties, see Pedersen & Bille, 1991. Cf. also Bille, 1997.
17 The municipal reform of 1970 has not completely changed older organization patterns within the older parties. In 1995 there still existed within the four "old" parties almost 2,000 local branches, which should be compared with the number of municipalities, 275. Bille, 1997, provides a rich data base as well as discussions of these numbers and the trends.
18 For further details, see Bille,1993 and Bille,1997. A comprehensive dataset is also available in the chapter on Denmark (by Lars Bille) in Katz & Mair, 1992.
19 A recent example is the defeat of the Social Democratic Vice Chairperson (young, female, academic education, living in Copenhagen), who in vain tried to win a nomination in Jutland before the 1998 election.
20 An analysis of the relationship between home, constituency and the seat of parliament in the recruitment process can be found in Pedersen, 1975.
21 The only scholar who has studied the internal life of national Danish party organizations at any length is Lars Bille (Bille, 1997). He has, however, not yet conducted survey studies inside the parties. The internal life at the level of the municipality has been analyzed by Roger Buch Jensen (Jensen, 2000), cf. also Elklit & Jensen, 1997, various chapters.
22 The above mentioned female candidate who had such great success in the Funen

constituency in 1998 was widely criticized because some of her campaign activities had crossed the boundaries of the nomination districts. Several examples of this kind of interference were reported during the 1998 campaign.

23 Suffrage rights for women were introduced by a constitutional amendment in 1915.

24 The Conservative leader Asger Karstensen, quoted from *Folketingstidende* 1919/20, B. Col. 953.

25 To the following see Pedersen, 1966. Another accessible source dealing with the system of preferential voting is Johansen,1979. A valuable analysis can also be found in Johansen & Kristensen, 1979. These studies are, however, partly outdated due to changes in the constituency formats, the party system, as well as the nomination practices and the voters' utilization of their voting options.

26 The small left wing party, the Unity List, is the only party which utilizes all the options provided by the electoral law. The party does, however, use the party-controlled "party list option" in most of those constituencies where it was probable that the party might win a seat.

27 During the same period the use of the "party list option" which is really a technical variation of the "nomination district option" has decreased from 24 percent to 10 percent, mainly due to the fact that a number of left wing parties, including the Communists, have refrained from putting up candidates, but instead have combined their diminishing strength in the Unity List.

28 An analysis of the effects of preferential voting and nomination behavior etc. during the 1993 municipal elections suggests that electoral and nomination effects are very complex and almost impossible to disentangle (Kjær, 1997). At the level of municipal politics the voters do, however, tend to disfavor the female candidates slightly, while the parties try to favor the women during the nomination phase.

29 Approximately 10 percent of the whole population are members of political parties (see Pesonen, Sänkiaho & Borg 1993, 208).

30 A survey questionnaire was sent to party district officials in January 1995. Almost 90 percent (88.6) of the target group returned the questionnaire. Party rules and all information on the aspirants and on the results of party primaries were gathered with the party district survey. This data was supplemented by official electoral statistics. As a result of the project, three different studies focusing on slightly different aspects of nominations were accomplished (Helander 1997; Helander, Kuitunen and Paltemaa 1997 (eds.); Kuitunen 1998).

31 It was as early as the 1970s, during the stage of incomparable expansion of Finnish parties, that the political parties themselves along with the media became anxious about the eroding effects on the internal party activities resulting in centralization, bureaucracy, etc. During the summer of 1998 this debate intensified again mostly due to the report published by the most circulated newspaper, *Helsingin Sanomat*. According to this report, the number of the party members has declined by ⅕ during the 1990s.

32 A particularly illustrative example of using outsiders as vote collectors is to be discovered in the candidate nominations for the 1999 parliamentary election. Two persons in highly influential positions in Finnish politics in general and party politics in particular (both are chairpersons of their party) have decided to seek candidature in the constituency of capital city, Helsinki, outside their actual place of residence.

33 The primary aim of these telephone interviews conducted with the party district officials in 1998 was to shed light on the reasons for deselection of previous candidates and legislators in candidate selection.
34 A total of 11 telephone interviews with party district officials were accomplished in order to study the reasons for deselection in a more qualitative manner. Interviews were loosely structured dealing with different aspects of turnover, for instance the significance of internal party disputes, the demands of constituency and supply of candidates in explaining the turnover of both sitting members of parliament and previous candidates.
35 This chapter was written before the 1999 parliamentary election in Iceland. Before that election a new electoral alliance, the United Front, was formed, composed of four political parties: the People's Alliance, the Social Democratic Party, the Women's Alliance, and the People's Movement. The United Front used open primaries to select its candidates in five electoral districts, including the largest ones. Around 30,000 people voted in these primaries (nearly 80% of the vote received by the United Front parties in the 1995 election in the districts holding primaries). Thus the trend towards the open primary as the most legitimate nomination method employed by the main political parties was completed, whatever future elections may hold.
36 We would like to thank Leiv Mjeldheim, Jo Saglie, Kaare Strøm, Paul Thyness and Bernt Aardal for comments, and Ingunn Opheim and Erik Bolstad Pettersen for technical assistance.
37 The seminar was directed by Mr. Einar Löchen. The idea was that a number of students should write their theses for the Magister degree about nominations at the 1949 *Storting* election. Actually, only two dissertations were completed: Tim Greve (1953) on the Conservative Party and Henry Valen (1954) on the Labor Party.
38 A community study of voters and political leaders in the Stavanger area in southwest Norway.
39 A postal questionnaire was sent to all members of nomination committees throughout the country. The response rate was 60 percent.
40 A postal questionnaire was sent to all members of the nomination conventions as well as to nominated candidates in three large constituencies: Akershus, Hordaland and Nordland. The response rate was 76.4 percent.
41 See *Valgordningskommisjonen* of 1917. Inst. 2. See also *Stortingsforhandlingene* 1920, 3a. Ot. prop. nr. 1-50.
42 One may wonder why primary elections were not considered. A reasonable explanation is that the character of the political system, above all the parliamentary form of government, conditioned the choice. From the debate during 1905-1918 (Mjeldheim, 1978) we may infer that the political community tended to emphasize the need for relatively strong and unified parties. The convention model was seen as more likely than primaries to promote compromises and cooperation within the individual parties.
43 The number of seats is not directly proportional to population size, partly because sparsely populated provinces are intentionally overrepresented compared to central areas, partly because the number of seats for each province has been stable for long periods, while the size of the population is affected by migration. In 1988 eight adjustment seats were introduced in addition to the 157 seats elected from the

provinces. This amendment improved the territorial proportionality of the *Storting* (see Matthews and Valen, 1999; Aardal, 1997).
44 By-elections are unknown in Norway. If an elected representative becomes a member of government or leaves office as a result of death, illness, travel abroad, etc., the next candidate on the list who then becomes the 'alternate representative' succeeds him or her.
45 The electoral law, section 44, states: 'When the number of seats for each list has been decided by the electoral results, a new count is undertaken for candidates on the list. The candidate who has gained most votes as number 1 is elected.' If some voters prefer candidate number 2 to candidate number 1, the name of the latter has to be crossed out by 50 percent of the voters plus 1. Since this system was introduced in 1920 it has never happened that the voters have successfully changed the parties' rank ordering at *Storting* elections.
46 According to section 3 of the Nomination Act, the number of delegates is defined as follows: 20-150 votes at the preceding *Storting* election: 1 delegate. For a greater number of votes up to 1900: 1 delegate for every 400 or fraction thereof. And when the vote exceeds even this figure: 1 delegate for every 700 or fraction thereof.
47 The right of the nomination meetings to make final decisions is normally not challenged. Nonetheless, to our knowledge three exceptions have occurred in recent years. One in 1985, when the Labor Party in Sogn og Fjordane did not nominate a female candidate in one of the top positions on the list, and the women's movement demanded that the nominations should be canceled. In two cases the nominations of the Progress Party have triggered conflicts within the provincial party organization (the provinces of Østfold 1989 and Oppland 1997). In both cases the party chairman has sided with the opposition and supported the demands for new nominations, which have then taken place. Of course, this decision implied that the Nomination Act was not followed.
48 According to the Iron Law of Oligarchy (Michels, 1913), it would be a reasonable hypothesis that national party leaders might affect decision-making by exploiting their control of the communication lines in the organization.
49 Apparently, they are intentionally uninformed because the constituencies seek to avoid interference from party headquarters. In their study of nominations in 1985 Valen and Matthews (1998) turned to the party headquarters for help in identifying members of the nomination committees, but they were told that lists of names were not available at the national level. National leaders would not take the risk of infuriating the provincial organizations by asking about the names. Thus, the questionnaire had to be distributed through the provincial secretaries of the respective parties.
50 An attempt was made at the party's national congress of May 2001 to alter party statutes regarding nominations to the effect that if the chairman or deputy chairman sought nomination, they should automatically receive the top place on the list. However, the party congress defeated this proposal.
51 In a very stimulating paper on the Progress Parties in Denmark and Norway Harmel and Svåsand (2001) have discussed the character of leadership in relation to political and organizational change in recent years within the two parties.
52 In an article in *Aftenposten* (October 10, 2001), Heidi Borud has described in detail the hostile feelings towards Mr. Hagen among FRP dissidents.
53 For more than one year all Norwegian newspapers were greatly concerned with

the internal conflicts in the Progress Party, including those that were evident during the 2001 parliamentary nominations. See e.g. comments by Arne Strand in *Dagsavisen*, Februrary 27, 2001: "Standretten settes i FRP" (*Kangaroo Court set up in the Progress Party*), and February 14, 2001: "Carl I. Hagens endelikt?" (*The end of C.I. Hagen?*). In addition, May 8, 2001, the leading newspaper in Norway, *Aftenposten*, published a report by Gunnar Magnus on how the turbulence affected party nominations. The situation in the province of Vest-Agder attracted most attention, where the incumbent candidate Vidar Kleppe, an ardent anti-immigration spokesman, was removed from the list – apparently by the order of Mr. Hagen. Subsequently, Mr. Kleppe presented a separate list in competition with the Progress Party list. The newspaper's report refers explicitly to an interview with one of the local party leaders in the town of Kristiansand, Mr. Messel, who claimed that Mr. Hagen had indicated opposition to the renomination of Mr. Kleppe. Mr. Messel, who was also chairman of the local nomination committee, revealed that he had previously attended a national party summit with other local committee chairmen, where Mr. Hagen had also been present. Such a meeting is unheard of at nominations in Norway.
54 The three provinces were the city of Oslo and the provinces of Hedmark (East Norway) and Sogn og Fjordane (the West Coast).
55 In the Stavanger study the political leaders were asked: 'To what qualities would you attach the strictest requirements in a person whom you would nominate to the electoral list?'
56 'Let us go in the other direction. Which qualities in a candidate would you consider to be particularly unfortunate for the party's representation amongst the voters?'
57 In the literature on the origins of political parties, a distinction is often made between those parties generated initially inside the legislature, and those born as social movements or interest groups outside it, the latter frequently but not invariably moving into the legislatures at a later stage. Notable examples of the former type are the Liberal and the Conservative parties in 19th Century Europe, whereas socialist parties and the parties representing the working class are examples of the latter. Moreover, the different origins of political parties are frequently characterized in terms of their organization, the former type being cadre parties, which is more or less synonymous with Rational-Efficient parties, and the latter being mass membership parties, which is equivalent to the Party Democracy type of parties. See e.g. von Beyme, 1987; Hine, 1987.
58 The members of the nomination committees were asked: 'Here is a list of characteristics attributed to candidates for the *Storting* election. Concerning top candidates, which one of these characteristics do you consider most important, and which are most important for lower candidates?'
59 The 1985 sample consisted of members of the nomination committees from all parties all over the country. In 1993 the respondents were the delegates to the nomination conventions in three constituencies. Moreover, the relevant questions differ. In 1985 an open-ended question was applied, in 1993 the respondents were asked to react to fixed response alternatives (see Skare, 1994; Matthews and Valen, 1999).
60 These figures represent the parties that obtained representation in the *Storting* in the respective years. A number of minor parties have been slightly more inclined to nominate 'alien' candidates.

Notes 235

61 In recent years there has only been one alien candidate in a top position outside Oslo and Akershus. In 1989 the Socialist Left Party wanted to see their new leader, Erik Solheim, elected to the *Storting*. Solheim lived in Oslo, but in this constituency the party had only one safe seat, and renominated the popular incumbent candidate at the top of the list. The party leader now turned to the party branch in the province of Sør-Trøndelag (mid-Norway) and asked for nomination. His demand was successful, and as a result Mr. Solheim was elected to parliament. However, this incident was very unusual, and it triggered substantial public debate as well as some uproar among local activists.

62 We use the term 'new' parties for those parties that emerged after the Second World War, i.e. the Socialist Left Party and the Progress Party. The 'old' parties are then the parties that emerged before the war, i.e. the Conservatives, the Liberals and Labor before the turn of the century, the Center Party in 1920 and the Christian People's Party in 1933.

63 Observe, that in Table 5.4 we have defined as 'lawyers' only those who practiced law (as a job) at the time they were elected. Hence, people with a law degree, but working as a civil servant, professor, journalist etc. are defined by their profession and not by their education.

64 In contrast to Table 5.4 the figures in Table 5.5 are based on information from survey data (self-classification). Moreover, since the categories used to classify occupation and sector are broader in Table 5.5, the two tables are not directly comparable.

65 In a nationwide survey the sample was asked to indicate agreement or disagreement with the following statements: (1) 'People should keep their political opinions to themselves, it only results in difficulties when informing everyone about your own view.' (2) 'When meeting people who belong to another party than your own, it is best to avoid talking about politics.' (3) 'It would be best if people stopped talking about differences among the parties and rather focused upon what they agree about.' These items were combined in a Guttman-scale (reproducibility = .94; scalability = .73) that expresses four levels: 0 marks highest and 3 least conflict avoidance.

66 In its original form this hypothesis was formulated by the late Stein Rokkan, but unfortunately he never analyzed the data.

67 The study, which was conducted by Lars Bauna (1997), was modeled on Richard Fenno's analysis of members of the American House of Representatives, who were re-interviewed a number of times. Bauna selected 9 MPs from three constituencies, Oslo, Hedmark and Finnmark, belonging to the Labor Party (5), the Conservatives (1), the Center Party (2), and the Socialist Left Party (1). The analysis focused upon the activities of the representatives in four different arenas: the *Storting*, the party organization, the constituency, and the media.

68 The contrast between the two levels is reflected in the title of the thesis: 'Fighting for Oslo does not qualify for a cabinet minister position.' This sentence is quoted from one of the interviews.

69 The former president of the *Storting*, Mr. Guttorm Hansen, was among those observers pointing to the increased tendency to deselect top candidates due to regional demands (*Aftenposten*, January 1997).

70 Observe that prior to 1953 urban and rural areas were organized in separate con-

stituencies. In our data we have made adjustments for this reform and counted candidates by province for the entire period. Minor parties, which did not obtain representation in the *Storting*, have been excluded from this presentation.

71 This tendency is evident in the published biographies of elected representatives in 1945, in which great attention was given to the war record of the MPs. According to the biographies most of them had served in the resistance movement during the war and quite a few had been exposed to torture and imprisonment in concentration camps. The remaining number had served outside the country or had been involved in the work of the exile government in London.

72 Top candidates were those who were either elected or ranked in the next two places on the list. For lists that did not obtain representation, the first two names are classified as top candidates.

73 Conceivably, the parties might turn informally to the electorate for advice, but so far such attempts have been unsuccessful. The most notable attempt to involve the voters in the nomination process was made by the Liberal Party in the 1950s and 1960s. Liberal voters were invited to send proposals for candidates to the party's constituency organizations. But almost without exception, the proposals received came from active party members.

74 According to data from the election studies at the Institute for Social Research (Aardal and Valen, 1995). The data are available at the Norwegian Social Science Data Services (NSD). Observe, that membership figures reported by the extra-parliamentary party organizations tend to be higher than those obtained through voter surveys (Heidar, 1988; Svåsand, 1985). We firmly believe that the voter reports are the most reliable.

75 In 1985 up to five names were recorded. For the sake of comparability, however, Table 8 only reports up to 3 names. Those who mentioned more than 3 names in 1985 have been put into that category.

76 When the same question was asked in the Stavanger study of 1957, 56 percent of the voters were able to mention one or more candidates (Valen and Katz, 1964:140). It is not correct, however, to make direct comparisons between a local study of 1957 and the nationwide studies. Nonetheless, all three studies indicate low candidate awareness. The figures for 1985 and 1997 are only slightly higher than those of 1957, despite the increasing level of general education during the intervening period, and despite the fact that the nomination process was opened up to the public at the end of the 1960s (Narud, 1991).

References

Aftenposten, "AP-ordførere marsjerte mot partiledelsen." November 12, 1999.
Allum, P. 1995. *State and Society in Western Europe*. Cambridge: University Press.
Almond, G. and J. Coleman 1960. *The Politics of Developing Areas*. N.J.: Princeton University Press.
Aardal, B. 1997. "Electoral systems in Norway 1814-1997." Paper presented at the UCI conference on Evolution of Electoral Systems and Party Systems in the Nordic Countries, Laguna Beach, Ca., Dec. 13-14, 1997.
Aardal, B. and H. Valen 1995. *Konflikt og opinion*. Oslo: NKS-forlaget.
Barkfeldt, B., D. Brändström, U. Simm, and L. Zanderin 1971. "Partierna nominerar." *Den kommunala självstyrelsen* 3. Uppsala.
Bauna, L. 1997. *Å slåss for Oslo blir man ikke Kirke- og undervisningsminister av. En case studie av representasjon med særlig fokus på representasjon av valgkretsen*. Hovedoppgave. Institutt for statsvitenskap, Universitetet i Oslo.
Bergman, T., W. C. Müller and K. Strøm 2000. "Parliamentary Democracies and the Chain of Delegation." *European Journal of Political Research* vol. 36:255-260.
Best, H. and M. Cotta 2000 (ed.), *Parliamentary Representatives in Europe 1848-2000*. Oxford: Oxford University Press.
Beyme, K. von 1987. "Functions of political parties." in V. Bogdanor (ed.), *The Blackwell Encyclopaedia of Political Institutions*. Oxford: Blackwell: 412-416.
Bille, L. 1993. "Candidate Selection for National Parliament in Denmark 1960-1990. An Analysis of the Party Rules." Pp. 190-204 in Bryder, T. ed. *Party Systems, Party Behaviour and Democracy*. Copenhagen: Copenhagen Political Studies Press.
Bille, L. 2001. "Democratizing a Democratic Procedure: Myth or Reality? Candidate Selection in Western European Parties, 1960-1990." Special issue of *Party Politics* vol. 7 no. 3:267-276.
Bille, L. 1997. *Partier i forandring*. Odense: Odense University Press.
Blondel, J. 1980. *World Leaders*. London and Los Angeles: Sage.
Bochel, J. and D. Denver 1983. "Candidate Selection in the Labour Party: What the Selectors Seek." *British Journal of Political Science* 13:45-69.
Borg, S. 1997. "Kansalaisten suhde politiikkaan murroksessa." In Suhonen, P., (ed.), *Yleinen mielipide*. Helsinki: Tammi.
Brockmeyer, V., P. B. Mortensen and N. Preisler 1983. *Folketingsvalgloven*. Copenhagen: Jurist- og Økonomforbundets forlag.
Brändström, D. 1972. *Nomineringsförfarande vid riksdagsval*. SOU 1972:17.
Burns, J. McG. 1978. *Leadership*. New York: Harper and Row.
Christensen, T. 1976. "Kvinnen som politisk trekkplaster." *Tidsskrift for samfunnsforskning* 17:135-157.
Christensen, T. 1974. *Mange er kallet, men få er utvalgt*. Magistergradsavhandling i statsvitenskap. Universitetet i Oslo.
Christoffersen, H. 1992. "Udviklingen i selektionen af Folketingspolitikere 1966 til 1988." Pp. 342-75 in Andersen, J. G. et al. *Vi og vore politikere*. Copenhagen: Spektrum.
Czudnowski, M. 1972. "Sociocultural Variables and Legislative Recruitment." *Comparative Politics* 4:561-587.

Czudnowski, M. 1975. "Political Recruitment." *Handbook of Political Science*, Vol 2. Micropolitical Theory.
Dahl, R. A. 1990. "The Myth of Presidential Mandate." in *Political Science Quarterly* 105:3.
Danielsen, R. 1964. *Det norske Storting gjennom 150 år*. Bind II. Tidsrommet 1870-1908. Oslo: Gyldendal.
Denver, D. 1988. "Britain: centralized parties with decentralized selection." in Gallagher, M. & Marsh, M., (ed.), *Candidate Selection in Comparative Perspective*. London: Sage Publications.
Dybdahl, V. 1969. *Partier og erhverv – Studier i partiorganisation og byerhvervenes politiske aktivitet 1880-1913*. Vol. 1-2. Aarhus: Aarhus Universitetsforlag.
Eliassen, K. and M. N. Pedersen 1978. "Professionalization of Legislatures: Long-Term Change in Political Recruitment in Denmark and Norway." *Comparative Studies in Society and History* 20:286-318.
Eliassen, K. 1985. "Rekrutteringen til Stortinget og Regjeringen 1945-1985." i T. Nordby (ed.), *Storting og regjering*. Oslo: Kunnskapsforlaget.
Elklit, J. 1988. *Fra åben til hemmelig afstemning. Aspekter af et partisystems udvikling*. Aarhus: Politica.
Elklit, J. and R. B. Jensen, (ed.) 1997. *Kommunalvalg*. Odense: Odense University Press.
Epstein, L. D. 1980. *Political Parties in Western Democracies*. New Brunswick, N.J.: Transaction Books.
Esaiasson, P. and S. Holmberg 1996. *Representation from Above*. Dartmouth: Aldershot.
Fearon, J. D. 1999. "Electoral Accountability and the Control of Politicians: Selecting Good Types versus Sanctioning Poor Performance." in A. Przeworski, S. C. Stokes & B. Manin (ed.), *Democracy, Accountability and Representation*. Cambridge: Cambridge University Press.
Fenno, R. F. 1978. *Home Style: House Members in their Districts*. New York: Harper and Collins.
Folketingsvalget den 21. september 1994. Copenhagen: The Ministry of the Interior, 1995.
Folketingsvalget den 11. marts 1998. Copenhagen: The Ministry of the Interior, 1999.
Foverskov, P. 1979. "Den politiske rekrutteringsproces omkring folketingsvalget 1973." Pp. 206-23 in Pedersen, M.N. (ed.), *Dansk politik i 1970'erne*. Copenhagen: Samfundsvidenskabeligt Forlag.
Gallagher, M. and M. Marsh 1988. (ed.), *Candidate Selection in Comparative Perspective. The Secret Garden of Politics*. London: Sage Publications.
Greenwood, J. 1988. "Promoting Working-Class Candidatures in the Conservative Party: The Limits of Central Office Power." *Parliamentary Affairs* 41:456-68.
Greve, T. 1953. *Nominasjon ved stortingsvalg*. Bergen: Christian Michelsens Institutt.
Grímsson, Ó. R. 1979. *Network Parties*. Reykjavík: Félagsvísindadeild Háskóla Íslands.
Hardarson, Ó. 1999. "Iceland." in G. de Lury (ed.), *Facts on File Publications*. New York.
Hardarson, Ó. 1995. *Parties and Voters in Iceland*. Reykjavík: Social Science Research Institute.
Harmel, R. and L. Svåsand 2001. "Party Life Cycles and Changing Leadership Needs. The Progress Parties at Middle-Age." Paper presented at APSA, San Fransisco, September 2001.
Hatting, J. and K. Winding 1950. "Rigsdagen og Vælgerne." Pp. 7-155 in Fabricius, K. et al., (ed.), *Den danske Rigsdag 1849-1949. Vol. III*. Copenhagen: J. H. Schultz Forlag.
Heidar, K. 1988. *Partidemokrati på prøve*. Oslo: Universitetsforlaget.

Heidar, K. 1997. "Roles, Structures and Behavior: Norwegian Parliamentarians in the Nineties." *Journal of Legislative Studies*, 3:91-109.
Helander, V. 1997a. "Ehdokkaat ja heidän eväänsä: Turun eteläisen vaalipiirin ehdokkaat vuoden 1995 eduskuntavaaleissa." in Helander, V., Kuitunen, S. & Paltemaa, L., eds., Kansalaisesta aktiiviksi, aktiivista edustajaksi. *Turun yliopiston valtio-opin laitoksen julkaisuja* 51.
Helander, V. 1997b. "Finland." in Norris, P. (ed.), *Passages to Power*. Cambridge: Cambridge University Press.
Helland, L. and J. Saglie 1997. *Strategisk koordinering i fire stortingsvalg: 1909-1918*. Forskningsrapport 03/97. Oslo: Institutt for statsvitenskap.
Hellevik, O. 1969. *Stortinget – en sosial elite?* Oslo: Pax Forlag.
Hernes, G. and W. Martinussen 1980. *Demokrati og politiske ressurser*. Oslo: Norges Offentlige Utredninger.
Hernes, G. and K. Nergaard 1989. *Oss i mellom*. Oslo: Fafo-rapport nr. 090.
Hine, D. 1987. "Development of Political Parties." in V. Bogdanor (ed.), pp. 410-412 in *The Blackwell Encyclopaedia of Political Institutions*. Oxford: Blackwell.
Jensen, R. B. 2000. *Lokale partiorganisationer*. Odense: Odense University Press.
Johansson, J. 1999. *Hur blir man riksdagsledamot? En undersökning av makt och inflytande i partiernas nomineringsprocesser*. Stockholm: Gidlund Förlag.
Johansen, L. N. 1979. "Denmark." Pp. 29-57 in Hand, G., J. Georgel & C. Sasse, (ed.) *European Electoral Systems Handbook*. London: Butterworths.
Johansen, L. N. and O. P. Kristensen 1979. "Sikre kredse og personlig stemmeafgivning ved folketingsvalgene i 1960'erne og 1970'erne." Pp. 151-205 in Pedersen, M. N., (ed.), *Dansk politik i 1970'erne. Studier og arbejdspapirer*. Copenhagen: Samfundsvidenskabeligt Forlag.
Jupp, J. 1968. *Political Parties*. London: Routledge & Kegan Paul.
Jääsaari, J. and T. Martikainen 1991. *Nuorten poliittset valinnat: tutkumus nuorden aikuisten poliittisesta suuntautumisesta pääkaupunkiseudulla*. Helsinki: Gaudeamus.
Katz, R. S. and P. Mair, (ed.) 1992. *Party Organizations. A Data Handbook*. London: SAGE Publications.
Katz, D. 1973. "Patterns of Leadership." in Jeanne N. Knutson (ed.), *Handbook of Political Psychology*. Washington, San Francisco and London: Jossey-Bass.
Key, V. O. 1968. *Political Parties and Pressure Groups*. 5th. Edition. New York: Crowell.
Kiewiet, D. R. and M. D. McCubbins 1991. *The Logic of Delegation*. Chicago: The University of Chicago Press.
Koskiaho, T. 1972. "Edustajaehdokkaat ja valitut kansanedustajat." in Pesonen, P., (ed.), *Protestivaalit, nuorisovaalit*. Tampere: Tammer-Paino.
Kristinsson, G. H. 1996. "Parties, States and Patronage." in *West European Politics* 19/3:433-457.
Kristjánsson, S. 1998b. "Delegation and Accountability in Parliamentary Democracies: The Case of Iceland." Draft paper for the project on *Constitutional Change and Parliamentary Democracy*. Umeå: Department of Political Science.
Kristjánsson, S. 1998a. "Electoral Politics and Governance: Transformation of the Party System in Iceland, 1970-1995." in Lane, J.-E. & Pennings, P. (ed.) *Comparing Party System Change*. London: Routledge.
Kristvik, B. and S. Rokkan 1964. *Valgordningen*. Mimeo. Bergen: Christian Michelsens Institutt.
Kuitunen, S. 1997a. "Herroja vai narreja?" in Helander, V., Kuitunen, S. & Paltemaa, L.,

(ed.), *Kansalaisesta aktiiviksi, aktiivista edustajaksi. Turun yliopiston valtio-opin laitoksen julkaisuja* 51.
Kuitunen, S. 1997b. "Rekrytoitumisprosessin mysteeri: miten ehdokkaaksi ja edustajaksi valikoidutaan?" in Helander, V., Kuitunen, S. & Paltemaa, L., eds., *Kansalaisesta aktiiviksi, aktiivista edustajaksi. Turun yliopiston valtio-opin laitoksen julkaisuja* 51.
Kuitunen, S. 1997c. "Poliittinen rekrytaatio Suomen kunnallisvaaleissa." *Kunnallistieteellinen Aikakausikirja* 4: 323-343.
Kuitunen, S. 1988. "Naisten poliittinen rekrytoituminen vuoden 1995 eduskuntavaaleissa ja niiden ehdokasasetteluissa." *Politiikka* 2:22-37.
Laakso, M. 1980. "Edustuksellinen demokratia ja politiikan tutkimus." *Politiikka* 4:337-357.
Lane, J. E., T. Martikainen, P. Svensson, G. Vogt and H. Valen, "Scandinavian Exceptionalism Reconsidered." *Journal of Theoretical Politics* 5:195-230.
Lane, R. 1996. "Positivism, Scientific Relativism, and Poltical Science: Recent Developments in the Philosophy of Science." in *Journal of Theoretical Politics* 8/3:361-382.
Larsen, K. 1979. "Venstreorganisationerne 1866- 1929." Pp. 45-77 in Sørensen, K. (ed.) *Venstre 50 år for folke- styret*. Copenhagen: Forlaget liberal.
Loewenberg, G. and S. Patterson 1979. *Comparing Legislatures*. Boston: Little, Brown and Company.
Lupia, A. and M. McCubbins 2000. "Representation or Abdication? How Citizens Use Institutions to Help Delegation Succeed." *European Journal of Political Research* vol. 36:291-307.
Matland, R. E. and D. T. Studlar 1996. "The Contagion of Women Candidates in Single-member District and Proportional Representation Electoral Systems: Canada and Norway." in *The Journal of Politics* 58/3:707-733.
Matthews, D. 1985. "Legislative Recruitment and Legislative Careers." in Loewenberg, G., Patterson, S. & Jewell, M., (ed.), *Handbook of Legislative Research*. Cambridge: Harvard University Press.
Matthews, D. and H. Valen 1999. *Parliamentary Representation: the Case of the Norwegian Storting*. Columbus: Ohio State University Press.
Meyer, P. 1965. *Politiske partier*. Copenhagen: Nyt Nordisk Forlag – Arnold Busck.
Michels, R. 1962. [1911], *Political Parties*. New York: Free Press.
Ministry of the Interior, 1996. *Parliamentary Elections and Election Administration in Denmark*, Copenhagen: Ministry of the Interior.
Mitchell, P. 2000. "Voters and their Representatives: Electoral Institutions and Delegation in Parliamentary Democracies." *European Journal of Political Research* vol. 36:335-351.
Mjeldheim, L. 1984. *Folkerørsla som vart parti*. Bergen: Universitetsforlaget.
Mjeldheim, L. 1978. *Parti og Rørsle*. Bergen: Universitetsforlaget.
Müller, W. C. 2000. "Political Parties in Parliamentary Democracies: Making Delegation and Accountability Work." *European Journal of Political Research* vol. 36:309-333.
Narud, H. M. and H. Valen 2000. "Does Background Matter? Social Representation and Political Attitudes." Ch. 4 in P. Esaiasson and K. Heidar (ed.), *Beyond Westminister and Congress: The Nordic Experience*. Columbus: Ohio State University Press.
Narud, H. M. 1991. "Fra oppgjør på kammerset til spill for åpen scene: Rekruttering av kandidater til stortingsvalg." *Norsk Statsvitenskapelig Tidsskrift* 3:155-172.
Narud, H. M. 1994. "Nominasjoner og pressen." in K. Heidar og L. Svåsand (ed.), *Partiene i en brytningstid*. Bergen: Alma Mater: 287-326.

Narud, H. M. 1999. "Norwegen: Professionalisierung zwischen Parteien- und Wahlkreisorientierung." In J. Borchert (ed.), *Politik als Beruf. Die politische Klasse in westlischen Demokratien.* Opladen: Leske & Budrich.

Narud, H. M. 1988. *Pressens dekning av nominasjoner. En innholdsanalyse av en del avisers omtale av nominasjonene foran stortingsvalget i 1965 og 1985.* Master thesis. Oslo: Institutt for statsvitenskap.

Noponen, M. 1964. *Kansanedustajien sosiaalinen tausta Suomessa.* Porvoo: WSOY.

Noponen, M. 1989. "Kansanedustajan valitsemisprosessi ja poliittinen ura." in Noponen, M., (ed.), *Suomen kansanedustusjärjestelmä.* Juva: WSOY.

Norris, P. and J. Lovenduski 1993. "If Only More Candidates Came Forward: Supply-Side Explanations of Candidate Selection in Britain." *British Journal of Political Science* 23: 373-408.

Norris, P. 1996. "Legislative Recruitment." in L. LeDuc, R. Niemi and P. Norris (ed.), *Comparing Democracies. Elections and Voting in Global Perspective.* Thousand Oaks, CA: Sage.

Norris, P. 1997. (ed.), *Passages to Power.* Cambridge: Cambridge University Press.

Norris P. and J. Lovenduski 1995. *Political Recruitment. Gender, Race and Class in the British Parliament.* Cambridge: Cambridge University Press.

Nousiainen, J. 1992. *Suomen poliittinen järjestelmä.* Juva: WSOY.

Oksanen, M. 1989. "Poliittinen sosialisaatio kiinnostuksen herättäjänä ja asenteiden kehittäjänä." in Noponen, M. (ed.), *Suomen kansanedustusjärjestelmä.* Juva: WSOY.

Paltemaa, L. 1997. "Kunnalliset luottamustoimet – ponnahduslauta edustajaksi?" in Helander, V., Kuitunen, S. & Paltemaa, L., (ed.), Kansalaisesta aktiiviksi, aktiivista edustajaksi. *Turun yliopiston valtio-opin laitoksen julkaisuja* 51.

Pedersen, M. N. 1993. "Eine kurzgefasste Übersicht über die Entwicklung des dänischen Parteiensysteme." pp. 91-108 in Pappi, F. & H. Schmitt, (ed.), *Parteien, Parlamente und Wahlen in Skandinavien.* Frankfurt/New York: Campus Verlag.

Pedersen, M. N. 1994. "Incumbency Success and Defeat in Times of Electoral Turbulence: Patterns of Legislative Recruitment in Denmark 1945-1990." Pp. 218-50 in A. Somit, R. Wildenmann, B. Boll and A. Römmele (ed.), *The Victorious Incumbent. A Threat to Democracy?* Aldershot: Dartmouth.

Pedersen, M. N. 1965. "Kvindernes mobilisering i dansk politik." *Danske Økonomer* vol. 12:531-39.

Pedersen, M. N. 1972. "Lawyers in Politics: The Danish Folketing and American Legislatures." in S. C. Patterson and J. C. Wahlke (ed.), *Comparative Legislative Behavior Research.* New York: John Wiley & Sons.

Pedersen, M. N. 1966. "Preferential Voting in Denmark: The Voter's Influence on the Election of Folketing Candidates." *Scandinavian Political Studies* vol. 1:167-187.

Pedersen, M. N and L. Bille 1991. "Public Financing and Public Control of Political Parties in Denmark." Pp. 147-72 in Wiberg, M., (ed.) *The Public Purse and Political Parties.* Jyväskyla: The Finnish Political Science Association.

Pedersen, M. N. 1987. "The Danish 'Working Multiparty System': Breakdown or Adaptation?" Pp. 1-60 in Daalder, H., ed. *Party Systems in Denmark, Austria, Switzerland, The Netherlands and Belgium.* London: Frances Pinter.

Pedersen, M. N. 1975. "The Geographical Matrix of Parliamentary Representation: A Spatial Model of Political Recruitment." *European Journal of Political Research* vol. 3:1-19.

Pedersen, M. N. 1977. "The Personal Circulation of a Legislature: The Danish Folke-

ting 1849-1968." in W. O. Aydelotte (ed.), *The History of Parliamentary Behavior*. Princeton: Princeton University Press.
Pedersen, M. N. 1984. "Velgerbevægelighed og politisk rekruttering: nogle spekulationer og nogle foreløbige resultater." pp. 60-85 in O. Berg and A. Underdal (ed.), *Fra valg til vedtak*. Oslo: Aschehoug.
Pekonen 1997: Kansa ja puolueet nyt: puolueiden toimintaympäristön muutos. Teoksessa Borg, Sami (toim.): *Poolueet 1990-luvulla. Näkökulmia puoluetutkimukseen*. Turun yliopiston valtio-opin tutkimuksia 53/1997.
Pennings, P. and R. Y. Hazan, 2001. "Democratizing Candidate Selection: Causes and Consequences." Special issue of *Party Politics* vol. 7 no. 3:267-276.
Pesonen P., R. Sänkiaho, and S. Borg 1993. *Vaalikansan äänivalta. Tutkimus eduskuntavaaleista ja valitsijakunnasta Suomen poliittisessa järjestelmässä*. Juva: WSOY.
Pitkin, H. 1967. *The Concept of Representation*. Berkeley: University of California Press.
Prewitt, K. 1970. *The Recruitment of Political Leaders: A Study of Citizen-Politicians*. New York: The Bobbs-Merrill Company, Inc.
Przeworski, A. and H. Teune 1970. *Logic of Comparative Social Inquiry*. New York: John Wiley & Sons.
Putnam, R. 1976. *The Comparative Study of Political Elites*. New Jersey: Prentice- Hall.
Ranney, A. 1981. "Candidate Selection." in D. Butler, H. R. Penniman and A. Ranney (ed.), *Democracy at the Polls: A Comparative Study of Competitive National Elections*. Washington D.C.: AEI publications.
Ranney, A. 1983. *Channels of Power. The Impact of Television on American Politics*. New York: Basic Books.
Ranney, A. 1978. *The Federalization of Presidential Primaries*. Washington D.C.: American Enterprise Institute.
Ranney, A. 1977. *Participation in American Presidential Nominations, 1976*. Washington D.C.: American Enterprise Institute.
Ranney, A. 1965. *Pathways to Parliament. Candidate Selection in Britain*. Madison and Milwaukee: The University of Wisconsin Press.
Rasmussen, E. and R. Skovmand 1955. *Det radikale Venstre 1905-1955*. Copenhagen: Det danske forlag.
Reiter, H. 1985. *Selecting the President: The Nominating Process in Transition*. University of Pennsylvania Press.
Riker, W. 1986. *The Art of Political Manipulation*. New Haven: Yale University Press.
Ruostetsaari, I. 1999. "From Political Amateur to Professional Politician and Expert Representative. Recruitment of the Parliamentary Elite in Finland 1863-1995." in Best, H. & Cotta, M., (ed.), *The European Representative. 150 years of Parliamentary Recruitment in Comparative Perspective (1848-1998)*. Oxford: Oxford University Press.
Raaum, N. 1995. (ed.), *Kjønn og politikk*. Oslo: Tano.
Schattschneider, E. E. 1942. *Party Government*. New York: Farrar and Rinehart.
Schlesinger, J. 1966. *Ambition and Politics: Political Careers in the United States*. Chicago: Rand McNally and Co.
Schlesinger, J. 1994. *Political Parties and the Winning of Office*. Ann Arbor: The University of Michigan Press.
Scott, R. and R. Hrebenar 1979. *Parties in Crisis*. New York: John Wiley.
Sejersted, F. 1984. *Høyres Historie* vol. 2. Oslo: Schibsted.
Seligman, L. G. 1967. "Political Parties and the Recruitment of Political Leadership." in L. Edinger (ed.), *Political Leadership in Industrialized Societies*. New York: Wiley.

Seligman, L. 1961. "Political Recruitment and Party Structure: A Case Study." *American Political Science Review* 55:77-86.
Seligman, L. 1971. *Recruiting Political Elites*. New York: General Learning Press.
Sjöblom, G. 1986. "Problems and Problem Solutions in Politics." in Castles, F. and Wildenman (ed.) *Visions and Realities of Party Government*. Berlin: deGruyter.
Skard, T. and E. Haavio-Mannila 1986. "Equality between the Sexes – Myth or Reality in Norden?" In S. Graubard (ed.), *Norden – the Passion for Equality*. Oslo: Norwegian University Press.
Skare, A. 1996. "Kandidatutvelging – mer enn riktig kjønn fra rett sted. Politisk utvelging og politiske endringer i en brytningstid." *Tidsskrift for samfunnsforskning*, 37:328-362.
Skare, A. 1994. *Nominasjoner. Kandidatutvelgingens politiske innhold*. Master thesis. Oslo: Institutt for statsvitenskap.
Skjeie, H. 1997. "A Tale of Two Decades: The End of Male Political Hegemony." in K. Strøm and L. Svaasand (ed.), *Challenges to Political Parties*. Ann Arbor: The University of Michigan Press.
Skjeie, H. 1992. *Den politiske betydningen av kjønn*. Report 92:11. Oslo: Institutt for samfunnsforskning.
Skjeie, H. and H. Hernes 1997. "Mellom fag og feminisme. Kvinneforskning i statsvitenskap." *Norsk Statsvitenskapelig Tidsskrift* 13:363-381.
Skovmand, R. 1964. "Folkestyrets Fødsel 1830-1870." in *Danmarks Historie* vol. 11 (ed.), John Danstrup & Hal Koch). Copenhagen: Politikens Forlag.
Sköld, L. 1958. *Kandidatnominering vid andrakammarval*. Rapport til författningsutredningen, SOU 1958:6.
Somit, A., R. Wildenmann, B. Boll, and A. Römmele 1994. (ed.), *The Victorious Incumbent: A Threat to Democracy?* Darthmouth: Aldershot.
Stortingsforhandlingene 1920. 3A Ot.Prop. nr. 1-50.
Strøm, K. 2000. "Delegation and Accountability in Parliamentary Democracies." *European Journal of Political Research* vol. 36:261-289.
Strøm, K. 1999. "Voter Sovereignty and Parliamentary Democracy." Pp. 49-69 in H. M. Narud & T. Aalberg (ed.), *Challenges to Representative Democracy: Parties, Voters and Public Opinion*. Bergen: Fagbokforlaget.
Styrkársdóttir, A. 1999. "Women's Lists in Iceland-A response to political lethargy." in Bergqvist, C. et. al. (ed.) *Equal Democracies? Gender and Politics in the Nordic Countries*. Oslo: Scandinavian University Press.
Sundberg, J. 1999. "The Enduring Scandinavian Party System." *Scandinavian Political Studies* vol. 22:221-242.
Sundberg, J. 1989. *Lokala partiorganisationer i kommunala och nationella val*. Helsinki: Finnish Society of Sciences and Letters.
Sundberg, J. 1995. "Organizational Structure of Parties, Candidate Selection and Campaigning." in Borg, S. & Sänkiaho, R., (ed.), *The Finnish Voter*. Tampere: The Finnish Political Science Association.
Sundberg, J. 1996. *Partier och partisystem i Finland*. Esbo: Schildts Förlag AB.
Svåsand, L. 1985. *Politiske partier*. Oslo: Tiden.
Sänkiaho, R. 1995. "Cleavages and Party System Dimensions." in Borg, S. & Sänkiaho, R., (ed.), *The Finnish Voter*. Tampere: The Finnish Political Science Association.
Tarasti, L. and H. Taponen 1990. *Suomen vaalilainsäädäntö*. Helsinki: VAPK.
Tarasti, L. and H. Taponen 1996. *Suomen vaalilainsäädäntö*. Helsinki: Oy Edita Ab.

Tarkiainen, T. 1971. *Suomen kansanedustuslaitoksen historia osa IX*. Helsinki: VAPK.
Timonen, P. 1972. "Edustajaehdokkaiden valikoituminen puoluejärjestöjen jäsenäänestyksessä." in Pesonen, P., (ed.), *Protestivaalit, nuorisovaalit*. Tampere: Tammer-Paino OY.
Timonen, P. 1981. "Esivaalien edustavuus." *Politiikka* 17:166-176.
Timonen, P. 1981. Puolueiden ehdokkaiden asettaminen eli kansanedustajavaalilain 26 §:n ja 26 f:n syntyä, soveltamista ja seurauksia. *Tampereen yliopiston politiikan tutkimuksen laitoksen julkaisuja* 58.
Valen, H. 1969. "Continuity of Political Leadership in the Norwegian Storting." Paper presented at the Conference on Comparative Legislative Behavior Research. University of Iowa, May 1969.
Valen, H. and D. Urwin 1985. "De Politiske Partiene." in T. Nordby (ed.), *Storting og regjering 1945-1985*. Vol. 2. Oslo: Universitetsforlaget.
Valen, H. 1958. "Factional Activities and Nominations in Political Parties." *Acta Sociologica* 3:183-199.
Valen, H., H. M. Narud & O. Hardarsson 2000. "Geographical Representation." Ch. 5 in P. Esaiasson and K. Heidar (ed.), *Beyond Westminister and Congress: The Nordic Experience*. Columbus: Ohio State University Press.
Valen, H. 1954. *Nominasjon av stortingskandidater i det norske Arbeiderparti*. Magister dissertation. Oslo: Institutt for statsvitenskap.
Valen, H. 1956. "Nominasjon ved stortingsvalg", *Statsøkonomisk Tidsskrift*, 70 (2) 1956:115-152.
Valen, H. and D. Katz. 1964. *Political Parties in Norway*. Oslo: Universitetsforlaget.
Valen, H. 1966. "The Recruitment of Parliamentary Nominees in Norway." *Scandinavian Political Studies*. Vol. 1:121-166.
Valen, H. 1986. "The Storting Election of September 1985: The Welfare State under Pressure." *Scandinavian Political Studies*. Vol. 9:177-88.
Valgordningskommisjonen av 1917. Innstilling nr. 2.
Vallance, E. 1979. *Women in the House: A Study of Women Members of Parliament*. London: Athlone Press.
Wallin, G., H. Bäck, and M. Tabor 1981. "Kommunalpolitikerna. Rekrytering – arbetsförhållanden – funktioner del 1." *Ds Kn* 17.
Ware, A. 1996. *Political Parties and Party Systems*. Oxford: Oxford University Press.
Weber, M. 1958, [1918]. "Politics as Vocation." Pp. 77-128 in H. H. Gert and C. Wright Mills (ed.), *From Max Weber*. New York: Oxford University Press.
Wiberg, M. and M. Mattila 1997. "Committee Assignments in the Finnish Parliament: 1945-1994." in Isaksson, G., (ed.), Inblickar i nordisk parlamentarism. *Meddenlanden från ekonomisk-statsvetenskapliga fakulteten vid Åbo universitet* Ser A:470.
Winter, L. de 1988. "Belgium: Democracy or Oligarchy?" in Gallagher, M. & Marsch M., eds. Candidate Selection in Comparative Perspective: London: Sage Publications.
Wright, W. E. (ed.) 1971a. *A Comparative Study of Party Organization*. Columbus: Charles E. Merril.
Wright, W. E. 1971b. "Comparative Party Models: Rational Efficient and Party Democracy," in W. E. Wright (ed.) (1971a), *A Comparative Study of Party Organization*. Columbus: Charles E. Merril: 17-54.
Wyller, T. Chr. 1959. "Om nominasjoner ved offentlige valg som statsvitenskapelig problem." *Statsøkonomisk Tidsskrift* 73:122-139.

References

Party statutes
The NCP 1993.
The CP 1989.
The SDP 1993.
The LWA 1994.

Interviews
The CP district officials 14.12.1994, 16.3.1998, 24.3.1998.
The LWA district officials 11.3.1998, 16.3.1998, 17.3.1998.
The NCP district officials 16.3.1998, 17.3.1998.
The SDP district officials 15.12.1994, 24.3. 1998, 28.3.1998.

Newspapers
Helsingin Sanomat 7.8.1998; 9.7.1998
Kansan Uutiset 8.7.1998
Suomenmaa 8.7.1998
Turun Sanomat 8.7.1998

Contributors

SVANUR KRISTJÁNSSON is professor in political science at the University of Iceland. He has published books and articles in the fields of Icelandic politics, political recruitment and democratic theory.

SOILE KUITUNEN is research director at Taloustutkimus, Finland. She has published several articles about political recruitment and representative democracy.

HANNE MARTHE NARUD is professor at the Department of Political Science, University of Oslo. Her recent works have been in the fields of elections, coalition governance and political representation.

MOGENS N. PEDERSEN is professor in political science at the University of Southern Denmark. He has published books and articles about parties, elections, political institutions and legislative recruitment.

AUDUN SKARE was research fellow at the Department of Political Science, University of Oslo. He worked in the fields of nominations, parties and the welfare state. Audun Skare passed away in January 1998.

HENRY VALEN is professor emeritus in political science at the University of Oslo, and is presently senior researcher at the Institute for Social Research in Oslo. He is one of the pioneers in the study of parliamentary nominations, and has a number of publications in this field as well as on elections, public opinion, political leadership- and representation.

Index

accountability 16, 21, 225, 229; Finland 65, 102; Iceland 110, 160, 162-163, 165-166; Norway 208; ex ante 109-110, 161, 163-164; ex post 109-110, 161, 163-164
agency loss 16, 22, 227, 229
agency model 18
agency theory 11, 224
agent 16-21, 23, 46, 63, 108-110, 112, 160, 163-164, 171, 223-225, 230
agent problems 109
aggregation of interests 189
Agrarian Liberal Party, Denmark 32, 40-42, 51, 56
Agrarian Party, Finland 93
Akershus 178, 191, 203-204, 215, 232, 235
Almond, G. 190
Althingi, Iceland 107, 113, 115, 140, 142, 147, 151, 157, 166, 222; members 113

Barkfeldt, B. 85
Bauna, L. 235
Bergman, T. 229
Best, H. 222-223
Beyme, K. von 234
Bille, L. 13, 38-39, 42, 226, 230
Bjerregaard, R. 230
Blomgren, M. 229
Blondel, J. 183
Borg, S. 70, 101, 231
Bochel, J. 79
Borud, H. 233
Brockmeyer, V. 230
Brändström, D. 25
Burns, J. McG. 183

cadre party 111, 115, 119, 133-135, 141, 156, 234
Canada 117
candidate knowledge 211-212
candidate selection 9, 11-13, 16-23, 25, 217-220, 226-227, 229, 232; Denmark 29, 42, 52; Finland 63-67, 69, 75, 77-79, 81, 84, 86, 88-89, 94, 98-102; Iceland 107, 109-110, 115, 123-124, 128-131, 135-137, 153, 161, 163; Norway 169-174, 176, 178-179, 181-185, 189-190, 193-194, 202, 207, 209-211, 214-215
candidate supply 87, 99, 222
career politician 24, 194
carpetbaggers 130
Center Democrats, Denmark 38, 40-43, 51, 56
Center Party (CP), Finland 71-75, 77-78, 80, 82
Center Party, Norway 179, 187-188, 210, 235
Center Party, Sweden 159
centralization 19, 231; degree of in candidate selection 12-13, 18, 21, 42, 67, 110, 129-130, 132-133, 225
central-local conflict 33
certification 14, 23, 184, 188, 220
chain of parliamentary delegation 16, 63, 225
Christensen, T. 170
Christian League, Finland 67
Christian People's Party, Denmark 42-43, 51
Christian People's Party, Norway 179, 188, 210, 235
Christoffersen, H. 54
citizen control 226
Coleman, J. 190
Communist Party, Denmark 231
Communist Party, Iceland 114
conflict avoidance 199-201
Conservative Party, Denmark 32, 40, 42-43, 51, 56
Conservative Party, Finland 93
Conservative Party, Iceland 114

Conservative Party, Norway 172-173, 179, 180, 188-189, 203, 210, 232, 235
Conservatives, Sweden 157
constituency 9, 12, 22, 25, 217-220, 230-236; Denmark (*amtskreds*) 29, 31-34, 36-41, 43-46, 48, 50-51, 53, 56-57, 60-61; Finland 66-75, 77, 79, 82-84, 86, 98, 103; Iceland 107-108, 113, 130; Norway 171-178, 183, 186-187, 190-193, 202-203, 205, 211, 214-215; local 25; multi-member 68, 174
constituency bond and contacts 23, 99, 190, 225
constituency convention 171
constituency interest 20, 203, 214
constituency party 12, 173, 177, 192, 219, 236
contract design 17, 25, 65
control 10, 13, 17, 20-21, 217, 223-226, 229, 233; Denmark 34, 39, 42, 61; Finland 63, 68; Iceland 111, 117, 119, 125, 135-136, 151, 155-156, 162-164; Norway 175, 178, 203
control mechanism 24; ex ante 16-17, 226; ex post 16-17, 226
convention method 122, 127-128, 137, 152, 155, 162, 173, 222, 226
convention model 175-176, 218-219, 232
Copenhagen 31-32, 45, 56, 230
Cotta, M. 222-223
critical pluralist school 166
Czudnowski, M. 78, 80, 85

Dahl, R. A. 166
Danielsen, R. 171, 174
Danish People's Party, Denmark 39, 42
decentralization 163; degree of in candidate selection 13, 20, 25, 63-64, 75, 78, 99, 133, 166, 169, 176, 178, 180, 214, 217-218, 225
decisive ballot 41-42
delegation 16-17, 19, 21-22, 24, 223, 225, 229; Finland 63, 65, 101; Iceland 110, 159, 163, 166; Norway 171, 202, 208
delegation mechanisms 70, 109
democracy 10; Denmark 30, 47; Finland 67, 101; Iceland 107, 110-111, 117, 133, 162, 164- 166; Norway 217; party 101, 155, 226; representative 9, 16, 170, 223, 226
democratization, degree of in candidate selection 13, 22, 173, 226-227
demographic representativeness 197
Denver, D. 79
deselection reasons 98, 232
district interests 192
district magnitude 158-159
district meetings 173
Dybdahl, V. 33, 230

Eduskunta, Finland 82, 92
election 9, 13-18, 22, 24, 218, 222-224, 226, 229-234, 236; Denmark 29-32, 34-39, 41, 43-48, 50-61; Finland 63-65, 67-68, 70, 72, 74, 81, 83-97, 99-104; Iceland 107-109, 113, 115-125, 127-132, 138-152, 154-155, 157, 159-161, 163-164; Norway 170-178, 181, 185, 191, 193, 195, 199-212, 214
Electoral Act, Finland 71-72, 81; (1969) 67-68, 82; (1975) 65, 68-69, 77
electoral alliance 33, 66-67, 73, 126, 128-129, 232
electoral campaign 17, 36, 45, 67, 157
electoral colleges, Norway (*valgmannsting*) 171-172
Electoral Commission, Norway 175
electoral district 232; Finland 69; Iceland 107, 113-114, 116-118, 120-121, 123, 125-127, 129-132, 135, 137, 141, 145, 151, 159, 161-162, 164; Norway 191
electoral law 11, 17-18, 218, 231, 233; Denmark 34, 37, 48; Finland 64-65, 68-69, 100-101; Norway 175, 189
electoral reform 21, 66, 68, 172, 174, 217
electoral system 11-12, 17-18, 22, 24-25,

217, 226; Denmark 29-30, 32, 34, 47, 53, 58; Finland 64-65, 70, 94, 100; Iceland 107, 112-114, 120, 123, 126, 130, 134-135, 156, 158-159, 162; Norway 169, 171-174, 198, 214
electoral volatility 24, 53, 139, 141-144, 207, 209, 224
Eliassen, K. 24, 59, 194, 197
élitist bias 86-87, 222
Elklit, J. 230
Esaiasson, P. 24

factional activity 181, 190, 193
factional affiliation 15
factions 15, 81, 84, 117, 221; ideological 15, 23, 194; interest 15; political 23, 170
Farmer's Party, Iceland 120
Fearon, J. D. 18, 229
feminist mobilization 198
Fenno, R. 235
Finnmark 235
Finnish People's Democratic Union (FPDU), Finland 68
Fjordane 192, 233-234
flash parties 60
Folketing, Denmark 31, 33, 35, 38, 60; election 34, 43-44, 46; members 32, 55
Foverskov, P. 43, 54
Funen 34-36, 44-45, 230
fylker, Norway 176
Fælles Kurs, Denmark 60

Gallagher, M. 10, 12, 14, 20, 25, 64, 72, 75, 79, 81
gatekeeper 13, 31, 131, 144, 176, 229
gatekeeping control 61
gender quota 192, 205
geographical balancing 191
geographical representation 220
Germany 63
Glistrup, M. 39
Great Britain 12, 229
Greece 13

Greve, T. 170, 232
Grímssom, Ó. R. 131
group affiliation 17, 19-20, 79, 183
group interest 20, 169, 176, 187, 214
group representation 23, 78, 81, 85, 189, 193, 198, 210, 212, 214-215, 220-221

Haavio-Mannila, E. 90-91, 221
Hagen, C. I. 181, 233-234
Hansen, G. 235
Hardarson, Ó 108, 113
Harmel, R. 233
Hatting, J. 32, 230
Hazan, P. Y. 12, 226
Hedmark 234-235
Heidar, K. 191, 194, 236
Helander, V. 11, 68, 71, 73-74, 76, 83, 86-87, 231
Helland, L. 172
Hellevik, O. 194
Helsinki 83, 231
Hernes, G. 191, 196
Hernes, H. 198
Hine, D. 234
Holmberg, S. 24
Hordaland 203-204, 232

Icelandic Federation of Labor 114
inclusiveness, degree of in candidate selection 13, 19, 21, 217, 226
incumbency 14-15, 58, 91-92, 144, 202, 205, 208
incumbents 17-20, 22, 24, 223-225, 230, 234-235; Denmark 35-37, 40, 45-46, 52, 58-60; Finland 63, 65, 87, 92-96, 98-99, 103; Iceland 122, 151-152, 162; Norway 202-203, 208-209; defeated 35, 94-95, 152, 208, 223
incumbents' success rate 59, 95
Independence Party (IP), Iceland 108, 114-119, 123, 127, 129-130, 132-134, 141, 143-145, 152-153, 156, 158-159, 164
indirect elections 171-172, 174

institutional change 77, 101, 172
institutional setting 19, 21, 217
interest group 15, 166, 234
interest organizations 10, 188, 190
interest representation 20, 223
intraparty conflict 67, 98, 117, 124-125, 140-142, 144-145, 147, 151-152, 154-155, 223
involuntary removal 94, 224
Iron Law of Oligarchy 233

Jensen, R. B. 230
Johansen, L. N. 52-54, 231
Johansson, J. 25
Jutland 230
Jääsaari, J. 92

Karstensen, A. 231
Katz, D. 171, 180, 183-184, 219, 236
Katz, R. S. 12, 38, 42, 229-230
Key, V. O. 11
Kiewiet, D. R. 16
Kjær, U. 231
Kjærsgaard, P. 39, 42
Kleppe, V. 234
Koskiaho, T. 67-68
Kristensen, O. P. 52-54, 231
Kristiansand 234
Kristinsson, G. H. 136
Kristjánsson, S. 165-166, 222, 246
Kristvik, B. 172
Kuitunen, S. 71, 79, 85-86, 222, 231, 246

Labor Party, Norway 173, 179-180, 185, 188, 192, 204, 210, 229, 232-233, 235
Landmandsforbundet, Norway 174
Lane, J.-E. 11
Lane, R. 112
Lange, A. 181
Larsen, K. 31-32
Left Party, Sweden 159
Left Wing Alliance (LWA), Finland 71-75, 77, 80, 85
Liberal Party, Iceland 114

Liberal Party, Norway 172-173, 179-180, 187-189, 210, 235-236
Liberal People's Party (LIB), Finland 68
list manipulation 72, 86-87
list system 64; closed 17-20, 100, 227; long 67; open 70, 100; PR 47
list turnover 95-97, 205
local autonomy 40
local connection 14, 17
local experience 83
local interests 162, 190-191, 215
local residency 130
Loewenberg, G. 86
London 236
Lovenduski, J. 14-15, 65, 117, 132, 157, 198
Lupia, A. 229
Löchen, E. 232

Magnus, G. 234
Mair, P. 12, 38, 42, 229-230
Marsh, M. 10, 12, 14, 25
Martikainen, T. 92
Martinussen, W. 196
mass media 17, 22-23, 227, 231, 235; Denmark 37, 54; Finland 76, 78, 91, 99; Iceland 136-137, 166; Norway 170, 181-185, 191-192, 214
mass political party 110-111, 115, 120, 122-123, 126, 133-134, 136, 156
Matland, R. E. 156, 158-160, 221
Matthews, D. 21, 24, 78, 85, 171, 187, 189, 194-195, 211, 233-234
Mattila, M. 93
McCubbins, M. D. 16, 229
Michels, R. 233
Mitchell, P. 17, 225
Mjeldheim, L. 171-173, 232
Müller, W. C. 229

Narud, H. M. 15, 24, 170, 182-183, 185, 191-192, 194, 197, 236, 246
National Coalition Party (NCP), Finland 68, 71-75, 77, 80
Nergaard, K. 191

Index   251

New Zealand 157
Nomination Act, Norway (1920) 171, 175-176, 192, 233
nomination committee 177-179, 189, 208, 232-234
nomination convention 177, 182, 184, 189, 192, 210, 218, 232
nomination district, Denmark (*opstillingskreds*) 34-35, 38-39, 41, 43, 45-48, 50-56, 230-231
nomination method and procedures 11-12, 17, 217-218, 222-223, 225-226, 232; Denmark 34, 42; Finland 65-66, 72; Iceland 107, 112, 114-115, 117-119, 122-124, 127-130, 132-135, 138, 152-156, 158, 162, 164; Norway 171, 174, 214
nominations, distribution of influence 39; major patterns of 51; party control of 111, 117, 135, 155, 162, 164, 224
nomination system 12-13, 20-21, 23, 25, 217, 219, 227, 236; Denmark 30-33, 37, 39, 41, 44, 47, 53-54, 61; Finland 63-70, 75, 79, 81-82, 88, 94, 98, 100-101; Iceland 107, 109-110, 112-113, 117, 119-123, 127-138, 144, 152-154, 158-166; Norway 169-173, 180-181, 184, 191, 214-215
Noponen, M. 79, 82, 86, 95
Nordland 203-204, 232
norm 10, 14, 21, 23, 25, 217, 219-220, 223, 225, 229; Denmark 36, 46; Finland 84, 91; Norway 184, 186, 192; of "non-intervention" 46
Norris, P. 12, 14-15, 25, 65, 117, 132, 157, 198, 229
Nousiainen, J. 66, 82

occupational groups 81, 213, 221
Oksanen, M. 84
open polls 121
Opheim, I. 232
Oppland 233
organizational process 169, 177-178, 214
Oslo 176, 178, 191, 210, 215, 229, 234-235
Otterup 230

Paltemaa, L. 83, 86, 231
participation 121, 187, 198, 218, 225; degree of in candidate selection 13, 107, 116-118, 122-124, 128-133, 163, 210-211, 225
participation rates 72-75
Party Act, Finland 67
party activist 18, 22, 108, 163, 181, 192, 205, 211
party branch, local 13, 34, 36, 38-39, 63-64, 66, 69, 73-74, 76, 78, 81, 98, 102-103, 115, 217, 226, 229, 230; regional 217
party constitutions and statutes 15, 25, 233; Denmark 37; Finland 64, 67-69, 71-72, 78; Iceland 112-113, 115-116, 121, 123-124; Norway 184, 190, 192; United States of America 14
party convention 73, 107-108, 119, 131, 155, 162, 164; national 115-116, 123-124, 155, 164, 192; regional 131, 161-165
party decline 76, 78, 126; hypothesis of 134, 136
party democracy party type 185, 234
party discipline 161, 225
party district executive 75, 81, 86, 102
party dominance 63, 169
party government 162
party institutions 77, 119-120, 122, 124-125, 126, 128, 131, 153, 155-157, 165; local 121, 125, 130; national 120
party leaders, central 20, 181, 192, 214-215, 219; local 19, 33, 66, 120, 161, 170, 184, 194, 225, 234; national 25, 33, 108, 112, 116, 130, 160, 162, 164, 170, 175-176, 178-181, 214, 218, 233; regional 19, 108, 112, 160-161, 164-165
party leadership, central 34, 39-40, 181, 192, 217, 225, 229; local 29, 191, 225; national 29, 33, 40, 64, 66, 76, 121, 145, 170
party list option 39, 51, 231
party loyalty 80, 184-185
party members, participation in candidate selection 13, 218, 236; Denmark

42, 61; Finland 64, 66, 69, 72-79, 81, 86-87, 98-100, 102; Iceland 115-116, 118, 121-123, 129-134, 156, 161-164; Norway 170, 175, 177, 210-211, 215
party organization, central 32-33, 36, 40; district 63-64, 69, 76; local 33, 40-41, 58, 116, 119-121, 123, 126-127, 171, 177, 179, 184, 189; national 102; provincial 233
party primaries 19, 63, 72-75, 77, 81, 86, 96, 102, 104, 231; closed 66; open 22
party procedure 25, 72
party rule 13, 64, 67-68, 107, 112, 117, 135-136, 160-162, 166, 231
party system 10, 30, 33, 53, 58-59, 65, 114, 157, 190, 230-231
party units, local 123, 131-132, 171, 175, 177, 218
party unity 15, 173, 182, 190
PASOK 13
Patterson, S. 86
Pedersen, M. N. 11, 24, 36, 38, 45, 50, 52, 54, 57, 59, 194-195, 224, 230-231, 250
Pekonen 101
Pennings, P. 12, 226
People's Alliance (PA), Iceland 108-109, 114-115, 126-131, 133, 149-152, 155-157, 232
People's Movement, Iceland 232
personal abilities 14
personal qualities 19-20, 23, 183
personal vote 17-19, 22, 35-36, 50, 52-53, 61, 113-114, 135-136, 161, 237; effective 50, 52; ineffective 50, 52
Pesonen, P. 81, 231
Pettersen, E. B. 232
Pitkin, H. 9
platform abilities 23, 184-189
pre-election 92, 127-128, 151
preferential vote 22, 35, 48, 52, 56, 61, 113
preferential voting system 47, 70, 226
Prewitt, K. 36
primaries 13, 218-219, 222-223, 225-226, 232; Finland 66-72, 87, 92, 101; Iceland 115-125, 128, 131-132, 145; Norway 172-173, 175; closed 13, 77, 127, 133, 152, 155-156, 219; open 13, 19, 219, 222, 224-225, 232; Finland 66; Iceland; 107, 109-110, 112, 117-119, 121-126, 131-137, 142, 153-156, 163-166
principal 16-21, 24, 224-226, 230; Denmark 29; Finland 63, 102; Iceland 108-110, 112, 160-164; Norway 170-171, 209
principal-agent relation 11, 16, 18, 20, 64-65, 102, 170-171, 224-225, 230
Progressive Conservative Party, Iceland 117
Progressive Party (PP), Iceland 108, 114-115, 119-123, 127, 129-130, 133-134, 141, 145-147, 152, 154, 156, 158
Progress Party, Denmark 39-40, 43-44, 51, 60, 233
Progress Party, Norway 179-181, 188-189, 192, 204-205, 214, 233-235
proportional representation electoral system 47, 113, 156-157, 159, 171, 174
Przeworski, A. 11
Præstø 31
Putnam, R. 15, 85, 221

quota system 141, 192

Raaum, N. 194, 198
Radical Liberal Party, Denmark 33, 40, 51, 56
Ranney, A. 10-14, 81, 87, 175, 182, 202, 227
Rasmussen, E. 34
rational-efficient party type 185, 234
recidency rule, Norway (bostadsbånd) 190
recruitment 15, 23, 217, 224-225; Denmark 36, 53, 58, 60; Finland 78, 82-83, 90, 98; Iceland 133, 135, 137, 139, 141, 143, 151-153, 155-158, 162, 165; Norway 198, 204-205, 215; of party leadership 204
recruitment process 14, 24, 52, 61, 83, 87,

99, 104, 156, 171, 222, 229
re-election rate 92-93, 96-97
referendum 175; EU 208
Reiter, H. 10
renomination 45, 98, 131, 140-142, 162-163, 177, 202-203, 207, 234
representation, according to gender 84; district 20, 191; of occupational groups 213; of youth 193, 213; political 9, 198, 214
requirement for selection 79
responsible party school 162, 166
retirement rate 59
retirement reasons 140, 144-150
reward 16, 64, 92, 96, 137, 162-163, 202
Reykjanes 124-125, 158-159
Reykjavík 113-114, 124, 127, 131, 151, 158-159, 161
Riker, W. 17
Rokkan, S. 172, 235
Ruostetsaari, I. 81-82, 93-94
rural legislators 82

safe seats 56, 60, 141, 222
Saglie, J. 172, 232
sanctions 16-18, 19, 64, 89, 92, 102, 137, 202, 227; ex post mechanism 103
Schattschneider, E. E. 10
Schlesinger, J. 65
screening 21-23, 165, 219-220, 222, 227
Sejersted, F. 180
selection criteria 14, 20, 23, 78, 102, 193
Seligman, L. G. 14, 23, 79, 184, 220
simultaneous nomination option 50-55
Sjöblom, G. 165
Skard, T. 221
Skare, A. 170-171, 193,-194, 234, 246
Skjeie, H. 194, 198
Skovmand, R. 34, 230
Sköld, L. 25
social bias 23; iron law of 15
Social Democratic League of Workers and Smallholders (SDL), Finland 67-68

Social Democratic Party (SDP), Denmark 31, 33-35, 38, 41, 43, 46, 50-51, 56
Social Democratic Party (SDP), Finland 66-68, 70-75, 77, 80-81
Social Democratic Party (SDP), Iceland 108, 114-115, 123-126, 129-130, 133-134, 141, 147-149, 152, 154-156, 232
Socialist Left Party, Norway 179, 188, 204, 210, 235
Socialist People's Party, Denmark 41-42, 50-51
socio-demographic composition 79, 81, 85-86, 194
Sogn 192, 233-234
Solheim, E. 235
Somit, A. 87
Stavanger 232, 234, 236
Storting, Norway 169, 196-197, 203, 205-206, 212-213, 234-236; election 170-171, 175-176, 181-182, 193, 203, 207, 209-210, 214, 232-234; members 179-180, 209
Strand, A. 234
Strøm, K. 16-17, 229, 232
Studlar, D. T. 156-160, 221
Styrkársdóttir, A. 115
Sundberg, J. 11, 66-68, 71, 73, 76, 79, 81, 84, 102
Svåsand, L. 211, 233, 236
Sweden 157-159
Swedish People's Party (SPP), Finland 68
Sänkiaho, R. 84, 231
Sør-Trøndelag 235

Taponen, H. 63-69, 79
Tarasti, L. 63-69, 79
Tarkiainen, T. 66-67, 79
territorial conflict 84, 193
territorial representation 23, 81-82, 85, 190-191, 215
"test" elections 172-173
Teune, H. 11
Thyness, P. 232

ticket balancing 25, 70, 79, 81, 84, 189-192, 214-215
Timonen, P. 64, 67, 70, 73-75, 102
Turkey 12
turnover 21, 24-26, 223-224, 232; Denmark 58-59, 60; Finland 64, 92-100, 103-104; Iceland 128, 138-139, 141-147, 149-156; Norway 169, 202, 204-209
Turku 83
turnover rate 53, 59-60, 64, 92-93, 96, 103, 142, 144, 147, 204-206, 223-224

United Front, Iceland 232
United Socialist Party (USP), Iceland 126-127
United States of America 9-14, 63, 66, 117, 119, 174-175, 227, 229
Unity List, Denmark 42, 50-51, 231
Urwin, D. 207

Valen, H. 14-15, 20-21, 23-25, 75, 78-81, 170-171, 175, 178-180, 184-187, 189-192, 194-195, 197, 200-201, 207, 210-211, 219, 232-234, 236, 246
Valgordningskommisjonen, Norway (1917) 232
Vest-Agder 234
veto right 40
voluntary retirement 98, 104, 154

Wallin, G. 85
Ware, A. 12-13
West Germany 12
Wiberg, M. 93
Winding, K. 32, 230
Winter, L. de 75, 79
Women, recruitment of 24, 220-223, 230-233; Denmark 35, 43-45, 53-58; Finland 65, 76, 78, 81, 84-93, 96-98, 102; Iceland 115, 138, 140, 153-160; Norway 191-192, 194, 196, 198-201, 204-205, 208-209, 212, 214-215
Women's Alliance (WA), Iceland 115, 140, 157, 160, 232
women's movement 192, 198, 221, 233
women's organizations 191
women's quotas 23-24, 84, 155, 158, 160, 191-192, 205, 223
Wright, W. E. 185
Wyller, T. Chr. 170

Østfold 233

Aardal, B. 207, 232-233, 236
Aarestrup, E. 230